The

BOSS's Survival Guide

The *For Paul —*

BOSS's Survival Guide SECOND EDITION

Workplace 911
for the toughest problems today's managers face

with thanks & best wishes —

Bob Rosner and Allan Halcrow

Allan Halcrow

New York   Chicago   San Francisco   Lisbon
London   Madrid   Mexico City   Milan   New Delhi
San Juan   Seoul   Singapore   Sydney   Toronto

The *McGraw·Hill* Companies

1 2 3 4 5 6 7 8 9 0   WFR/WFR   0 1 0 9

ISBN 978-0-07-166808-8
MHID   0-07-166808-X

McGraw-Hill books are available at special quantity discounts to use as premiums and sales promotions, or for use in corporate training programs. To contact a representative, please e-mail us at bulksales@mcgraw-hill.com.

This book is printed on acid-free paper.

To Hallie and Frankie, I hope this will help to create a saner workplace for you.

—BR

To my father, Douglas Halcrow, for setting the example.

—AH

Contents

Special Acknowledgments

The authors especially want to thank Alan Levins of Littler Mendelson for his contributions to this book and *The Boss's Survival Guide*. Alan's knowledge of labor and employment law, and his ability to crystallize and simplify the legal questions at issue, were critical to the success of *The Boss's Survival Guide* and served as the underpinnings of this edition. Alan practices in Littler Mendelson's San Francisco office. He is the "go-to" person with respect to any labor or employment law question.

The authors appreciate all the advice and counsel that we received from WorkplaceFairness.org in the course of writing this revision. *PC Magazine* called WorkplaceFairness.org one of the Web sites "that you can't live without." The site is consistently ranked at or near the top of Google's searches on workplace legal issues. The Web site has been nominated for a Webby and most other Web awards that matter. Their information is easy to understand and digest. Paula Brantner is a true leader in her field—visionary, committed, and always willing to go above and beyond the call of duty. But don't take our word for it; check out WorkplaceFairness.org yourself.

AUTHORS' NOTE

All the material in this book reflects the views of the authors. Although we've made every effort to be legally accurate, it should not be construed as legal advice.

In the interest of improving readability, we decided not to use the cumbersome "he or she" and "his or hers" construction of sentences when we are not referring to specific people. We also chose not to break the rules of grammar and use "they" when referring to a single person. Instead, we've used "he" or "she" throughout the book. The choice of which we used in any given place is entirely random, and should not be construed as a political statement. Really.

Acknowledgments

Anyone who says that writing is a solitary venture clearly doesn't understand how much support stressed-out, creatively blocked, multitasking writers need. Our lengthy list of key people will give you some idea.

To my family and friends who help to keep me on my toes. To Allan Halcrow, who is the greatest coauthor you could hope to have. To Paula Brantner and everyone at WorkplaceFairness for all their legal insight. To my unpaid board of advisors (Jay, Joanna, Susan, Andy, Chris, Tom, Denise, Dennis, Gifford, Pam, Mike, James, Erik, Joanne, Bob, Chance, Sharon, Gianni, Rene, Steve, Serni, Dana, Dee, Suma, Lisa, Saul, Theresa, Brian, Paula, Sherrie, and all those who will be brainstorming with me in the not-too-distant future). To everyone who has ever written to either WorkingWounded.com or Workplace911.com with either problems or solutions. To Mary and Knox and everyone at McGraw-Hill. To all the hardworking bosses out there who create healthy, sane, and productive environments for their people. Finally, to the Boss, Bruce Springsteen, just because that's what guys from Jersey do.

—BR

First, last, and always, my thanks to Brian Gillet for making every day worthwhile, keeping me sane, holding me accountable and being my best friend (just for starters). My thanks, too, to the rest of my family (Doug, Eileen, Marie, Nathalie, Ron, and Helene) and especially to my sister, Cheri, who (even when in Malta or Thailand or somewhere) is a great friend, too. Thanks to Bob Rosner for being the best coauthor a guy could have. Thanks to Lynne Gabriel for letting me work with her and for making every minute of it fun. Thanks to the gurus out there who inspire me and who said "Sure" when I asked for input for the book, especially Ann Perle and Rebecca Ryan. Thank you Mary and Knox at McGraw-Hill. Thank you to all the friends who make life a lot more fun and much more interesting, especially Shari Caudron, Brian and Sandy Alters, Jana and Rick Perkal, and Charlene Solomon. And last (but certainly not least) thank you to all the people who shared their workplace stories.

—AH

The Forgotten Four

What's it like to be a boss today? The Beirut Commodore Hotel immediately leaps to mind.

A hotel? Yes. During the Lebanese Civil War the Commodore was the hotel of choice for journalists covering the war. When you checked in, the front-desk staff would smile and ask, "Shelling side or sniper side?"

Sound familiar?

Today's bosses get sniped from below by employees and vendors and shelled from above by their bosses, customers, and the economy in general. We're not exaggerating when we say that there has never been a tougher time to be a boss. It's so bad that today there aren't many people out there eager to admit that they *are* the boss. The confident swagger of the corner-office crowd has been replaced by the furtive scurry that used to be reserved for politicians caught in a scandal.

In fact, we did a poll asking which movie title best described your relationship with the boss. One in five said *Little Shop of Horrors*. One in four said *It's a Wonderful Life*. But the number one movie describing the relationship between bosses and employees? *House of Games*, the choice of 55 percent of those polled. Ouch!

How did "the Boss" fall so far—so fast—in the national hierarchy? Just as a few high-profile druggies have tarnished all of professional sports (and Bernie Madoff gave all financial advisors a black eye), a handful of boneheaded CEOs behind some spectacular flameouts have undermined the Captain America image of corporate leadership. Lehman Brothers, Enron, Circuit City, AIG, WorldCom—the ever-expanding list of corporations run into the ground through greed, incompetence, and stupidity have made CEOs an easy target.

Don't believe us? Then take note of Hollywood, that great zeitgeist thermometer. From James Bond to *Wall-E*, corporate executives have replaced Russians, third-world tyrants, and mafia dons as the villain du jour at today's multiplex.

And why not? There's a certain vicarious thrill in seeing a CEO suffer a fantasy comeuppance. If we can't get in the face of the CEO who gambled away our retirement, did away with our job, and flew the corporate jet to ask Congress for a bailout, at least 007 can. This time, it's personal: we've all suffered because of wretched corporate excess.

And if you're a boss somewhat lower on the totem poll, it's probably not news to you that you've suffered doubly. After all, you're the one left to clean up the mess—to show up every day as the face of management, to watch morale fall off a cliff, to throw a few people under the bus yourself, and, oh yes, to be thanked for it all by wondering when the hatchet will fall on *you*.

The only thing worse than hearing that miserable phrase, "Do more with less" at work? Being stuck saying it.

And wait—there's more! Add a volatile mix of baby boomers, Gen X-ers and Millennials, all approaching work with their own values and style. Do battle in a hyper marketplace in which new competitors can emerge overnight from a country halfway around the world or from a previously unknown entrepreneur's kitchen table. Toss in a tsunami of government regulations and a never-ending threat of lawsuits. And if your stress level isn't already off the charts, consider increasingly complex technology that makes you long for the days when you used to tease your parents about the blinking 12:00 on their VCR. If you pay attention to the business and financial news, you can reasonably ask whether our organizations have become unmanageable—too big and too complex to weather this storm.

No wonder we aren't having fun. And there are some doom-and-gloomers arguing that it may not get back to "normal" before the Octomom's brood is ready for middle school. Or college. Sure we'll recover, but not without fundamental changes to our economy. And to ourselves. Think of it all as the "new" normal.

Maybe you think we're exaggerating—that the picture for bosses isn't as bad as we've painted it to be, that organizations are inherently manageable, that what worked before will continue working. We would respectfully disagree. Just as your old investment strategy tanked—leaving you with only a fraction of your previous investments—you've also got to be prepared to let go of outdated approaches to management. The old rules, and leadership style, just won't cut it any longer.

Which brings us to the most honest e-mail we've ever received from a boss. Given that we've personally responded to more than

50,000 e-mails from bosses and employees, that's really saying something. "I've been a supervisor at a variety of Fortune 500 companies," he wrote. "In my opinion, I wouldn't want to work for me." Beyond being one of the most honest people ever, he raises the difficult question we all need to ask ourselves: Do we get results because of our leadership style, or in spite of it?

Take the media's descriptions of our financial meltdown. First they called it a subprime crisis, then a credit crisis, next a financial crisis. Somehow, they never called it what it really was: a leadership crisis. Until we focus on the thinking that got us in trouble (yes, we're talking to all you monogrammed-shirt-wearing MBAs out there), we're all part of the problem. U.S. Army General Eric Shinseki summed it up best: "If you don't like change, you're going to like irrelevance even less."

We've coined a name for this new era in business. Heck, we're authors, speakers, and consultants. What did you expect us to do? Welcome to the "Humble Pie" era, in which all managers and leaders need to take a step back and accept that we're all tarnished by recent business history. We've all acquired bad habits, elevated assumptions, an infatuation with our insight, and the unwavering belief that we'd built an escalator that only went up.

Even though this book is called a "survival guide," we believe that organizations can go beyond survival and actually thrive. But only if we all focus on repairing the key building block in every organization: the boss-employee relationship. That relationship is broken, and yet it is still not finding a top slot (or even a medium slot) on our daily to-do list. It should.

Really? With everything complicating business today we want you to focus on the boss/subordinate relationship? Yes, because

rebuilding any shattered structure must start with the foundation—
the core element—and slowly work its way to the top.

Business guru Peter Drucker said it best: "So much of what we
call management consists of making it difficult for people to work."
What makes it so difficult? Bosses struggle to listen, employees struggle to speak up, and both sides have precious little empathy for the other.

We believe that the rift between most bosses and their employees is getting worse, not better. And this has massive consequences
for every organization and each and every one of us. We're not suggesting that work become a never-ending coffee klatch, that we all
need to hug more often, or that anyone should sing "Kumbaya"—ever!

Perhaps you remember a famous scene from a *Pink Panther*
movie. A guy is standing on a street corner next to a dog. Inspector
Clouseau walks up and asks the man if his dog bites. The man says
no. Clouseau bends over to pet the dog. The dog bites him. Clouseau
gets upset and yells at the man, who turns to him and says, "But it's
not my dog."

Like Clouseau, we can't become better leaders until we ask the
right questions, about our organizations, our people, but mostly about
ourselves. Whether you read this book from cover to cover or use it
as a reference guide when a crisis presents itself, our goal is simple:
to give you a new approach to solving your top problems at work.
That's a tall order, but that's why we'll start off with an overview of
how to turn things around. We call it the Forgotten Four.

THE FORGOTTEN FOUR

Before we tell you how to become a better boss, let's explore the
opposite end of the spectrum: how to be a really lousy leader. Jack

Zenger and Joseph Folkman examined 11,000 360-degree evaluation forms of executives (*Harvard Business Review*, June 2009). They compared the top 10 percent to the bottom 10 percent and found the following traits distinguished the worst managers. They

- Lack energy and enthusiasm
- Accept their own mediocre performance
- Lack clear vision and direction
- Have poor judgment
- Don't collaborate
- Don't walk their talk
- Resist new ideas
- Don't learn from mistakes
- Lack interpersonal skills
- Fail to develop others

Somehow, we doubt we'll see any of the bosses in the bottom 10 on the cover of *BusinessWeek* anytime soon.

But there's hope for the rest of us. After reviewing many studies—and our own in-box—we determined that there are four primary ways to escape this dungeon and become an effective leader. We call them the Forgotten Four:

- Fairness
- Flexibility
- Leverage
- Empathy

For each of these four areas, we'll outline three strategies to develop your skills, including one strategy for each that you can implement immediately. Let's start with three strategies for Fairness.

FAIRNESS

Part 1: Multitasking?

We all know that multitasking is a requirement today. We're all trying to get so much done that who has the luxury of doing just one thing at a time? But let's look at it another way. If we were to tell you that 2007 studies from Microsoft and Oxford University showed that when we multitask we double our mistakes *and* the length of time it takes to do an assignment, would that change your view of multitasking? Looking at it that way, who can afford to multitask with our most important assignments?

It goes even deeper than that. Brain research shows that our brain is capable of doing amazing calculations, but only sequentially. It can't do two tasks at the same time. Don't believe us? Check out John Medina's book *Brain Rules*.

Beyond that, multitasking is rude and unfair. Yet we do it all the time, for example, when using our PDAs while an employee is sitting across the desk from us. As a manager pointed out in one of our seminars, we routinely do things to the people who report to us that we'd never do to a customer.

We all need to take the *multi* out of tasking and to demand the same of others. Single-task our most important work: what a concept.

Strategy: Single Task.

Part 2: Accountability and Authority?

Remember when you were an employee and you were given accountability for getting a job done but no authority? Frustration doesn't begin to capture that feeling. Yet, many of us do that consistently to our people. A better alternative is the greatest management philosophy that no one has ever heard of: the Waterline Principle.

Embraced by W. L. Gore and Associates (the folks who make Gore-Tex), the idea is simple. Your organization is like a boat. If it is damaged above the waterline, the boat will still float. If it is damaged below the waterline, well, you know what happened to the *Titanic*. The Waterline Principle states that everyone in an organization needs to know where the waterline is. When the challenge is above the waterline, employees can make their own decisions, learning and growing in the process. When it is below it, others must be called in before any decisions can be made.

Here's another real-world example: At Ritz-Carlton Hotels, every employee can spend as much as $2,000 to solve a customer's problem. There's no need to get approval from a supervisor; anyone— starting with housekeeping staff and custodians—can take action to make a dissatisfied guest a satisfied one. Ritz-Carlton's people know where the waterline is for their company. Do your people know where your waterline is?

Why should you care? Well, if your people don't know where the waterline is, they either see every problem as above the waterline (and just tell the orchestra to play louder so no one will notice), or they treat every problem as if it's a below-the-waterline crisis— and run to you to give the order to lower the lifeboats.

Strategy: Establish the Waterline.

Part 3: Tasks?

How do you begin each day? Checking your e-mails, text messages, and voice mail? Join the club.

Which means we often notice that it's 2 P.M. and we haven't done anything actually important because we've been putting out fires. That's why it's so important to distinguish between the "urgent" and the "important." We're not suggesting you spend an hour contemplating your navel; just start each day with a few minutes reviewing your goals. You'll be amazed at how productive your day can be when you focus on the big-picture stuff from the start.

Which reminds us of the Gravina Island Bridge. Doesn't ring a bell? You might recognize the name it's more commonly known by, "the Bridge to Nowhere." The bridge was intended to replace the ferry that connects the town of Ketchikan, Alaska, to the Ketchikan International Airport and 50 residents—for the bargain price of only $398 million. Planned to be nearly as long as the Golden Gate Bridge, it was eventually stricken from the budget as a classic case of pork-barrel politics.

How many Bridges to Nowhere are currently on your to-do list? Start a regular not-to-do list of things that you, and your team, shouldn't do at all, so you can focus your efforts on the important stuff.

Strategy: Not To-Do List. (Why wait? This strategy can be implemented immediately.)

FLEXIBILITY

Part 1: Feedback?

Ken Olsen was the founder and CEO of Digital Equipment Corporation, one of the leading computer companies in the early days of the industry. In 1977 he said in a presentation to the World Future Society: "There is no reason for any individual to have a computer in his home."

We all say dumb things occasionally. But for a top executive at a top computer company to say this in 1977—when there were already thousands of hobbyists with computers in their homes— shows the danger of being out of touch. His company missed a huge opportunity and eventually had to merge with another company.

Unfortunately, many of us are more like Mr. Olsen than we'd like to admit. We see feedback as something that is good for the gander, but not the goose. But there is an even better way to foster a lively dialogue at work. Marshall Goldsmith, CEO coach, has coined the term *feed-forward*. Rather than just beating people up for past sins, he suggests focusing on the type of behavior you'd like to see in the future and let your employees do the same for you.

Strategy: Feed-Forward.

Part 2: Leadership Style?

Daniel Goleman did a fascinating study on leadership for the *Harvard Business Review*. He wanted to discover the most successful leadership style. First he identified six different styles using the words a leader would use practicing that style.

What was the most effective leadership style? "Let's work on this together." But Goleman didn't stop there. He discovered that the most successful leaders don't try to form committees to tackle every workplace problem. The best leaders have a full tool kit and take out the right leadership style based on the circumstance.

Which reminds us of the famous phrase, "We're going to be in the Hudson." Chesley Sullenberger, the US Airways captain who managed to crash-land his plane into New York's Hudson River with no fatalities, reminded us that complete engine failure shortly after takeoff is no time to call a meeting.

Strategy: Leadership Styles.

Part 3: Bad News?

Movie mogul Samuel Goldwyn summed up the way many of us view our employees: "I don't want any yes-men around me. I want people to tell me the truth, even if it costs them their jobs."

Goldwyn could have learned a few things about human nature from Winston Churchill. Churchill knew that people instinctively filter information when they are dealing with the person signing their paychecks. That's why when he created the Central Statistical Office to collect data during World War II, he did not have it report directly to him. That way, the data wouldn't be skewed to what the boss wanted to hear.

How do you ensure that the information you're getting is truthful? It won't just happen; you have to lay the groundwork. Our technique is called Cassandra's Toss. Before each meeting, participants wad up a piece of paper and put it in front of them. If anyone, including the boss, says something that you disagree with, you toss the paper at them. This turns disagreement and dissent into something acceptable and, dare we say, entertaining.

Strategy: Cassandra's Toss. (Again, why wait? This strategy can be implemented immediately.)

LEVERAGE

Part 1, Control?

According to an engineer quoted in the *Wall Street Journal*, up to 90 percent of thermostats in corporations aren't connected to anything. They even have a name for it: "an illusion of control." You just can't make this stuff up.

That's how many of us manage. Instead of giving people the tools to do their jobs, we give them an illusion of control—to our own, and our organizations', detriment. Which brings us to Jack Stack's *The Great Game of Business*. This is a book about how a management team took over a factory that was hemorrhaging money. The new leadership team made two commitments. First, to teach finance to every employee. Second, to give each employee a say in how the business was run. Radical, yes. But there is also an inescapable logic to this approach.

When one employee learned how much a particular piece of steel cost, for example, instead of using it to make one stamping, he figured out how to get two stampings from the one piece. Employees can dramatically add to the bottom line, but only when they have the insight, tools, and permission to do so. That's why we believe employees should know the key metrics for their jobs, so they can monitor and improve their own performance.

Strategy: Their Key Metrics.

Part 2: Hiring?

When hiring new staff, organizations tend to be very concerned about whether a prospective employee will fit in with the rest of the team. We believe there is an equally important quality to consider: the ability to speak up. New employees need to be able to disagree appropriately with the status quo so the organization can adapt to changing times.

Consider the battle between Coke and Pepsi. For many years Coke had its iconic bottle. Pepsi spent a long time trying to create its own distinctive bottle. Eventually, someone realized that the key issue wasn't the shape of the bottle, but its size: Pepsi introduced the two-liter bottle and changed the rules of the game.

So, the key question to consider when hiring: Would your new employee continue to try to create a new shape for the Pepsi bottle, or would she get past that kind of thinking and suggest a different size bottle? After all, isn't that the kind of new energy and insight that your organization really needs? If you come across a potential hire who appropriately challenges the way you're doing business, make an offer.

Strategy: Hire for New Thinking.

Part 3: Innovation?

Today, innovation seems to be the answer, no matter what the question. But we all have to do battle with the Corporate Immune System—the tendency to embrace the status quo. Unfortunately, many of us boost the Corporate Immune System's idea-killing tendencies whenever an employee makes a suggestion and we respond, "No, because . . ." "We tried it before. . . ." "We couldn't raise the capital . . ." We've all said these things.

Look at this from your employees' point of view. What if every time you suggested a new idea, the first thing you heard was "No"? That's why we prefer a more positive approach: "Yes, if . . ." Anything is possible if all the *ifs* can be satisfied. For example, consider all the *ifs* that NASA engineers had to resolve before astronauts could land on the moon. Initially, the idea was rejected as impossible. But then they went through the *ifs*—*if* we can launch a rocket that carries astronauts, *if* we can get the rocket out of Earth's atmosphere, *if* we can get the rocket to the moon, *if* we can get the rocket in orbit around the moon, and so on—and then resolved them one at a time. Sure, it takes a bit more work on your end to come up with what follows the *if,* but we believe this is a small investment in time and energy that will pay off for you many times over. Another famous "yes, if " thinker, Walt Disney, famously observed, "It's kind of fun to do the impossible."

One employee wrote to us saying that he felt his company had focused a lot of attention on the people who'd quit and left. He thought it would be wise to focus instead on the people who quit and stay. Unfortunately, we believe that some of these people who quit and stay didn't get there on their own—they were "no, because" there.

Strategy: "*Yes, If . . .*" (This is another strategy that can be implemented immediately.)

EMPATHY

Part 1: Energy?

$E = mc^2$. Recognize that formula? It's Einstein's way to calculate energy. Ken Blanchard tweaked it to focus on how to increase energy inside an organization. His equation is: Energy equals Mission times Cash times Congratulations. We agree.

People want to feel like they're making a contribution, that they're being paid fairly, and that their work is appreciated. It's easy to forget when you are trying to tap-dance through the minefield of your average day.

There is another key consideration when it comes to energy at work. It's a quote from motivational speaker Keith Harrell: "A dead battery can't charge a dead battery." If we want our people to bring more energy to work, we first need to take a look in the mirror to see how much energy we bring to work each day.

Strategy: $E = mc^2$.

Part 2: Results?

We once interviewed Jim Moore, director of Executive Education for Sun Microsystems. We asked him what it was like to be responsible for the educational advancement of his bosses. He took out a pen and drew two circles on a cocktail napkin (now you've learned our favorite place to conduct interviews), one inside the other. He pointed to the inside circle and said, "This is their comfort zone. If I don't get them out of here they don't grow and they don't learn." We asked about the second circle. "That's their limits. If I take them outside of here I become the *former* director of Executive Education."

Most of us talk about getting results out of our people, but we have no idea where their comfort zone or limits are at all. See the problem?

It's not unlike a tin can. Really. The tin can was revolutionary in 1810. It allowed sailors to undertake long voyages without getting scurvy, because they could pack fruits and other important foods. There was only one problem. Do you know what year the can opener was invented? In 1858! For 48 years the only way to get the food out of the tin can was to hit it with a hammer and chisel, and spray much of the contents on the wall and floor. Are we any more sophisticated when it comes to getting the most out of our people?

Strategy: Comfort Zone and Limits.

Part 3: Retaining Top Talent?

Don't think it's that important to retain your top talent? We have four words for you: Circuit "51 Cent" City. This once prosperous electronics chain went out of business exactly 20 months after it decided to fire its most expensive (read: most experienced) staff. Anyone who earned more than 51 cents over the company average was let go— 3,400 people in all.

You already know the moral to this story. Customers deserted the chain in droves when they figured out that Circuit City salespeople could no longer explain things well. Top talent matters.

Circuit City self-destructed, but the rest of us have the benefit of an early-warning system. We call it the Pronoun Test, and we learned it from former Secretary of Labor Robert Reich. Just listen to your people talk about the company. Do they use *us* and *we* or *they* and *them*? If you overhear key staffers using *they* and *them*, you need to reconnect with them ASAP.

The best way we know comes from business consultant and author Bev Kaye. She says that leaders should ask their most valuable people, "What would it take to keep you working here?" After all, if they're that important, do you really want to let another day pass without knowing the answer to that question? Of course, if they say they want their salary tripled and vacation time quadrupled, you can say you'll work on it during the next budget cycle. But, according to our e-mails and research, most will ask for something totally reasonable.

Strategy: Ask: "What would it take to keep you working here?"

FORGOTTEN FOUR SUMMARIZED

Many leaders bring a simple philosophy to work, the Golden Rule: Do unto others as *you* would have them do unto *you.*

Sure the Golden Rule has been around for centuries, but we believe it's time to retire that kind of thinking. Because your employees don't care what *you* want done unto *you.* To them what matters is the Platinum Rule: Do unto others as *they* would have done unto *them.*

We all customize our products and services for our customers. Doesn't it make sense to do the same with our employees?

How do you do this? Let's all take a lesson from the Queen of Thailand. Many years ago the queen was riding in a boat with hundreds of servants on board and many more citizens waving to her from the shore. The boat started to sink. Although there were many people who could have saved her, the queen died. How could this happen? The answer: in Thai culture, no one can touch the queen.

Which raises the question: Have you become untouchable at work? We hear what you're thinking. "Of course not, I have an open-door policy." We're going to level with you: too many managers with an open-door policy have a closed-mind policy. To paraphrase Jack Nicholson in *A Few Good Men*, "Can you handle the truth?"

A quick real-world example. We facilitated an open town hall for a large insurance company that was suffering morale problems. The general manager was newly promoted into management, but had worked with most of the people for 20 years. When people really started to speak up about what was bothering them at work, she realized how much of a wall had sprung up between her and her former colleagues. It was an invisible wall to the GM, but plainly visible to everyone else in her organization.

Sniper side and shelling side—sure, it's tough to be a boss in today's workplace. But follow these strategies and you'll have the tools, and insight, to get the most out of your people. And yourself.

DO THE RIGHT THING

This book contains hundreds of ideas that you can use to save time, increase profits, reduce costs, solve problems, and stay out of jail. But it doesn't stop there. It's designed to help you maximize your strengths as a leader. What is a leader? Someone with a fancy office and a title? Someone with a wall full of awards? Someone who gets coffee delivered right to her desk?

No, we take a simpler view. A leader is someone with follow-ers, and this book is dedicated to giving you the tools and insight to keep your people engaged and focused no matter what is happening around them.

Let's face it: even under the best circumstances, work is tough. And hardly anyone we know would call our recent history the best of circumstances. But it goes far beyond that. We'll start with a question: What do you like to do? Photography, dancing, cooking, working out, watching movies are just a few of the things people tell us in our pre-sentations. Now, pick your favorite and do it for eight or nine hours tomorrow. Repeat it the next day. And the next. Do it at least 40 hours the next week, and 160 hours the next month. You get the idea.

Sustaining any effort over the long haul is tough, even when we love it. Just ask Lance Armstrong, the Rolling Stones, or Michael Phelps. But it's far easier when we find meaning and community. If people feel like they're making a contribution and they're part of something bigger, they'll be more engaged. More involved.

Achieving that is even tougher for this generation of leaders because we need to manage in a tougher environment. No more of the "my way or the highway" kind of stuff that we heard when we were first starting out our careers. No, today we have to be a coun-selor, guide, and cheerleader. It's tough to have to learn a new way to lead on the fly.

This book explains in great detail how to foster meaning and community across a broad range of your biggest headaches. Not only to solve your problems, but to do so in a way that engages the heart and soul of your people.

If, at this point, you're thinking, "Meaning? Community? Heart? Soul? Are these guys nuts? I'm running a warehouse in Cleveland, not an organic bakery on the Crazy Coast. My people are lucky to have jobs. Who has time for all that feel-good stuff?" then stay with us.

It's true that most people today *do* feel fortunate to have jobs, especially given what we've all been through. And it is easier to just get the work done, take steps to keep out of court, and go home. Easier, but what's the point? Is there any other area in your life in which you're happy to just get by? If you're a parent, is your only job to make sure that your kids are alive and not in prison at the end of the day? If you play on any kind of sports team, do you show up for each game just hoping not to drop the ball and lose the game for the team?

The economy goes up and down and back up again in an endless cycle. When it's up, do you want to pursue that promotion or next job saying that you managed a crew of malcontents well enough to keep the doors open? Or do you want to be able to say that you led a team of satisfied high performers who surpassed expectations and thrived despite the odds?

It's easy to feel cynical, that your efforts don't matter, that you're just a replaceable cog. But you need to remember that every boss casts a big shadow, over all the people who depend on him. And you can do one thing, make your corner of the bureaucracy the most knowledgeable, prepared, and focused within the organization. Within any organization. You might not be able to change the world, right now, but you can put your team in a position to win.

We think of that as leadership. It's the right thing. The right thing for your customers, for your people, for you. We hope this guide will help you in your journey.

2

The Essential 10: A Short Course in Management

Ever see the movie *In Like Flint*? It's a late '60s spoof of the James Bond 007 movies. James Coburn played the suave and sophisticated Derek Flint. There is a famous scene in which Flint is showing someone his multistoried library, containing thousands of books. The visitor asks how Flint—as a raconteur, scientist, and secret agent—could possibly have time to read all those books. Flint replies, "I didn't read them. I wrote them."

Those were the days. Now, we barely have the time to read or write a text message, let alone the avalanche of e-mails, memos, and reports that we need to read each day. And don't even get us started on LinkedIn, Facebook, and Twitter. Reading industry publications, the business press, and strategic plans feels like a luxury from the era of barbershop shaves.

That's why we've created a sort of guided tour through this book. We started with the most common problems that people write to us about. Then, for each of those problems, we've identified the sections throughout the book that offer the most effective relief. Together, they offer a crash course in successful management.

But don't overlook the ultimate power tool at work: energy. Consider the journey of the Olympic torch to the games in Atlanta. At one point the rider carrying the torch fell off his bike and the torch went out. Fortunately, the rider was followed by a truck carrying the Mother Flame. Officials relit the torch and the journey resumed.

We think that's a great metaphor for work. When people first start a job, they carry their passion like the torch. And what happens? It gets blown out. How do we respond? Usually by hiding our passion. If we bring it to work at all, we keep it locked up in our desk.

That's why it's so important for us, the corner-office crowd, to be the Mother Flame at work: to look for people who need a spark and to give it to them.

SURVIVING TOUGH TIMES: THE ESSENTIAL 10

1. Innovation: How to Get Creative in Tough Times

2. Alternatives to Layoffs: How to Keep Top Talent (and Still Cut Costs)

3. Conflict Management: How to Resolve Disagreements (Without Bloodshed)

4. Fear and Mistrust: How to Overcome Negative Emotions That Infect the Workplace

5. Stress: How to Cope with Workplace Pressure

6. Apologizing: Why Managing Often Means Having to Say You're Sorry

7. Working with HR: How Human Resources Can Help You Get the Most Out of Your Team

8. Layoffs: How to Cut the Risk of Lawsuits

9. Virtual Employees: How to Manage the People You Can't See

10. Negligent Supervision: How What You Don't Do Can Cost You

HAVING A BIGGER IMPACT AT WORK: THE ESSENTIAL 10

1. 360-Degree Feedback: How to Get the Truth (and Improve Your Performance)

2. Managing 101: How to Be the Boss Today's Employees Need

3. Mission, Goal Setting, and Finding Opportunities: How to Sort Out the "Where To?" of Work

4. Time Management: How to Make the Most of Every Hour

5. Managing Up: How to Keep *Your* Boss Happy

6. Meetings: How to Get Things Done (Without Wasting Time)

7. First Days on the Job: How to Lay the Groundwork for Success

8. The Generation Gap: How to Help Everyone Get Along (and Get Things Done)

9. Documenting Performance: How to Be Fair, Complete, and Legal

10. Texts, Tweets, and the Next New Technology: How to Stay Connected (Without Losing Your Mind)

STAYING OUT OF JAIL: THE ESSENTIAL 10

1. Performance Reviews: How to Keep Employees on Track
2. Discipline: How to Change Problem Behavior
3. Termination Letters: How to Write a Document That Protects Your Company
4. Cultural Values: How to Get Past Race and Ethnicity
5. Sexual Harassment: How to Recognize and Prevent Inappropriate Behavior
6. Overtime/Comp Time: How to Pay People
7. Training: How to Keep People Learning and Growing
8. Privacy: How to Balance the Rights of Employees and Your Company
9. Medical Problems and the FMLA: How to Help an Employee Through a Personal or Family Medical Crisis
10. Job Offers: How to Structure and Negotiate a Win-Win Package

KEEPING YOUR BEST PEOPLE: THE ESSENTIAL 10

1. Leadership: How to Vary Your Style to Get Results
2. Walk the Talk: How to Align What You Say and What You Do
3. Keep Employees in the Loop: How to Fill the Information Vacuum
4. Emotional Intelligence: How to Recognize and Use the Data in Your Emotions
5. Listening Skills: How to Hear What People Really Have to Say

3

Managing Yourself

If you've ever actually paid attention to the airline safety video shown before each flight (and—just an aside—you should), then you've heard that if oxygen masks drop from the compartment above you should secure your mask first and *then* help others with theirs. After all, if you help a toddler first you may run out of oxygen before you can help yourself—and the toddler won't be able to return the favor.

It's like that in management, too. Although your job is mostly about *them*, it also needs to be at least some about *you*. Not only are you a role model for everyone else, but if you aren't keeping your own skills current, working to improve your performance, and managing all the pressures on you (such as time and stress), then you aren't being the best boss you can be.

Given that, you can't relegate responsibility for your own job performance to *your* boss. Sure, you need your boss to help set expectations and partner with you in working with the rest of the organization. But you also need to actively manage yourself. Yes, that means your head count just got one bigger. But unless you need a therapist much more than you need this book, when you manage yourself, you won't be dealing with someone who talks back, complains, whines, stabs you in the back, or refuses to do what you ask.

In other words, managing yourself can be especially rewarding, and before we get into how to manage others, we'll make sure you're doing a good job of managing yourself.

MANAGING UP: HOW TO KEEP *YOUR* BOSS HAPPY

Know the Issue

If you live under the iron fist of a homeowner's association (as a growing number of people do), then you have been trained to keep the board (or rules committee) happy. You ask permission before making major changes to your home—and even then only after developing a plan and winning the assent of your neighbors. You respond promptly to problems. You anticipate maintenance issues and stay ahead of what needs to be done. In short, you make the neighborhood—and by extension the association—look good.

In business we call this managing up. It's the process of managing your boss's expectations, being responsive, and maintaining a good relationship. ("Managing up" should not be confused with "kissing up." Managing up is being proactive about what you should be doing anyway, and demonstrating that you are on top of things. Kissing up requires putting the boss's ego ahead of the needs of the business, and involves a nauseating amount of insincerity and loss of dignity.)

Managing up is always important (the bottom line is that one of your most important jobs is to make your boss look good), but especially in tough times. After all, if layoffs loom, do you want to be seen as an indispensable team player or as someone your boss can't rely on?

Take Action

- *Know your boss.* It sounds like a no-brainer—of course you know your boss! But you'd be surprised how often we hear, "I don't know what my boss wants," or some similar refrain. Yes, in a perfect world your boss should tell you what he or she wants—and how. But we don't live in a perfect world, and if your boss isn't forthcoming, make it your business to find out. You should know what your priorities, deliverables, and deadlines are. You should also understand your boss's personality and style and (within reason) accommodate it.

- *Take ownership.* Unless you work for a control freak (our sympathy if you do), you don't have a job in which you should sit at your desk until you're told what to do. *You* should decide what to do—what the priorities are, how to allocate resources and make assignments, how to meet your deliverables. If you're uncertain about a course of action, don't just plop into a chair in your boss's office and say, "What should I do?" Instead, come up with a plan, or options, and ask your boss for feedback. Think about it this way: If your boss has to figure everything out, why does he or she need *you*?

- *Advocate.* There's a reason that every industry and special interest has lobbyists in Washington: somebody has to fight for attention and resources if, say, the honey industry is ever to get on an agenda dominated by, say, war and the economy. Although your boss presumably has less on his or her plate than the President or the Speaker of the House, you should still assume that you are not his or her only priority and, well, lobby accordingly.

Advocate for your department or team by focusing on your contribution to the bottom line. Remind your boss what you've done today, or this week, to make the organization stronger. Advocate for the resources (money, equipment, supplies) that you need to be effective. If you see opportunities, advocate for exploiting those opportunities; don't settle for the status quo. And advocate for your team. Celebrate their accomplishments (collective and individual) and offer credit where credit is due. Watch your team's commitment increase exponentially if they believe you are fighting for them. And remember that the better they look, the better you look: No one ever thought less of a coach if he developed a team of all-stars.

- *Avoid surprises.* As you advocate for your team, your boss should advocate for you. But he or she can't do that (or help you through a rough patch) without being in the loop. Is your team or department going to miss a deadline or exceed your budget? Tell your boss *before* that happens. Have you had to discipline an employee? Tell your boss. Are you exceeding your goals? You get the idea. The last thing you want is your boss's boss, or the CEO, or HR, or your boss's peer, to ask about something happening under your watch and have your boss respond with a blank, clueless stare.

- *Be a good soldier.* Your boss will make decisions you don't like. But once the decision is made, fall into line and offer your public support. Sometimes, that means implementing policies that you don't agree with or following a path that doesn't feel right to you. Still, it's important to present a united front. Unless, of course, your boss is asking you to do something illegal or unethical, in which case you have even bigger concerns to address. If you openly disagree with your boss ("I don't think this is right, but I have to do it"), then you undermine your boss's authority. Ultimately, your team will be harder to manage because those who agree with you will continue to search for ways to undermine the boss's decision. If you find that you're often holding your nose and doing things you don't believe in, then it may be time to look for another job.

Real-Life Example

The sales manager's boss checked in regularly to see how things were going, and the sales manager's answer was always the same: "Fine." And to her things *were* fine—the team was on target to meet its goals, problems had been resolved, and she felt it would waste her boss's time to recap daily minutiae.

But to her boss, "Fine" was like fingernails on a chalkboard. The boss was a realist who knew that problems happen, that clients offer a lot of feedback, and that salespeople need a lot of attention. Hearing that things were fine left her wondering whether the sales manager was clueless about what was going on or was too inept to be doing anything. Knowing that things couldn't really be fine, she began micromanaging and doing end runs around the manager to get information directly from the sales force. The pattern inevitably resulted in a confrontation, and both parties were shocked by how the other saw the situation. Together, they worked out a compromise. The boss stopped micromanaging when the sales manager stopped answering "Fine," and instead offered a summary of the issues that had arisen, the action she had taken, and the scuttlebutt she was hearing from the field. Now the boss was getting information, and she felt confident she knew what was happening and wouldn't look bad to *her* boss.

Get More Information

> *The Courageous Follower: Standing Up to & for Our Leaders,* 3rd. ed., Ira Chaleff, Berrett-Koehler, 2009.
>
> *Managing Up: How to Forget an Effective Relationship with Those Above You,* Rosanne Badowski, Currency, 2003.

YOUR CAREER: HOW TO STAY COMPETITIVE IN THE JOB MARKET

Your career and Madonna's are alike in one very important way: Without constant attention, they will wither and die.

You don't want that to happen. Nor do you want it to be something that you define at the end, when you're ready to retire and your "career" is nothing more than a list of the jobs you've held. Why? Because unless you own a business, you're just borrowing your job— your career is what you own. You alone chart its path, maneuver its ups and downs, and make course corrections as needed. You alone will reap the rewards of a career well managed—or wonder what might have been.

We hope that sounds like opportunity, not pressure. If so, you're ready to make the most of what lies ahead. Here's how.

Take Action

- *Decide what career path you want to pursue.* If you're reading this book, odds are that you are either already a boss or about to be a boss. Congratulations! But now what? Do you want to be a boss at this level forever? (It's okay if you do; it's just important that you know the answer to the question.) Are you eager to move up the ladder and get more responsibility and greater rewards—perhaps, ultimately several steps up the ladder? Or would you prefer to get off the boss track and work instead at honing specialized skills? (Perhaps you just want to be a great nurse and not manage other nurses.) Picture yourself in two years, five years, ten years. What would you like to be doing at each of those milestones?

- *Identify potential obstacles on your path.* Once you've evaluated where you are and where you want to be, consider what you need to do to get from here to there. Do you simply need more (or different) experience, or do you need to learn new skills? Do you need a degree that you don't currently have? Whatever it is you need, devise a plan for getting it. Keep in mind that reaching your long-term goal may mean a short-term detour. For example, in some organizations international experience is a definite plus. In that situation, you'd be better off pursuing a two-year assignment overseas even though it would take you out of the corporate office for a while. It may also be that you need related experience in a related department. For example, to get to the top of the sales organization you may need to spend time in marketing.

- *Decide what you're willing to do.* Are you truly willing to do whatever it takes to reach your goal, or are there some deal breakers? For example, what if your path requires that overseas assignment? Or relocating to another state? What if it means a stint doing something you actively dislike? Now is the time to figure out what you will compromise and what you won't. If there are things you won't do, now may be the time to reassess the path you've outlined.

- *Ask yourself 12 questions.* If you're unsure about whether you're in the right place, the Gallup organization has identified 12 questions (based on 80,000 in-depth interviews) to help you assess whether your workplace fosters effective performance. (See "12 Questions to Measure Your Effectiveness" later in the chapter.) If your organization doesn't score well, it may be time to seek a better environment.

- *Know yourself.* The more you know about yourself the better. Do what you can to find out. Subject yourself to a 360-degree feedback (we will get to this later in the chapter) and use the results. Find out what your emotional intelligence is (see "Emotional Intelligence: How to Recognize and Use the Data in Your Emotions" in Chapter 6) and develop the skills that are especially relevant to your work. In general, pursue opportunities that will help illuminate your strengths so you are clear about what you have to offer and where your real value lies. And work now to overcome your flaws so you are prepared for what lies ahead.

- *Keep current in technology.* Like it or not, technology is a big part of the work environment today, and that isn't going to change. You'll be less marketable if you aren't technosavvy. Be readily familiar with basic programs like word processing and spreadsheets, but knowledge of other programs is helpful, too. (And if there is technology unique to your industry, pay particular attention to that.) Beyond that, explore consumer technology, such as Twitter, smart phones, and augmented-reality applications. Without that knowledge, you run the risk of seeming out of touch. And you never know when being able to use such devices may help you better connect with a target market or find a new way to solve a business problem.

- *Keep current in your industry.* Assuming you intend to stay in the field you're in now, commit to being well-informed on what's happening. Visit industry Web sites, join industry associations (and don't forget to go to their meetings), and check out the latest books on the subject. It can only help you to be seen as the expert in the field. (And if you're not planning to stay in your current field, why are you still in it?)

- *Pursue opportunities.* With your career at stake, don't sit back and wait to be handed opportunities. Pursue them—aggressively. Volunteer to head special projects or task forces. Ask for new assignments. Seek training.

- *Be visible.* Think of your workplace as the *Cheers* bar—everybody should know your name. You don't want to be obnoxious about it, but make an effort to be friendly. Volunteer for things that get you noticed by people outside your department. Make sure your boss (and his or her boss) knows what you are up to and what you're accomplishing. Take the time to promote what other people are accomplishing, too; it helps keep you focused on what's working, and it builds a lot of goodwill.

- *Maintain your network.* You'll never know everything, and sooner or later you'll want to call in favors or seek expertise.

That will be much easier if you have an extended network. Start with key people in your organization, but network in industry groups, too. And don't forget such social networks as LinkedIn or Facebook. When you accomplish something significant, let people know.

- *Talk to competitors.* It used to be that the competition was the enemy. Today, competitors could just as well be collaborators or colleagues. So take opportunities to get to know your competitors—not to give away company secrets, but to explore possibilities.

- *Keep your résumé current.* You never know, unfortunately, when you may need it. Beyond that, keeping it current will help you focus on what you've accomplished and what you have to offer. In other words, it will help you think about yourself from a marketing perspective.

- *Take off your rose-colored glasses.* The economy—and your company's prospects—are less predictable than ever. That's why it's important to develop worst-case scenarios as well as best-case scenarios. Contingency plans should be just that: thoughts about what you'd do in a wide range of scenarios.

- *Be willing to follow a path.* Life happens. Sometimes we get to a milestone along our path and figure out we've been on the wrong path. What looked good from afar doesn't look good at all when we're in it. If that happens, be willing to accept that your career path isn't right for you and begin developing a new one. Of course, if you're miserable in a situation you know will end soon anyway, then you may be better off sticking it out. But a more general unhappiness is a good reason to look around. The odds of a major shift in how you feel if you just wait long enough are slim.

Get More Information

Gray Matters: The Workplace Survival Guide, Bob Rosner, Allan Halcrow, and John Lavin, Wiley, 2003.

The Pathfinder: How to Choose or Change Your Career for a Lifetime of Satisfaction and Success, Nicholas Lore, Fireside, 1998.

We Are All Self-Employed: How to Take Control of Your Career, 2nd ed., Cliff Hakim, Berrett-Koehler, 2003.

What Color Is Your Parachute?2009 A Practical Manual for Job-Hunters and Career-Changers, Richard N. Bolles, Ten Speed Press, 2008.

---

12 Questions to Measure Your Effectiveness

After 80,000 in-depth interviews with managers in more than 400 companies, the Gallup organization says that measuring the strength of a workplace can be simplified to just 12 questions. You can use this list two ways. First, assess how well the work environment fosters what you're trying to do. Second, use it (answer honestly) to assess how effectively you're creating a positive environment for the people who report to you. Are there some things here that you could be doing better?

1. Do I know what is expected of me at work?
2. Do I have the materials and equipment I need to do my work right?

continued

3. At work, do I have the opportunity to do what I do best every day?

4. In the last seven days, have I received recognition or praise for doing good work?

5. Does my supervisor, or someone at work, seem to care about me as a person?

6. Is there someone at work who encourages my development?

7. At work, do my opinions seem to count?

8. Does the mission/purpose of my company make me feel my job is important?

9. Are my coworkers committed to doing quality work?

10. Do I have a best friend at work?

11. In the last six months, has someone at work talked to me about my progress?

12. This last year, have I had opportunities at work to learn and grow?

Source: First, Break All the Rules: What the World's Greatest Managers Do Differently, Marcus Buckingham and Curt Coffman, Simon & Schuster, 1999.

360-DEGREE FEEDBACK: HOW TO GET THE TRUTH (AND IMPROVE YOUR PERFORMANCE)

Know the Issue

Top executives (read: high-profile CEOs) in big, publicly traded companies routinely get feedback from all sides. Their performance draws comment (often very public comment) from others in the organization, the board of directors, Wall Street analysts, the press, and a lot of anonymous people posting on Internet bulletin boards. If they don't have a sense of how they're perceived, they just aren't paying attention.

The rest of us can often muddle through happily oblivious to how we are perceived—and to our biggest flaws as managers. It happens because everyone thinks we already know, because they are afraid to confront the boss, or because nobody asked. Yet without feedback from all sides we can continue to work with blind spots, holding ourselves back.

Fortunately, it's pretty easy to get the feedback you need—stay with us—through a 360-degree feedback process. Yes, we know that 360-degree feedback has a bad reputation in many places. That's because the concept is good but the execution quite often is not.

That's really too bad, because it's actually pretty easy to do 360-degree feedback well. And done well, it can be the best tool you have for improving your performance and getting ahead. (And yes, using 360-degree feedback to develop your subordinates is a good idea, too.)

Take Action

- *Follow the Four Commandments.* Leadership guru Marshall Goldsmith has developed what he calls the Four Commandments of 360-degree feedback, and they are well worth following:

  1. Let go of the past.
  2. Tell the truth.
  3. Be supportive and helpful—not cynical or negative.
  4. Pick something about yourself to improve—so everyone is focused more on "improving" than "judging."

- *Disconnect 360-degree feedback from reviews or compensation*. Unfortunately, some employees see a 360 as a way to reward their friends or punish their enemies. One way to reduce this problem is to separate the results from performance reviews or compensation in any way. Simply use them as a tool to get feedback and improve performance—you'll reduce the odds of vindictive behavior.

- *Don't limit 360-degree feedback to lower levels*. In our experience, 360s are used less often the higher up you go in an organization. But unless you believe that people learn everything they ever need to know early in their careers—and we don't—the need for feedback does not diminish. The 360-degree feedback is valuable for lower-level supervisors but essential at the highest levels.

- *Explain the process before you start*. It isn't helpful when a 360-degree evaluation form simply appears in someone's in-box. When that happens, people are uncertain about what it is, how it will be used, or what's expected of them. People are in a better position to provide valuable feedback when they are well-informed up front. Take the time to outline the process and, yes, sell the value. After all, if the feedback they offer results in real behavior change, then all employees stand to benefit from the process.

- *Keep it confidential*. To give honest feedback, people need to be sure their comments will be kept confidential. When it comes to keeping things hush-hush, most companies resemble Swiss cheese, so don't be surprised if people are initially skeptical of the process.

- *Provide structured feedback and action plans.* This is our biggest complaint about how 360s are handled in most companies: It's all about data collection and very little is done about changing behavior based on the feedback. Put your emphasis on improvement and it won't be feedback at all—it will become feed-forward.

Real-Life Example

One of Marshall Goldsmith's favorite examples of how to use a 360 concerns the feedback he got to change his behavior. "How do we stop making destructive comments? That was my problem several years ago," he reports. "I had my staff do a full 360-degree evaluation of my behavior. The feedback said I was in the eighth percentile on 'avoids destructive comments'—meaning that 92 percent of the people in the world are better at it than I was. I had failed a test that I wrote!

"So I talked to my staff. I said, 'I feel good about much of my feedback. Here's one thing I want to do better: Quit making destructive comments. If you ever hear me make another destructive comment about another person, I'll pay you $10 each time you bring it to my attention. I'm going to break this habit.'

"This policy was in force in our office for several weeks. And it cost me money. But eventually I brought up my score to the 96th percentile."

Get More Information

The Art and Science of 360° Feedback, Richard Lepsinger and Anntoinette D. Lucia, Pfeiffer, 1997.

High Maintenance Employees, Katherine Graham Leviss, Sourcebooks, 2005.

What Got You Here Won't Get You There: How Successful People Become Even More Successful, Marshall Goldsmith (with Mark Reiter), Hyperion, 2007.

MISSION, GOAL SETTING, AND FINDING OPPORTUNITIES: HOW TO SORT OUT THE "WHERE TO?" OF WORK

Know the Issue

If you're like most people today, chances are good there is a water bottle within arm's reach as you read this. Take a moment and check out its label. You'll probably see something you've never noticed before: an expiration date. Yep, water can go bad—at least according to an article in the *Wall Street Journal*.

An expiration date for water seems downright silly. But some expiration dates are appropriate, such as those for your organizational and departmental goals. So often we assume that our mission and goals are fixed in stone that we rarely pause to even think about them, let alone reevaluate whether they still make sense. And if we're not thinking about our overall purpose, it's pretty hard to spot—or grab—new opportunities as they come along.

This sort of vigilance is especially important in tough times. Without it, you can be blindsided by new developments or changes in your market, or you could miss some chances to break away from the pack. So take a moment to step back and think about where you're going—and why.

Take Action

- *Know your mission.* Chances are good that your organization has a mission. But most departments within it don't. See the problem? Identifying a unique and important mission for each department keeps everyone focused and helps give meaning to what people do each day. Don't currently have a mission for your team? Set aside time in your next staff meeting to create one.

- *Ask yourself regularly what you're trying to accomplish.* It's so easy to lose your way at work today. Or to get sucked into someone else's agenda. That's why it's so important to ask yourself, and your team—on a regular basis—who you are, what you do well, where you want to be going, and how you are going to get there.

- *Write down your goals.* Ask most managers and they'll say that they know their goals. Many will then point to their heads, saying they are firmly planted in their brains. To be effective, goals need to be written down. It's going to be a lot harder to meet your goals if you're the only one who knows what they are.

- *Describe the desired outcome.* Most of us think of our goals in negative terms—we'll decrease costs, we'll reduce turnover, and we'll be more timely on meeting our deadlines. But it's always best to phrase them in positive terms, because it's more effective to remind yourself of the behavior that you want to see—for instance, we'll increase savings or strengthen employee retention.

- *Keep goals measurable.* Keeping your goals nebulous robs you of the opportunity to see your progress toward achieving them. That's why it's important to be specific; for example, "Each week we'll contact 20 new prospects" instead of "We'll increase sales contacts."

- *Create deadlines.* Let's face it: most of us need a deadline to get anything done. It's no different with your individual or organizational goals.

- *Keep your goals realistic, but also a stretch.* Goals that are too easy or impossible to achieve effectively aren't goals at all. You've got to hit the sweet spot: not so easy they don't get you anywhere, but not so hard that they wear you down.

- *Keep your eyes on the horizon for new opportunities.* A company that sold tackle boxes started getting calls from "one-named women" in New York ordering their product. You probably guessed what was happening: fashion models liked the boxes for storing their makeup. Soon, the makeup boxes became the most profitable part of the company.

    New opportunities are out there, but only if you are looking for them. Spotting them often takes the same mindset that facilitates innovation. Foster creative thinking in yourself and others (see "Innovation: How to Get Creative in Tough Times" in Chapter 6).

- *Celebrate your successes.* Reaching well-constructed goals will take hard work, cooperation, and creativity. So when you reach the goal, celebrate. That means do something more impressive than a few "attaboys." Mark the occasion as a group, and celebrate the innovations and insights that got you there. If you don't make a big deal about meeting goals, watch how hard it is to generate interest in your next set.

Manage Up

Share your department mission and goals with your boss. Goals and mission statements have a funny way of becoming infectious. Once one group does it, others tend to join in.

Real-Life Example

"This past New Year's Eve, I got together with significant people in my life to talk about what we wanted to materialize in the coming year," wrote a Workplace911.com reader. She explained that she had plenty of magazines, construction paper, glue sticks, and poster board. The goal, by the end of the evening, was to complete a poster that had pictures of what the partygoers wanted to achieve, along with motivating words.

Afterward, people were asked to put the poster in a visible place as a reminder of what they were working toward. "I've chosen images of physical exercise, spirituality, family, and relationship," she said. "We will meet in April, July, October, and December to see how we are doing in meeting our goals. I can tell you that I'm well on my way to achieving my goals, and it's only March! I've gotten a job that meets everything I've wanted, I've already lost 15 pounds, I'm practicing my spirituality, and things are improving with my family. Having a group to be accountable to makes a huge difference."

Get More Information

Managing Workplace Chaos: Workplace Solutions for Managing Information, Paper, Time and Stress, Patricia Hutchings, Amacom, 2002.

Never Eat Alone and Other Secrets to Success, One Relationship at a Time, Keith Ferrazzi, Currency, 2005.

TIME MANAGEMENT: HOW TO MAKE THE MOST OF EVERY HOUR

Know the Issue

If you're a television programmer, a week can seem like an eternity. There are all those hours to fill with episodes of something. And not just any something, either: something that will attract a large (and faithful) audience. If you've surfed channels lately you know how hard it is to pull that off.

For the rest of us, a week's worth of hours never seem anywhere near enough time in which to enjoy family activities, take care of the house, pursue our hobbies, exercise, run errands, sleep, or even begin to stay on top of everything we need to do at work. Juggling all those balls has never been easy, but in a tight economy it can be even harder. "Do more with less" may sound great to management gurus and stock analysts, but in the real world how do we pull that off? Although there is no silver bullet, there are some things you can do to deal with time on *your* terms.

Take Action

- *Know how you spend your time.* It's tough to manage the unknown, so understanding how you spend your time is a vital first step in getting control of it. That probably sounds obvious. But many people are surprised to discover that how they believe they're spending their time and how they're actually spending their time are very different.

  The best way to find out is to keep a time log, and there are several ways to do that. The lowest-tech option is simply to jot down what you do as you do it. You can make the list as general or specific as suits you, but to avoid turning the time tracking into a full-time job, you may just want to use check marks beside each primary activity to indicate each time you were interrupted. You can also track your time more generally, using five broad categories instead of individual activities. We like the categories developed by Small Business Canada: Putting Out Fires, Dealing With Interruptions, Doing Planned Tasks, Working Uninterrupted, and Uninterrupted Downtime. Log how much time each day falls under these headings.

There are also higher-tech options available. They range from job- and work-tracking software to iPhone applications, but they all offer means to keep track of your time.

Whichever method you pick, choose a typical work week. Track your time for at least two weeks to get a meaningful average of how you use your time. When you have that information, look for trends. Where are you spending too much time? Where are you not spending enough time? What can you *not* do to make room for what you do need to do? Make a not-to-do list (for more about that, see Chapter 1).

- *Pursue priorities.* If there were a *Billboard* chart of hit mantras, "Don't sweat the small stuff" would be near the top—ahead of "Don't worry, be happy" and neck and neck with "Brush after meals." So why do we sweat the small stuff? (Admit it—you do. Refer to your time log if you doubt it.) It's partly for the same reason that we're more likely to pay attention to a yapping poodle than to our spouse—it's noisier and more easily satisfied. But we also sweat the small stuff because we aren't sure what the big stuff is. Or, perhaps more accurately, we don't know which tasks best support the big stuff.

There are a couple of ways to find out. If you think like an engineer, you'll probably prefer creating a priority grid:

important	important	urgent and important
not important	neither urgent nor important	urgent
	not urgent	urgent

Put each task in the appropriate quadrant of the grid. Although too often we spend our time on tasks in the lower right (urgent but not important), we should spend more time in the upper right (urgent and important). If you focus on activities in that quadrant first—and do the rest only after those are complete—then you'll find that you are more productive.

If you don't think like an engineer, you'll probably prefer the Pickle Jar Theory popularized by marketing guru Jeremy Wright. The theory works like this: Imagine a large, empty pickle jar. Fill it with large stones. Is it full? No, because you can still get small pebbles into the jar. So do that. Now is it full? No, because you can still add sand to the jar. So now it's full. Except that it isn't, because you can still add water. *Now* it's full.

What does this have to do with your time? Nothing, unless you literally like to fill jars or you appreciate a good metaphor. The stones, of course, represent priorities—the really important stuff. The pebbles are things we actually enjoy doing. The sand is other stuff that we have to do. And the water is the annoying stuff that seeps in everywhere and clutters our lives. Unfortunately, most of us fill our jar with water first and then try adding the big stones. How well does *that* work? To put this theory more simply: do the important stuff first, fill in the open time with things you enjoy, and don't sweat the small stuff.

- *Know yourself.* When is an hour not an hour? If you have high energy and are in an environment you like, an hour can go by quickly—and you can get a lot done. When you have low energy and are in an environment you don't like, an hour can feel like three and you'll struggle to get anything done. The truth is, time is shaped by our biorhythms and personalities, and when we match the most demanding tasks with our peak times we are much more productive. Consider the following:

  - *Energy level.* When does your biological clock give you the most energy? Morning? Afternoon? Late at night? What factors give you energy (for example, sunshine, exercise, music, fruit)? What factors deplete your energy (cloudy days, heavy food, depressing news)?

  - *Optimal environment.* Consider light, noise level, music, level of clutter, color, and your work space.

Get More Information

> *Brain Rules: 12 Principles for Surviving and Thriving at Work,*
> *Home and School,* John Medina, Pear, 2008.
>
> *How To Be a Star at Work: 9 Breakthrough Strategies You Need*
> *to Succeed,* Robert E. Kelley, Times, 1999.

STRESS: HOW TO COPE WITH WORKPLACE PRESSURE

Know the Issue

Imagine being Michael Phelps arriving in Beijing in the summer of 2008, facing the worldwide expectation to swim better than you ever have before and, in the process, win more gold medals than any previous Olympian. Better yet, imagine being Captain Chesley Sullenberger, faced with having to successfully land US Airways flight 1549 on the Hudson River. Now, *there's* job stress. And although most job stress isn't that extreme, it may feel like it is during tough times.

That's because much of what happens in organizations—particularly during a down economy—acts like a shot of adrenaline in boosting stress. Among the contributors are layoffs (and the threat of layoffs), increased demands for overtime, pressure to work at your best all the time, and increased expectations that aren't matched by increased job satisfaction or rewards. The only thing worse than constantly being told to "do more with less"? Having to tell the people who work for you to do more with less. No wonder those knots in your shoulders feel bigger.

Stress was designed to get us out of immediate trouble—being chased by an animal or threatened by a storm. The biological reaction is designed to be fast, hence the term "fight or flight." But modern stress is usually anything but fast. It drags on for days, weeks, or even years. Our bodies just aren't designed to deal with this kind of chronic and debilitating reaction to the events around us.

Still, there's no reason to get stressed about how stressed you are. Although it's true that you often can't eliminate the causes of stress, you can almost always control how you respond to stress. And there are numerous things you can do to (exhale) breathe a little easier and create a healthier and more productive workforce.

Take Action

- *Don't multitask.* Sure, your kids make it look easy to do homework, surf the Internet, text their friends, and watch TV—all at once. In fact, the human brain is not well suited to multitask, and when we try, everything we do is slower and less effective. (Sorry, kids.) It also adds to our stress. So focus on one thing at a time and do it efficiently.

- *Learn your own stress signals.* Before a heart attack, our body often sends signals that our stress level is approaching dangerous levels. Unfortunately, most of us miss those signals. That's why it's important to learn your own signals, which may include sleep disturbances, stomachaches, or irritability. Putting your early warning system to work will not only help your health, but will also have a positive impact on the health of the people who work with and for you.

- *Cut yourself some slack.* The more you take on, the harder it is to do it all well. So don't. Accept that you can't do everything perfectly and focus your energy on those things that are most important. Unless you're an airline pilot or a brain surgeon,

85 percent is good enough for many projects. Better to get it done and move on than to agonize about that last 15 percent.

- *Avoid conflict.* You know who they are: the office gossips and drama queens who anticipate disaster, suspect everyone of hiding something, and love to stir up trouble. All the negativity they brew and feed on ratchets up the stress level. So avoid those people as much as possible and look for your drama on TV.

- *Get up earlier.* The "I'm late for work!" mad dash is a staple of TV and comic strip humor because we can all relate to it. But just because it's familiar doesn't make it a good idea. Skipping breakfast, fuming impatiently as we wait for the bus or subway or as we sit in rush-hour gridlock, and racing in at the last minute (or after) all add up to *starting* the day in a high-stress state. Giving yourself even an extra 10 to 15 minutes in the morning will give you time to settle in and start your day prepared.

- *Feel the burn.* Study after study shows that exercise reduces stress. Not surprisingly, the more you invest in exercise, the greater your return. That means that at least 30 minutes of activity that elevates your heart rate is ideal. But even shorter bursts of activity are better than nothing. No time to work out? Park farther away from the office. Take the stairs. Get up and go talk to a colleague instead of sending an e-mail.

- *Tune in.* You've heard the quote, "Music to soothe a savage beast." Well, the quote (by the English playwright William Congreve) is actually "Music hath charms to soothe a savage *breast*," (not *beast*), but his point is still valid. Music *does* help calm us down and alleviate stress. Happily, we live in the iPod age, where we can listen to music without subjecting everyone in the office to our taste.

- *Make friends*. Those sage philosophers the Beatles were on to something when they sang about getting by with a little help from their friends. At work, turning to friends for help when you're overwhelmed and need an extra hand can mean the difference between keeping your head above water and getting pulled under by the sharks. (Of course, you need to return the favor when called upon.) Away from work, having a friend who will listen as you vent about your day (and offer support and empathy as you do) is a proven stress reducer. And again, you should return the favor, too.

- *Eat better.* It's not your imagination that a big meal leaves you feeling lethargic. On the other hand, being hungry can make you irritable and make it harder to focus. A steady level of blood sugar is better for helping you feel better and, in the process, reduce stress. Try eating smaller portions more frequently, instead of larger meals. And be sure that those portions are more often a fruit smoothie than an order of fries.

- *Drink (and smoke) less.* A glass of wine or evening cocktail feels relaxing, so it's counterintuitive that alcohol actually isn't helpful in fighting stress. When the immediate effects of a drink wear off the result is often *higher* anxiety. And more than one drink in the evening can interfere with your sleep. As for smoking, the dangers are well-documented elsewhere. Beyond the long-term dangers, nicotine is a stimulant (yeah, that'll help cut stress), and having to step outside in a Chicago winter to sneak some puffs isn't going to reduce your stress, either.

- *Laugh.* One surefire way to cut through the stress in any situation is with a big laugh, so don't take the situation—or yourself—too seriously. Keep it clean, but find ways to bring some levity to the job. (Just don't make the joke at the expense of someone who reports to you—that's never funny.) Your shoulder muscles—and your colleagues—will thank you.

Get More Information

Love It, Don't Leave It: 26 Ways to Get What You Want at Work, Beverly Kaye and Sharon Jordan-Evans, Berrett-Koehler, 2003.

PROJECT MANAGEMENT: HOW TO STAY ON TOP OF WHAT YOU NEED TO DO

Know the Issue

Who are the patron saints of project management? Julia Child, Paula Deen, and Bobby Flay, for starters. Yes, really. That's because recipes are the greatest project management tool ever invented. Think about it. Recipes

- Have a clear purpose
- Itemize all the resources needed
- Spell out the timeline and ideal work environment
- Specify the correct tools
- Identify milestones
- Establish time frames
- Offer step-by-step instructions to achieve the desired results

What more you could ask of a project management tool?

And yet many people who wouldn't dream of making potato salad without a cookbook in front of them will rush into a major project without much (if any) preparation at all. Unless you're either incredibly brilliant or lucky, or both, that's a recipe for failure—or at least for costly errors along the way.

Given that project management is an important part of any boss's job, that's a recipe you can't afford to follow. Fortunately, you don't have to. Instead, try the following recipe for success.

Take Action

- *Define the project.* This step is akin to deciding what you want to make. What's the purpose of the project? What is the project objective? In other words, why are you doing this? You should be able to summarize the project in a single sentence. If you can't, the project is probably too vague or too big. Don't move forward until the definition is crystal clear. If you need to go back to your boss (or whomever) for clarification, do it.

- *Identify your resources.* Think of this as listing ingredients. What will you need to complete the project? Consider the people you'll need (both in terms of necessary expertise and man-hours), the budget required, and any materials. These materials may be tangible (for example, 500 three-ring binders) and intangible (access to certain computer files or a specified drive). If you were cooking, the ingredients list would only be the start; you'd also have to think about where to buy the ingredients. That's true in project management, too. Consider who (or which department) controls the resources you need. How can you best manage a relationship with those people?

- *List the key steps.* Break down the overall project into a series of crucial events. For example, suppose you were planning a new office tower. To get it done, there would be several key steps: raise (or earmark) the funds, identify the site, secure the site (through lease or purchase of the land), hire an architect, get a design, establish a budget, hire a contractor, get it built, and so forth. The idea is to give yourself an overview of what needs to be done.

- *List the detailed steps.* Once you have the overview, break it down into its component parts. Identifying the site, for example, might include evaluating the existing infrastructure, investigating zoning restrictions, doing an environmental impact report, and so forth. How detailed the list is will vary depending on how complex the project is.

- *Figure out your timeline.* Once you know what needs to be done, you can figure out how long it will take. Develop a timeline in increments that suit the project. The office tower, for example, will probably be measured in months (or even years); other projects might be measured in days. Identify key milestones in your timeline. (For example, the city must approve the plans by this date if construction is to begin on time.)

- *Develop a plan.* With the steps and timeline in place, put it all together as a plan. And then get feedback on the plan. Invite members of your team (and other stakeholders) to look it over. Does the plan seem workable? Or do they see potential trouble spots? Incorporate the feedback and adjust the plan as needed.

- *Expect the unexpected.* If your plan has no margin for error, you're in trouble before you ever get started. Anticipate that something will go wrong, and have an idea of how you'll deal with it when it happens. For example, suppose that an unexpectedly heavy rainy season delays construction. How will you get back on track? Work with the experts on your team to identify the areas where problems are most likely.

- *Remove obstacles early.* You can expect most projects to have insufficient budget, too few resources, too little time, or some combination of those factors. The project can be tweaked to adjust in response to some of those demands. But if some part of the plan is genuinely unworkable (an office tower simply can't be constructed in three weeks), then the time to raise the issue is at the outset. Put the problem on the table and work through it. Do not wait until well into the project to raise a red flag.

- *Monitor your progress.* Once the progress is under way, monitor your milestones and make sure things are happening as they are supposed to. If they aren't, find out why and, if need be, adjust the plan.

- *Document everything.* Don't depend on yourself or anyone else to remember everything that transpires. Document what happens: who, what, when, where, why, and how. Not only will you have a safety net if something goes wrong, but whoever does a similar project next will be able to take advantage of whatever you learned.

- *Prevent surprises.* Keep everyone who needs to know (or thinks they need to know) informed throughout. Don't let anyone come to you later and say, "Why didn't I know . . ."

Manage Up

Keep your boss in the loop. Make sure that your boss always knows what's going on. And be honest; don't paint an overly optimistic picture.

Get More Information

> *Absolute Beginner's Guide to Project Management,* 2nd ed., Greg Horine, Que Publishing, 2009.
>
> *The Fast Forward MBA in Project Management*, Eric Verzuh, Wiley, 2008.

WALK THE TALK: HOW TO ALIGN WHAT YOU SAY AND WHAT YOU DO

Know the Issue

"It's too late for me to quit," the father says to his son, lighting a cigarette, "but you're young. Don't you start."

What are the odds this son won't take up the habit?

Unfortunately, do as I say, not as I do, isn't very credible parenting—or managing. If you consistently say one thing and do another, your employees are guaranteed to follow your actions.

Granted, you can't always follow your own advice. Occasionally, you get new information, or change your mind, or forget. But if you can walk your talk most of the time, you'll be out ahead of the pack.

Take Action

- *Follow the rules.* You're looking for trouble if you believe there is one set of rules for you and a different set for your employees. If you insist on punctuality, for example, don't show up for work whenever you want to without explanation. If you ask people not to eat at their desks, don't let people catch you dropping sandwich crumbs into your keyboard. If you don't respect the rules, others won't either. They'll just break them behind your back.

- *Make decisions based on core values, not expediency.* Business gurus James C. Collins and Jerry I. Porras have built their careers on the simple premise that the companies that do best over the long haul are those that formulate core values, such as honesty, ethics, or continual improvement, and stick to them, even when it would be easier not to. Their book, *Built to Last*, cites examples that range from Procter & Gamble to Wal-Mart.

  This is good advice for individual managers, too. If you say you value honesty, then be honest, even if it means admitting that your competitor's product might better serve a client's need. If you say you value creativity, don't postpone your decisions so long that every new idea dies on the vine. Employees know that values are tested when times are tough, and they'll look to you to pass the test. If you do, they'll know they can count on you to support them when they rely on those values to make a decision.

- *Don't be careless.* Months have passed, and you can barely remember that you had to make this decision once before. You certainly can't remember what you decided. And if you can't, no one else will either, right? Wrong. You can count on at least one employee who will recall exactly what you decided.

Before you make a decision, stop and consider the precedent you've set. Then follow the precedent unless you have a really good reason not to. If you can't remember the precedent, ask.

- *When you don't walk the talk, explain why.* Times will occur when you'll have to do something that appears inconsistent with what you've said. For instance, suppose a core value is to ensure customer satisfaction. That may be a great overall philosophy, but you may have a customer who is never happy—one who demands endless corrections, custom options, and special treatment. Suppose you run the numbers and realize that the time invested in this customer is so great that you can't make a profit on his jobs.

  It would be a smart decision to decline further business from him. To your employees, however, that might seem like you've abandoned your values and that all the work they did to satisfy the customer was a waste of time. Save the situation by explaining why you've decided to walk away from his business. Employees may not agree with every decision, but they'll respect your integrity and the fact that you were open about your reasoning.

- *Face the music.* If you articulate values and then act in a way that contradicts them, it's only reasonable to expect employees to call you on it. When they do, pay attention. Strength will come from rethinking your actions and apologizing if need be. Don't be "right" just because you're the boss.

Stay Out of Jail

Enforce the rules. You don't want to find yourself in court listening to evidence proving that you enforced the rules inconsistently or didn't enforce them at all. Don't ignore the rules that are inconvenient or that you don't agree with.

Real-Life Example

"They say we should provide the best possible customer service," says Charles, an employee of a retail store that promotes its excellent service. "Service is the whole focus of the training we get. We hear the mantra every day, and they include examples of what they want in every employee newsletter. But they don't really mean it."

Charles points out that employees were docked pay if they were so much as a minute late from their break, even if a manager could see that they had stopped on the way to answer a customer's question. "You can imagine how many questions we answer now," he says.

He cites other examples, too. "We spent months developing a relationship with one of our customers, and he bought thousands of dollars in merchandise. It got to the point where he gave us his credit card number and trusted us to buy on his behalf. When we introduced a series of prints, he bought the whole set, with the understanding that he'd get one each month. Then, when it was time to ship him the last one, the manager decided to sell the print to a customer who was in the shop that day. So our best customer missed out on the last one. He returned the whole set, and we all felt like idiots. We felt that we violated his trust, and we won't be put in that situation again."

Manage Up

- *Never agree to something with your boss and then do something different.*
- *Never disregard something your boss says and then nail your employees for ignoring it.*

Get More Information

> *The Heart Aroused: Poetry and the Preservation of the Soul in Corporate America,* David Whyte, Currency, 1994.
>
> *Leading the Revolution,* Gary Hamel, Harvard Business School Press, 2000.

LISTENING SKILLS: HOW TO HEAR WHAT PEOPLE REALLY HAVE TO SAY

Know the Issue

"Stop. Look. Listen." We've all heard the classic advice to help children cross the street safely.

It's good advice for managers, too. Employees want to be heard, and a big part of your job is to listen. As the boss, you'll hear complaints, concerns, and fears. People will want rumors confirmed or denied, conflicts resolved, and questions answered. They'll need to vent, worry, and even cry. They'll also want you to understand that they are hardworking, smart, and creative, or that their coworkers are not.

All of which, believe it or not, shapes how you're perceived as a manager. If employees feel you're a good listener, you'll be seen as confident, compassionate, aware, and fair. If you're seen as a poor listener, employees will describe you as arrogant, mean, out of touch, and unfair.

Beyond that, if employees believe you're a poor listener, they'll stop talking to you. On some days that might be a very appealing idea. But in the long term it's not what you want. You need information to manage, and if employees don't talk to you, you'll never have enough.

So what does it mean to be a good listener? Here are some basics.

Take Action

- *Give employees your full attention.* You're busy. Your own boss is breathing down your neck. So when employees come with a question or concern, it's tempting to sort through your mail, sign checks, or approve expense reports while you listen. Resist the temptation. Set aside whatever you're doing and give the employee your undivided attention. It's important for the employee to see you listening:
  - Focus on asking questions instead of giving answers.
  - Focus on what they're saying, not what you'll say next.
  - Focus on what you can learn instead of what you can teach.
  - Focus on giving them the benefit of the doubt instead of doubting their benefit.

  If you're caught at a time when you can't be interrupted, make an appointment with the employee for the earliest available time.

- *Notice body language.* Watch employees when they talk. Is their body language consistent with what they're saying? For example, suppose you ask an employee if he knows anything about why the shipment didn't go out on time. If he looks straight at you, makes eye contact, and says that he knows nothing about it, what does that tell you? Is the message the same if he looks at the ground and shuffles his feet while making the same assertion? Be careful about jumping to conclusions, especially if the employee has different cultural values from the American business norm (see "Cultural Values:

How to Get Past Race and Ethnicity" in Chapter 7). But if what you hear and what you see don't correlate, that's your prompt to ask more questions.

- *Remember that silence is golden.* Yes, employees often want advice or information when they come to you, but they also want to be heard, so don't feel compelled to fill every pause in the conversation. Some people simply need more time to formulate a thought or to process what they've heard.

- *Keep tissues handy.* Sooner or later someone will cry. It's a natural expression of feeling. Nonetheless, it may be embarrassing for the employee, and you may feel very uncomfortable. When it happens, don't feel you need to do anything. Just reassure the employee that it's okay and hand her a tissue.

- *Repeat what you hear.* We all hear through the filter of our experience and viewpoint. It's important to be sure that what you hear is what the employee actually intended. To do that, pause occasionally and repeat back to the employee what you believe you heard. Say, "I want to be sure I understand what you're saying. What I heard is . . ." and then ask the employee whether you have it right. That gives the employee the chance to fix any misunderstandings or to add information. It also shows the employee that you're listening.

- *Think before responding.* Be sure you really want to say what you say before you say it. If an employee is critical, argumentative, or accusatory, it's natural to defend yourself or refute the exaggeration. Choose your words carefully so you don't say something you'll regret.

- *Make your response relevant.* Have you ever watched a political debate and wondered why the candidates rarely respond to the issue they've been asked to address? Instead, they talk about what they want to talk about. Show respect for employees by responding directly—without tangents, philosophical musings, or smoke screens—to their concerns.

- *Address the employee's expectations.* Occasionally, employees will talk to you with no expectation that you do anything. Usually, however, they expect some outcome from the discussion. Once you've heard what the employee has to say, decide what you're going to do. It may be that you'll do nothing. Either way, tell the employee what you're going to do and why. At the end of the conversation, he should have some sense of closure. Without it, he'll just be frustrated.

- *Make notes.* You don't need a record of every conversation. If an employee simply wants clarification about a procedure or a request you've made, there's probably no need to note it. There's also no need to document conversations in which employees share information about their personal lives, but you should make notes of some conversations:
  - Discussions of employee performance problems
  - Requests for training, promotions, or other career-related matters
  - Accusations of misconduct (such as charges that another employee is stealing or harassing others)
  - Requests for leave (particularly FMLA leave)
  - Requests for an ADA-covered accommodation

In these cases, make notes (see "Documenting Performance: How to Be Fair, Complete, and Legal" in Chapter 4) and put the notes in the appropriate file.

Stay Out of Jail

Unless something an employee tells you requires you to take action (such as investigating a complaint, for example) it's best to keep it to yourself. If you're unsure what to do about a situation, you may seek advice from HR, your boss, or another manager, but never gossip about employees or violate a trust.

Real-Life Examples

- A medical technician was called into her boss's office and counseled for being late to work. She had been late twice, in each case by one minute. Frustrated, the technician pointed out that she had often stayed late for patients, which the boss had never acknowledged. She was seeking to put her tardiness in some perspective and to clarify expectations: Were posted work shifts flexible or weren't they?

    Unfortunately, the boss proved to be less than helpful. "Well, Susan, it's like this," she responded. "Say I make a batch of brownies for my sons and I only put a little bit of dog poop in them. Do you think they will still eat them? There is only a little bit of dog poop in them."

    Susan was more than bewildered; she lost all respect for her boss. "I still, to this day, fail to see how dog poop was relevant to my situation," she says.

- The new manager, Juanita, had been told that one of the store's employees, Lisa, was "difficult"; Lisa was short-tempered, bossy, and often in conflict with other employees. So Juanita met with Lisa to address the problem.

  But it wasn't long before Alex, another employee, was in Juanita's office to complain about Lisa again. Juanita pumped Alex for information, but as she did so she sensed that Alex knew more than he was telling. Eventually, with a lot of prodding, Alex admitted that Juanita, herself, was part of the problem.

  Shocked, Juanita asked Alex to explain. He acknowledged that Lisa was difficult and prone to outbursts, but he said that Lisa's behavior had been aggravated by the perception that she and others thought Juanita was apathetic and didn't really understand what went on in the shop.

  Juanita was angry and hurt, but she kept her feelings to herself and simply asked if Alex knew why people felt that way. He offered examples of miscommunication and of issues that people felt weren't being addressed.

  Juanita listened carefully. She thanked Alex for his candor, admitted that she was surprised and disappointed, and promised to think about what he had said.

  The next day, she took Alex aside and shared some of the specific steps she was taking to improve. As a result, Juanita earned Alex's respect. He became her advocate to other employees and helped improve morale.

- A manager received a threatening telephone call. He was very concerned, and told a coworker what happened. The company decided that the matter would be dealt with confidentially.

Unfortunately, the manager's secretary overheard enough of the manager's conversation with his coworker to know that there was the potential for a serious problem.

After two sleepless nights, the secretary decided to confront a vice president. By watching and listening, it was clear to the vice president that the secretary was concerned about the manager, concerned for her own safety, and concerned about what she didn't know. The vice president asked the secretary to promise confidentiality, and she complied. He then told her the nature of the threat and generally what the company was doing to protect the manager. He reassured her that the threat was not directed at the company or at anyone other than the manager, and offered her time off.

The secretary was appreciative, informed, empowered, and fully willing to face the known risk. She did not take any time off because of the situation.

Manage Up

Use your best listening skills with your boss. Make a point of repeating back what you think you've heard to be sure you have it right.

Get More Information

The Zen of Listening, Rebecca Z. Shafir, Quest Books, 2000.

APOLOGIZING: WHY MANAGING OFTEN MEANS HAVING TO SAY YOU'RE SORRY

Know the Issue

"Love means never having to say you're sorry." In case you're too young to remember, that phrase comes from Erich Segal's chick-lit best seller, *Love Story.* No one understood what it meant, but that didn't keep it from becoming one of the catchphrases of the '70s.

Today the catchphrase might be, "Managing means never having to say you're sorry." It makes no more sense than Segal's phrase, but that doesn't stop managers from following its prescription—into trouble. Because even though some managers believe that apologizing is a sign of weakness and weakens their stature in the eyes of employees, the opposite is true. As novelist Jessamyn West observed, "It is easy to forgive others their mistakes; it takes more grit and gumption to forgive them for having witnessed your own."

Managers who never apologize are diminished. Employees know that no one is perfect and lose respect for managers who can't accept that. "Is it that he doesn't care when he screws up, that he's too dumb to know, or that he's too big a coward to admit it?" one employee asked about her boss. "Either way, I have no confidence that he's going to notice a problem and do something to fix it. And it's hard to respect someone who shows no respect for you."

Hardly a recipe for a happy, healthy workplace is it? Now, we're not asking you to whip yourself with a wet noodle or to go on *Oprah* to atone for your sins, but we are asking that when you blow it, you admit it and offer a sincere apology.

Take Action

- *Accept that you aren't perfect.* Yes, you're the boss. That doesn't make you infallible. In fact, as a boss you have more chances to goof up than anyone. Don't you feel better already?

- *'Fess up.* No screwup is worse than the mess you can get into pretending it didn't happen. (Nixon/Watergate. Clinton/Monica. Point made.) If you dropped the ball, say so and apologize. And when you apologize, do it sincerely.

- *Listen to your inner voice.* Adding numbers incorrectly is one kind of mistake; setting unrealistic deadlines is another. And then there are situations that just don't feel right, such as when you lose it in a meeting, snap at a colleague because you have the headache from hell, or stoop to sarcasm when you run out of patience. The little voice in your head will squawk enough to call your attention to most transgressions. When you hear it, heed it and apologize.

- *Don't wait to be asked for an apology.* Times will occur when you really don't know you blew it. When that happens and people call you on it, offer an apology with grace. More often, you'll know you made a mistake. Don't make people come to you and ask for an apology; that's more than a little manipulative.

- *Accept your role as apologist-in-chief.* You're the boss, which to your employees makes you the voice of the company. That means you'll be called upon to apologize for things you may have had nothing to do with. If an employee is shown to have been sexually harassed, for example, extend an apology on behalf of the company. Be sensitive to such situations. Your employees will feel like you're supporting them against the bureaucracy.

- *Don't play the blame game.* Finding blame is highly over-rated. It has only one possible outcome, which is to make everyone afraid of making mistakes. It's better not to blame anyone. Instead, see mistakes as learning opportunities.

- *Be honest with yourself.* When mistakes happen, you should first ask yourself what you may have done to contribute to the problem. Perhaps you've done nothing. Ask anyway. It's a good exercise to keep yourself honest. When you've blown it, admit it to yourself.

Stay Out of Jail

- *Don't make promises you can't keep.* Apologize for what's happened, but resist the urge to assure employees that "it will never happen again." You intend that it'll never happen again, but life is unpredictable.

- *If legal issues are involved, talk with an attorney before you say something that could come back to haunt you.*

Real-Life Examples

- The employees of a particular business report to work each morning two hours before the shop opens. That way, they have time to reconcile the cash registers, clean the shop, and put away stock. One morning they walked in to find so much new stock that they knew it would be a challenge to get it all put away. The situation was further complicated when the boss asked them to attend a morning meeting. One of the employees explained the situation and offered that if they attended the meeting the shop might not open on time. The manager agreed that it was all right if they opened late.

But after the meeting the boss gave them only a few minutes before he popped in and asked when the shop would open. The employees assured him they were doing their best. A few minutes later he was back. The third time he appeared, he stayed in the shop and began looking in the cases at the merchandise. Around him, employees put stock away and then opened the shop.

Afterward, one of the employees went to the boss. "I told him I didn't appreciate how things had gone," he said. "We had discussed the shop opening and agreed it would be late. Having him keep asking about it, and then stand around doing nothing, didn't help. I suggested that it would have been better if he had helped, or at least sent some other people in to help.

"He looked at me, and then he agreed. He said that we seemed so organized that he hadn't seen anything he could do, but he said he should have asked. And then he apologized. His apology went such a long way toward defusing the tension. It just stopped right then. Otherwise, we probably would have stewed about it all day."

- The CEO was having a monthly meeting with the management team. As usual, there was a long agenda. When it came time for new business, one manager—a newcomer to the team—shared some ideas she had for employee recognition.

She wasn't prepared for the response she got. The CEO flew into a rage, screaming at the manager, pounding on the table and shaking paper. He shouted that he had been recognizing employees, and that it was no longer up to him to do it. When the manager said quietly that she hadn't intended that the CEO implement her ideas, she was greeted with more screaming. Everyone at the table was shell-shocked.

Later, the CEO paid a visit to the manager. He explained that recognition had been an ongoing struggle, and that the discussion touched a raw nerve, but he didn't apologize. Nor did he apologize to any of the other managers who had been at the meeting.

The manager was appalled. "It was so inappropriate," she said. "I just felt abused. When there was no apology, I felt the CEO had no respect for us at all."

She and another manager at the meeting later cited the meeting as a turning point in their decisions to leave the company.

Manage Up

If you make a mistake, bring it to your boss's attention. And then apologize.

Get More Information

Resolving Conflicts at Work, Kenneth Cloke and Joan Goldsmith, Jossey-Bass, 2000.

4

Managing Performance

A company or a department with low morale is about as cheery as a seedy nightclub in 1930s Berlin. When you look around, everyone you see looks angry or depressed. You hear cynical comments and caustic laughter coming from the lunchroom. Cubicles sport posters that say, "You obviously have mistaken me for someone who cares." People are out "sick" in epidemic proportions. People get to work late and leave early. It's ugly.

It didn't get that way overnight. Low morale is the inevitable result of a lot of bad management. Decisions are second-guessed, mistakes are repeated, blame is assigned, poor work is ignored, training and performance reviews are not done, and recognition is overlooked. In short, low morale is a collective statement that employees feel adrift, ignored, and uninvolved.

Fortunately, high morale is within any manager's reach. It takes respectful leadership and a willingness to support employees. It takes sincere recognition of work done well, and finishing fair performance appraisals on time. It also takes giving employees the help they need when they need it.

Maybe that sounds like common sense. If so, you're halfway home.

LEADERSHIP: HOW TO VARY YOUR STYLE TO GET RESULTS

Know the Issue

Good chefs need knives—many knives. They need knives with long and short blades that are serrated and smooth, and heavy and light. Good chefs know when and why to use each knife, whether they are slicing carrots or bread, boning fish, or spreading frosting.

Good leaders need different styles of leading: demanding and mobilizing, harmonious and consensus-building, driven and developmental. Good leaders know when and why to use each style. One style works best in a crisis, and another helps forge a new vision; one helps heal, and another builds competencies for the long term.

Becoming a good leader who can use varied styles isn't easy. The only learning is trial and error. Good leaders are resilient and they look for options, so if one style doesn't work in a given situation, they try another. As they learn which style they're best at and which people respond to, they can draw on them as needed.

Getting to this point requires self-awareness, discipline, and a willingness to take risks. Ultimately, the leaders who are most comfortable with all six leadership styles are the leaders who get the best results. Isn't that what leadership is all about?

Take Action

- *Know the six styles.* It used to be that good leadership was like good art: no one could define it, but everyone knew it when they saw it. Research by the consulting firm Hay/McBer, however, has clarified what good leadership really is. The research drew on the experience of more than 3,800 executives worldwide and found that there are six basic leadership styles: coercive, authoritative, affiliative, democratic, pacesetting, and coaching. (See the sidebar "Leadership Styles: A Primer" later in the chapter.)

  Each style reflects underlying emotional intelligence competencies (see "Emotional Intelligence: How to Recognize and Use the Data in Your Emotions" in Chapter 6). Empathy, self-awareness, and the ability to develop others are the foundation of the coaching style, for example. Each style works best then when deployed in the appropriate circumstance, and doesn't work at all when used inappropriately. Using a coercive ("because I said so") style, for example, is disastrous when consensus is needed. Each style also has an impact on the organization's climate. Two of the six styles are negative.

- *Know yourself.* After even a quick review of the six styles, one style will probably feel right. That's the style that comes most naturally to you. Now pay attention to how you interact with your staff. Do you use solely that style, or do you use others as well? Do you use varied styles on your own, or only when your boss forces you to? Which style gets the best results, or does it depend on the situation?

- *Ask your employees.* Ask a few of your employees which leadership style you use, because it's hard to see yourself objectively. Ask employees whom you trust to be truthful, even though they are not necessarily your favorite employees. You want honesty, not fawning.

- *Observe your staff.* Just as we all use different leadership styles, we also respond to different styles. Someone with an affiliative personality, for example, won't feel warm and fuzzy toward a pacesetter-style leader. To which styles do members of your staff respond? It's unlikely that your employees all respond to the same style.

- *Challenge yourself.* Think about situations in your department that might benefit from different leadership styles and work at using some of the emotional intelligence skills required in those situations. If your style is affiliative, work on your collaborative skills to forge a more democratic style, or work at developing the potential in your employees to become better at coaching. Stretching yourself is important because even generally positive styles can become negative if they're used in every situation. Too much of an affiliative style, for example, can leave a group feeling rudderless. The group might feel good about each other, yet still fail.

  If your style is naturally coercive or pacesetting—the two leadership styles with negative impacts—you'll want to balance your approach with more positive styles.

- *Find mentors.* You can easily identify the leadership style of anyone you know. Pay attention to other people in your organization or even outside it. Single out those who use the styles you'd like to learn and observe them. Look for examples of how they get things done.

- *Experiment.* In the end, thinking and observing will get you only so far. To grow, you must take the plunge and actually try different styles in different situations and see what works for you in your company. Be bold. As William James once advised, "To change one's life: start immediately, do it flamboyantly—no exceptions."

Manage Up

- *Observe your boss's style.* What can you learn from her? Help your boss by using styles that complement her style. If your boss is a pacesetter, for example, being an affiliator can help balance this style and improve productivity and morale. Just don't do it in a way that undercuts her.
- *Discuss your leadership style with your boss.* Then share your plans to develop other styles and ask for candid feedback about your attempts.

Get More Information

> *Good To Great: Why Some Companies Make the Leap . . . and Others Don't,* Jim Collins, Harper Business, 2001.
>
> *Your Management Sucks,* Mark Stevens, Crown Business, 2006.

Leadership Styles: A Primer

Research by the consulting firm Hay/McBer found six basic leadership styles, though the most effective leaders use all the styles at least occasionally. Daniel Goleman, author of *Working with Emotional Intelligence* and *Ecological Intelligence*, has analyzed the six styles to determine their strengths and weaknesses, the situations in which

continued

they work best, and their overall impact on the climate of an organization or department. The most successful leaders are familiar with all six, and use each in different situations as appropriate, even if they rely most often on one of the most effective styles.

Authoritative

Basic approach. Mobilizes people toward a vision.

Catchphrase. "Come with me."

Underlying emotional intelligence competencies. Self-confidence, empathy, change catalyst.

Strengths. Helps people see how their work supports the broader mission; maximizes commitment; standards for success are clear, as are rewards; people have the freedom to innovate and take calculated risks.

Weaknesses. Leader may be seen as pompous or out-of-touch; the spirit of effective teams can be undermined.

When the style works best. When changes require a new vision; when a clear direction is needed.

Overall impact on climate. Strongly positive; it is the most effective of the six styles.

Affiliative

Basic approach. Creates harmony and builds emotional bonds.

Catchphrase. "People come first."

Underlying emotional intelligence competencies. Empathy, building relationships, communication.

Strengths. Has a markedly positive effect on communication; flexibility rises; people get ample positive feedback; people have a sense of belonging.

Weaknesses. Poor performance may go uncorrected; employees may feel that mediocrity is tolerated; employees must figure out how to improve on their own and may feel rudderless.

continued

When the style works best. To heal rifts in a team; to motivate people during stressful circumstances.

Overall impact on climate. Positive.

Democratic

Basic approach. Forges consensus through participation.

Catchphrase. "What do you think?"

Underlying emotional intelligence competencies. Collaboration, team leadership, communication.

Strengths. Builds trust, respect, and commitment; drives up flexibility and responsibility; people tend to be very realistic about what can and can't be accomplished.

Weaknesses. Endless meetings; consensus remains elusive; critical decisions may be postponed.

When the style works best. To build buy-in or consensus; to get input from valuable employees.

Overall impact on climate. Positive.

Coaching

Basic approach. Develops people for the future.

Catchphrase. "Try this."

Underlying emotional intelligence competencies. Developing others, empathy, self-awareness.

Strengths. Employees understand their unique strengths and weaknesses; employees set long-term career goals; plentiful instruction and feedback; excellent at delegating.

Weaknesses. May focus on long-term development at the expense of work-related tasks; fails if the leader lacks expertise.

When the style works best. To help an employee improve performance or develop long-term strengths.

Overall impact on climate. Positive.

continued

Pacesetting

Basic approach. Sets high standards for performance.

Catchphrase. "Do as I do, now."

Underlying emotional intelligence competencies. Conscientiousness, drive to achieve, initiative.

Strengths. Sets extremely high standards and exemplifies them; obsessed with doing things better and faster; demands a lot from people and replaces those who don't rise to the occasion.

Weaknesses. Employees feel overwhelmed; morale drops; people second-guess what the leader wants; flexibility and responsibility evaporate; work becomes routine.

When the style works best. To get quick results from a highly motivated and competent team.

Overall impact on climate. Negative.

Coercive

Basic approach. Demands immediate compliance.

Catchphrase. "Do what I tell you."

Underlying emotional intelligence competencies. Drive to achieve, initiative, self-control.

Strengths. Willing to make tough decisions; can break failed business habits; can shock people into new ways of working.

Weaknesses. Kills new ideas on the vine; people feel disrespected; sense of responsibility evaporates; damages the rewards system; employees become resentful.

When the style works best. In a crisis; when kick-starting a turn-around; with problem employees.

Overall impact on climate. Negative; it is the least effective of the six styles.

Source: "Leadership That Gets Results," Daniel Goleman, *Harvard Business Review,* March-April 2000.

MANAGING 101: HOW TO BE THE BOSS TODAY'S EMPLOYEES NEED

Know the Issue

True, Amazon's Jeff Bezos is smart and Xerox's Ursula Burns is dynamic, but our management role model is Glinda, the Good Witch.

Glinda? Yep. Think about it: Not only did Dorothy get home, but ultimately she figured out how to do it. Along the way she found strength and resourcefulness in herself she had never seen. She learned from her mistakes. She faced challenges with courage, and relied on her friends for support.

Yes, Glinda got results, but she was no micromanager. She simply pointed Dorothy in the right direction ("Follow the Yellow Brick Road"), gave her the resources she needed (the Ruby slippers), and removed a few obstacles (such as the Wicked Witch of the West's sleeping spell) when it was judicious to do so.

Most employees would be thrilled to work for Glinda. You can learn from her example.

Take Action

- *Expect the best.* No one goes to work to do a bad job. Teachers, directors, coaches, and generals will all tell you the same thing: people do what's expected of them. If you give an assignment and then stand back to wait for the screwup, you won't have to wait long. On the other hand, if you give an assignment that seems just beyond an employee's reach, people usually rise to the occasion.

  People occasionally fall short of their best, and when that happens they disappoint themselves and you. But people almost never fail intentionally. Give them the benefit of the doubt. As Abraham Lincoln observed, "It's better to trust and be disappointed occasionally than to distrust and be miserable all the time."

If you really believe that your people aren't capable, ask yourself two questions: Are they in the wrong job? Are you?

- *Put work in context.* People perform best when they feel they are part of something. Help people understand how they contribute to the overall mission and goals of the company. Do hotel laundry workers just wash sheets, or do they play a vital role in the guests' overall experience? Employees who don't see that connection wonder why it's important to do a good job.

  Once they know the overall mission, set goals to help them achieve that mission: How many guests do they need to please today?

- *Be clear.* When making those assignments, be clear. One boss routinely made assignments by scrawling instructions on scratch paper and leaving the scrawls on an employee's chair or in his in-box. Inevitably, employees would take the scrawl to a coworker for help in deciphering it. Sometimes large groups worked together to decode the messages.

  Why didn't they just ask? Because if they did, the boss would snatch back the assignment and yell, or she would tell them that they were paid to figure it out. It never seemed to occur to her that none of her staff could decipher what she wanted, and that an incredible amount of time was being wasted trying to figure it out or redoing tasks they'd misinterpreted.

If you write instructions, read them to yourself slowly. If you followed them literally, could you do what you're asking the employee to do? If you aren't sure, have someone else read them. If you give instructions verbally, ask employees to repeat them to you, and ask whether they have any questions.

- *Give employees the resources they need.* You wouldn't send a Boy Scout on a weekend camping trip without a sleeping bag, a canteen, and a compass. Don't ask employees to do a job without the resources either. Consider the following:
  - Are enough people assigned to the task?
  - Have you allowed enough time?
  - Do people have the appropriate equipment?
  - Do they have enough information?
  - Do they have your support?
  - Do they know where they can go for help?

- *Let employees do the work.* Once employees know the goal and have the resources they need, get out of their way. Resist any temptation you may have to micromanage. Nothing can be gained by standing over someone's shoulder, and a lot can be lost. Yes, employees will do it differently than you would. That's okay.

- *Remove obstacles.* Twelve Parisian streets come together in a star formation at Place d'Etoile. In the center is the Arc de Triomphe, and if you stand on top of it for five minutes, you're guaranteed to see at least one traffic accident. From that vantage point, you can see the big picture and anticipate where the accidents will happen. If you could somehow communicate with the drivers below, you could prevent many fender benders.

As the boss, you can communicate with the drivers if you see an accident ahead. Do it! But as a boss, you can do better than that. You have more clout in the organization. Use it! Picture yourself as a traffic cop in the Place d'Etoile. You can stop lanes of traffic, block cars from entering, or make drivers slow down. Do what you can to help your people maneuver through the traffic to get where they're going.

- *Don't give employees all the answers.* Employees will come to you for help, and if you're busy or tired, you'll tell them what to do. Don't. Every time you do it, you encourage them to come to you with the next problem. After all, it's easier to get the answer than it is to figure it out.

  But no one learns anything by getting the answer. Instead, ask employees what they've tried. Explore why it didn't work. Ask them what options they've considered. What do they see as the pros and cons of each? If they're not seeing some things, ask questions to gently open their eyes. Challenge sloppy thinking or miscalculations, but don't just tell employees what to do.

  If employees get to the solution themselves, they'll take greater responsibility and have greater ownership.

- *Vary your style.* We're not all the same. Not exactly a headline ripped from this morning's newspaper, is it? Yet many managers continue to treat their people as if they are all the same; everyone receives the same instruction, the same way, every time.

Manager Gilbert G. Bendix told Workplace911.com that it helps to think of employees as chefs. "One employee is like the chef who doesn't need a cookbook," he says. "Give him oral instructions once and know that the job will be done and done right. But another worker forgets simple instructions by the time he reaches his workstation. He needs different help: a detailed recipe with all the ingredients listed at the top."

Match your style to what employees need.

- *Don't stereotype.* We all have heard some stereotypes about performance: white men can't jump; women aren't good at math; older people are forgetful. Even though they're only occasionally accurate, and more often just plain wrong, that hasn't diminished their ubiquity. Still, you should be careful to avoid them.

   In a landmark study, Stanford University psychologist Claude Steele showed that it's the target of a stereotype whose behavior is most affected by it. Steele and his colleague Joshua Aronson observed that stereotypes make people so painfully aware of how they're seen that the knowledge affects their performance.

   For example, the University of Arizona's Jeff Stone found that women who were reminded of their gender even in the subtlest ways before taking an exam scored significantly lower than women who didn't get the reminder. Furthermore, stereotypes seem to affect star performers most strongly.

   Avoid stereotyping employees—even in a positive way and even in jest. There's nothing funny about a stereotype.

- *Let employees fail.* If we all had to be perfect the first time, no one would ever have seen a circus trapeze act. Sometimes employees fail. The solution is not to keep them from trying to catch the trapeze. The solution is to be sure they have a net beneath them and the confidence to climb the ladder and try again.

- *Help employees learn from their mistakes.* When employees screw up, count to 10 and resist the urge to get mad. Instead, use these talking points to help employees learn:
  - What went wrong?
  - When did it go wrong? Could they have seen the problem earlier?
  - Why did it go wrong? Was the mistake inevitable, or the result of a freak incident?
  - When did they notice something was wrong? Did they take action then or hope it would get better? Did they ignore their gut or warnings from others?
  - Were they lacking information? If so, where could they have found the information?
  - Does the incident remind them of any other mistakes they've made?
  - What will they do differently next time? Why?

- *Don't play favorites.* It's only natural to like some people better than others, but this is work, not a backyard barbecue. Don't make work decisions based on your personal feelings. Ask yourself who is best qualified to do the work. Be consistent in making assignments and bestowing privileges. (Don't take your favorites to lunch to talk about tasks while others get an e-mail.)

- *Think "we."* Here are some words to strike from your vocabulary: "I," "me," "my," "mine." (Put a quarter in a jar every time you use them and give them to your employees at the end of the year.) Don't refer to management as "us" and to employees as "you."

  Remember, you're all in this together. Talk about what we will do, what our customers expect, and so on. Never set yourself above or apart from the team.

  Don't stay above the fray either. If there's work to be done and you can do it, pitch in and help. Employees resent bosses who won't get their hands dirty stuffing envelopes, answering phones, or making copies occasionally. Is the work important, or isn't it?

Stay Out of Jail

Mistakes may be inevitable and excellent learning opportunities, but that doesn't mean you should avoid written warnings and discipline in all cases. Think of discipline as a form of education. Failure to take disciplinary action can lower the bar of employee expectations and lead to more mistakes.

Real-Life Examples

- When Kelly was appointed acting director of an emergency medical services coordinating system, her first challenge was dealing with the department's secretary, Rose. Rose was often seen painting her fingernails; she resisted deadlines and instructions; and she generally was seen as unwilling or unable. "No" was her favorite word.

Given her reputation, Kelly was surprised when Rose mentioned that she had figured out how to do mail merge on an outdated computer system with barely 64K of memory. Because Kelly was replacing the antiquated system, she asked Rose if she would like to have the new computers in her office. Rose's face lit up. "I saw that I was on to something," Kelly says.

They talked about rearranging the office to accommodate the new system. Kelly asked Rose where she thought everything should go and how it all should be arranged. "I took her advice on everything," Kelly says, "which apparently no one had ever done before. She became another person: willing, hardworking, dependable, totally 'with it.' She went from being an employee everyone barely tolerated to one who should have been employee of the year. It really taught me a lesson about managing people. The manager's true job is to serve those that work for her, in the sense that you give them the power and the assets they need to do their job, and permission to do it pretty much their own way, and you get happy, hardworking people who exceed all expectations."

- The CEO of a software firm called a meeting of the technical support department and proceeded to lecture them on what a poor job they were doing with his customers. "He actually used the phrase 'my customers' several times during this diatribe; in his mind, we clearly weren't part of the team," says Steve, an employee who was in the meeting. "He capped it off and lost any remaining respect we had for him when he told us that none of us cared about his customers. Now, you can tell me I have a thing or two to learn and I'll likely go

along with you. You can even tell me I need to work harder—
no one is 100 percent efficient. But don't tell me I don't care
about the people I've been doing my best to help for more than
a year, despite getting very poor training." Years later, the
employees who were there—now working elsewhere—still
talk about that meeting.

Get More Information

> *The Fifth Discipline: The Art and Practice of the Learning
> Organization*, Peter M. Senge, Currency, 1990.
>
> *12: The Elements of Great Managing*, Rodd Wagner and James
> K. Harter, Gallup Press, 2006.

KEEP EMPLOYEES IN THE LOOP: HOW TO FILL THE INFORMATION VACUUM

Know the Issue

The flight was scheduled to leave at 8:20. The sign at the ticket
counter shows that the flight is on time, but it's now 9:10 and it
hasn't even boarded. Why? Is the weather bad? Are passengers waiting for new safety instruction cards to arrive from the printer? Are
the pilots drunk? No one knows. As the minutes pass, passengers
grumble. Tempers flare. Shouts are exchanged. "Are we boarding in
two minutes, or can I go eat?" one passenger fumes. "I wish they'd
tell us what the hell is going on."

Your employees are the passengers on your airline. They want to
know what's going on. If they don't know, morale stays firmly earth-
bound. They aren't quiet about it either. Do you want your employees
venting to customers, "Management never tells us anything"?

Now, a dose of reality: it isn't possible to keep all the people happy all the time. (In fact, it's not even a sensible goal.) There always will be people who claim they didn't know, or didn't know soon enough, or found out the "wrong" way. Some employees will seek information, while others remain passive and expect to be spoon-fed. A few will claim they didn't know, even if they really did.

So why bother to keep employees in the loop? Because most employees will appreciate it, because keeping employees in the loop is too important to ignore, and because it's a big part of your job.

Take Action

- *Remember, it's about them.* Listen to the questions that employees ask when they get new information. Almost all of them will be some variation of, "What does that mean to me?" Employees naturally want to know what to expect and what's expected of them. Does it mean longer hours? A bigger bonus? No bonus? More responsibility? Different tasks? Focus on how employees will be most affected and be straight with them about it. If you don't yet know how they will be affected (and when senior management is scrambling in tough times, you often don't), admit that you don't know but commit to sharing the information as soon as you do know. An honest "I don't know" is always more effective than making something up or dodging the issue.

- *Provide context.* According to the polls we've taken in organizations, most employees say that management's decisions are arbitrary and poorly considered. That belief reflects the fact that employees are rarely given any context for the information they get. As abstractions, many decisions do seem arbitrary. Employees are more likely to reward you with patience and support if they understand the thinking behind decisions. Take a page from Journalism 101 and tell them:

○ Who made the decision and who will be affected by it

○ What the decision is and what it means

○ When it will happen

○ Where the company is going and how the decision contributes to progress

○ Why the decision was made

○ How the plan will be implemented

• *Don't sweat the small stuff.* Keep in mind that what employees want to know and what they need to know are two different things. Some employees want to know everything about everything, even if it isn't any of their business. Does everyone need an announcement that Linda is moving to a different cubicle?

Employees really only need information about things that affect the whole company (mergers, downsizing, purchases, product launches, key management changes, new policies) and those that affect their specific jobs.

• *Don't rely on one format.* People learn and process information differently. Some people learn by hearing, others by reading, and still others through action. Meet those needs, and take some pressure off yourself to do all communicating face-to-face, by sharing information several ways:

○ Hold meetings.

○ Send e-mail.

- Leave "broadcast" voice mail.
- Post information in break rooms or other gathering spots.
- Post information on the company intranet.

Don't use every media to convey every piece of information. Use more "active" media (such as e-mail) for more urgent or important information, and more "passive" media (such as an intranet) for less urgent information. Experiment to see to which media your employees respond best.

- *Expect some blowback.* Employees want to know what's going on, but that doesn't mean they will be happy about everything they hear. You should expect protests, complaints, and other responses that will not put you in your happy place. You don't need to take action in response to every complaint (and, let's face it, you can't), but you do need to listen respectfully and acknowledge what you've heard. Although you can't keep all the people happy all the time, opinions do change over time. And if you communicate consistently and honestly, then employees will learn to trust you, and that trust will be greater than any single situation.

- *Ask for feedback.* You've put the information out there, but did anyone notice or care? One way to find out is to ask for feedback. Are employees confused? Frustrated? Mad as hell? Indifferent? Asking the question increases the odds that they will pay attention, and the responses can tell you whether you need to communicate more.

Let employees know what you're going to do with the feedback. Share it? Act on it? Ignore it? Set realistic expectations.

- *Be proactive*. Don't wait to be asked before sharing information.

- *Get help*. You don't have to do all the communicating yourself. Ask employees working on specific projects or responsible for specific functions to communicate with their coworkers. Review their initial efforts before they share them to be sure they're complete and helpful. Offer coaching or training if employees need help with their communication skills.

- *Review the union contract*. If a union represents your employees, be sure you're familiar with the terms of the contract. Are you required to give specific notice of work assignment changes, changes in shifts, or other job matters?

- *Cut yourself some slack*. If every employee knew everything all the time, it would be a miracle. Feel good if most employees know most of what they need to know most of the time.

Stay Out of Jail

Be sure that employees are aware of any policy changes.

Real-Life Examples

- Laura Janke became the manager of 13 people who were dispirited and wary after working with an unsuccessful manager. To get things back on track, she implemented weekly meetings to discuss everything and anything. At first no one knew quite what to expect, and sometimes the meetings were little more than gripe fests, but ultimately they became an effective tool.

The meetings were a forum to discuss changes, deadlines, and activities in other departments that might have bearing on Janke's department. She also used the meetings for training, praise, and thanks. At the end of each meeting, everyone attending had a chance to share news.

Janke says the meetings were a success in part because they happened consistently. They were held at the same time each week, and she had a sign in her office as a reminder. Employees reminded Janke if she got busy or forgot; only twice in a year did she cancel the meeting.

"The meetings helped build a truly cohesive department that was fragmented and in disarray when I stepped in," she says.

- Chris was in a foul mood, and everyone knew it. After what seemed like a very long morning, a coworker took him aside and asked if everything was okay. It was not.

Chris had met the new manager the day before, and he was not happy. Oh, he had nothing against the woman, at least yet. He was just fuming because there was a new manager. After all, she was the fourth one in six months.

"I just figured out how to work with the last one, and now she's gone," he complained. "How long will this one be here?" True, the company was in the midst of change, but he was far from alone in his frustration. The entire department was up in arms. Each new manager had been introduced as the "new manager," only to be reassigned elsewhere after a few weeks.

The staff spent a lot of time commiserating about the changes and speculating about the next one. Morale had dropped; people had begun grumbling about leaving. "Why can't they just tell us what's going on?" Chris asked.

- "I left on vacation for three weeks to go on a long camping trip that everyone in my work group knew about," one software engineer said. "After I returned, I was at work for four days before my boss had any contact with me at all. No e-mail. No phone call. No visit to my office. No questions about the trip. No updates about what had happened while I was gone. No direction about what I should be doing. It left me feeling rather insignificant and unimportant."

Get More Information

10 Simple Secrets of the World's Greatest Business Communicators, Carmine Gallo, Sourcebooks, 2005.

You Are the Message: Getting What You Want By Being Who You Are, Roger Ailes, Currency, 1998.

JOB DESCRIPTIONS: HOW TO DRAFT BLUEPRINTS FOR RESULTS

Know the Issue

Many of us don't read the manual. We just plunge ahead, believing that trial-and-error learning will get our new Wi-Fi system working. Only later, after hours of fruitless labor when the laptop is still not connected to the network, do we resort to reading the instructions.

This aversion may explain why in many organizations job descriptions are sitting in files and are about as familiar to the rank and file as the schematic for the building's electrical system.

But job descriptions should be vital documents that you and your staff refer to often. Without them, the consequences are much greater than computers not connecting—people don't connect well. Jobs are harder to fill, employees often underperform, and you face greater risk of legal problems.

Take Action

- *Begin with the basics, whether you're writing a job description or revising an existing one:*
  - Job title
  - Department
  - Position to which the job reports
  - Fair Labor Standards Act (FLSA) status (exempt or nonexempt; see the sidebar "FLSA Status: A Primer" in this chapter)
  - Date the description was written
- *State the job's primary purpose.* This is not rocket science. We're talking about a sentence or two to summarize why the job exists in the organization. The statement should help you and the employee focus on what's most important. Some sample statements are:
  - Serve food and beverages to customers.
  - Process reservations and ticketing for passengers.
  - Provide noninvasive patient care as prescribed or requested.
  - Monitor and maintain product inventory.
  - Sell cars.
  - Write articles.

- *Outline the duties and responsibilities that support the over-all goal.* This is where you get into details. For example, we all know from personal experience that car salespeople swoop like vultures on hapless shoppers and trail customers with a resolve matching that of the CIA. Their job description might not include verbs like swoop or browbeat ("greet potential customers" is a touch more dignified), but you get the idea. Keep in mind that the goal is to list responsibilities (for example, "make sure that tables have complete place settings" for food servers), not every task that the employee might ever do ("fill salt shakers"). As you write, consider which tasks are essential job functions and which are a business necessity. (See below for examples.)

- *Define job requirements.* The books are filled with laws to protect employees (and job candidates) from discrimination. In addition, the Americans with Disabilities Act (ADA) protects disabled people and requires employers to make "reasonable accommodations" (see the sidebar "The ADA: A Primer" in Chapter 7) to permit disabled people to fulfill the essential functions of a job. Clearly stating your expectations and requirements in your job descriptions will show that all candidates and employees are assessed against a uniform set of standards. Include the following:

  - *Education and experience.* Does the job require a college degree? An advanced degree? A particular certification, such as an RN? Is special training a requirement? How much on-the-job experience is necessary?

  - *Language skills.* Take nothing for granted. If jobholders need to be able to read safety warnings or instruction manuals, say so. If they are expected to be able to write business letters or memos, say so. Also make note of any less common job requirements, such as public speaking or fluency in a second language.

○ *Math skills.* Most jobs require people to use basic addition, subtraction, multiplication, and division skills. Others require more advanced math skills. Either way, spell it out.

○ *Physical demands.* It's almost impossible to be too specific when outlining what employees must be able to do. Will they be required to sit for extended periods? To do any lifting? To walk? Focus on unusual requirements, but the description should be specific enough so that potential employees with disabilities (visible or otherwise) can decide for themselves whether they are able to fulfill the requirements of the job.

○ *Work environment.* Finally, talk about the work environment itself. Address noise, lights, stairs, walking distance, and so forth.

• *Have your organization's HR department review any job description before you make it public.* If you don't have an HR department, hiring a labor attorney to review it would be a worthwhile investment.

• *Revisit and, if necessary, update job descriptions.* Look at them whenever any of the following occur:

○ Job tasks are reassigned from one employee to another.

○ Job tasks are added to someone's job.

○ Job tasks are deleted from someone's job.

○ An employee is promoted or demoted.

- ○ An employee completes his or her introductory period.
- ○ The organization is downsized.
- ○ The organization is restructured, reengineered, or otherwise changed.
- ○ The organization merges or is acquired (unless your department is unaffected).

- *Encourage employees to keep tabs on their activities and to let you know if they feel their job is changing.* Employees are very aware of how they spend their time, and discussing changes as they happen will avoid confusion or disagreements when it comes time to do performance reviews. But be sure to discuss things; don't let employees change job descriptions on their own.

Stay Out of Jail

Because job descriptions define a job, they can be carefully scrutinized when a legal dispute arises. The courts want to be sure that some sort of discrimination hasn't been built into the job. To protect yourself, address the following two key areas.

The first idea is that each job has essential functions. These are those job responsibilities that provide the main reasons for the job's existence. To be protected under the ADA, an employee must have a disability and also be qualified to perform the essential job functions with or without reasonable accommodation.

For example, the essential job function of a food server is to serve food. He may also have to climb stairs to get condiments out of storage, or use the telephone or a broom, but those duties probably would not be considered essential or core functions. These are known as marginal functions. Therefore, you could not refuse to hire someone as a food server if the only reason for your refusal was that, due to a protected disability, he could not perform the marginal functions of the job, such as climbing, telephoning, or sweeping. On the other hand, if the server could not serve food even with the help of a reasonable accommodation, then you wouldn't be discriminating if you did not hire him. To avoid confusion, be sure that the essential job functions are clear in the job description.

The other concept is business necessity. Technically, that's the standard an employer must establish to enforce a company rule or policy that may adversely affect protected employees. An employer must prove that rules or requirements are job-related and necessary to the business. For example, a classic court case involved an employer in the South that was requiring all applicants for janitorial jobs to have a high school diploma. Eventually, the case was heard by the U.S. Supreme Court, which expressed concern that the rule was a pretext designed to eliminate African-Americans from the hiring process. The court held that the employer had failed to demonstrate it was a business necessity that janitorial applicants be high school graduates.

To protect yourself, make sure the requirements you make of applicants have a solid business rationale. If it's possible that the requirement adversely affects a protected class, be prepared to demonstrate how it's necessary to the business.

There are no shortcuts here; you must do this.

Manage Up

Review job descriptions with your boss. Make sure he or she doesn't have expectations that aren't addressed. Have the description reviewed by HR or legal counsel first, so your boss knows that the company will have no legal surprises.

Get More Information

Results-Oriented Job Descriptions: More Than 225 Models to Use or Adapt—with Guidelines to Create Your Own, Roger J. Plachy and Sandra J. Plachy, Amacom Books, 1993.

FLSA Status: A Primer

How employees are classified according to the Fair Labor Standards Act (FLSA) is crucial, because if you don't pay overtime to employees who are entitled to it, the penalties imposed by the government are severe. Understand the rules and designate people accordingly.

Exempt employers do not have to pay overtime for work performed by an exempt employee. The most common exemptions are executive, administrative, professional, computer employee, and outside salespeople.

Under federal law, an employee is exempt as an executive if compensated on a salary basis (as defined in the regulations) at a rate not less than $455 per week. Also, the employee's primary duty must be managing the enterprise, or managing a customarily recognized department or subdivision of the enterprise. The employee must customarily and regularly direct the work of at least two or more other full-time employees or their equivalent. Furthermore, the employee must have the authority to hire or fire other employees, or the employee's suggestions and recommendations as to the hiring, firing, advancement, promotion, or any other change of status of other employees must be given particular weight.

The requirements for an administrative employee are very similar, except that the primary duty of an administrative employee consists of office or nonmanual work that is related directly to the employee's policies or general business operations. The employee's primary duty includes the exercise of discretion and independent judgment with respect to matters of significance. Examples of employees in administrative categories who may be exempt include a human

continued

resources specialist, a buyer for a large department store, or the person in charge of marketing.

The professional exemption requires that an individual's primary duties consist of work that requires advanced knowledge in a field of science or learning, involves the exercise of creative talent, or entails teaching in a school or college, and which requires the consistent exercise of discretion and judgment; a salary of at least $455 per week is also required. Also, employees who have substantially the same knowledge and who perform substantially the same work as degreed employees may be exempt if they obtained such knowledge through a combination of work experience and intellectual instruction.

To be exempt as an outside salesperson, the employee must customarily and regularly be engaged in selling goods or services at locations away from the employee's place of business. This federal exemption has no minimum compensation requirement, but the employee may not devote more than 20 percent of a customary work week to activities unrelated to the employee's own sales.

Other exemptions (and partial exemptions) are more esoteric, such as agricultural exemptions, computer programmer exemptions, used car salesperson exemptions, truck driver exemptions, seaman exemptions, radio announcer exemptions, processors of maple syrup into sap exemptions, and others. Exemptions may vary under state law.

This point is of critical importance: to be exempt, an employee must be free from the obligation to be paid overtime under all three of the potential sources of overtime liability—federal law, state law, and employer promises (contract law). To compound the complexity, these three sources of the overtime obligation are often inconsistent, and each exemption under each of the three sources typically has many intricate subrequirements that must be met. Finally, it is typically the employer's burden to establish proof of exempt status.

Nonexempt. A nonexempt employee is one that the employer cannot prove is exempt and for whom the employer must pay overtime when the employee works beyond a number of hours specified by law. (Federal law requires paying overtime after an employee works 40 hours in a work week; California law requires paying overtime when

continued

an employee works more than eight hours in a day and when an employee works more than 40 hours in a work week.) The federal "overtime penalty" for hours worked over the maximum permitted is 1.5 times the employee's regular rate. Some states (including California) require double-time pay under certain circumstances (for example, when the employee works more than 12 hours in a work-day or more than eight hours on the seventh consecutively worked day in a work week).

BEHAVIORAL EXPECTATIONS: HOW TO DIRECT THE *HOW* OF THE JOB

Know the Issue

We've all faced enough cold soup and rude service to know that sim-ply getting food to the table isn't enough. That's why it's important to include behavioral expectations in a job description. Although the job description explains the "what" of the job, be sure to clarify the "how."

In setting expectations, clarify the how from two perspectives: how to do the job, and how to interact with you. Both are important.

Take Action

- *Tell your employees what the job demands.* Given enough time, most employees will figure out what's expected by watching what happens around them. It's more efficient—and kinder—to simply spell it out. Don't make assumptions. Don't ever assume that food servers know how often they should check with diners or that accurate orders are critical. Be prepared to discuss the following:

- ○ Will employees routinely be required to work extra hours? Are those extra hours scheduled predictably or unpredictably? How much notice will employees have?
- ○ How flexible are employees' work schedules?
- ○ Will the employee be required to travel? How often? For how long? To where?
- ○ Are employees permitted to telecommute? Under what circumstances?
- ○ How is vacation time scheduled? How far in advance should employees plan? How often are requests approved?
- ○ Are employees expected to check voice mail or e-mail on weekends or after hours?
- ○ How do employees get assignments? Formally? Informally?
- ○ How often are performance reviews conducted? Are they done on time?
- ○ What is the culture of the organization?

- *Make it clear that duties and requirements are subject to change.*
- *Tell employees how to win.* Employees are not mind readers. Most will adjust willingly to your preferences if they know what they are. Consider what's really important to you. Think about the following:
  - ○ *Personal space.* Do you object to employees leaving things on your desk? Taking things from your desk? Rearranging things on your desk?
  - ○ *Time.* Do you value uninterrupted stretches of time? Prefer quiet mornings when you first arrive? Prefer quiet evenings just before you leave?

- ○ *Communication.* Do you prefer structured meetings or impromptu conversations in the hall? Prefer voice mail, e-mail, or notes on your chair? Expect employees to check in while they are on the road, or to save information until they are back in the office? Interrupt you if your family calls?
- ○ *Status reports.* How often do you want to hear from people? Do you only want to hear when the project is complete, or do you want progress reports? Do you only want progress reports if a problem occurs? Is "Fine" an acceptable answer when you ask how things are going, or do you want specifics?

  These questions have no right or wrong answers. The point simply is to set employees' expectations.
- *Show that you respect employees by asking what's important to them.* You can't accommodate every foible, but you can accommodate many, and why keep doing something that you know drives someone crazy?

Stay Out of Jail

- *If certain behavioral expectations are so critical that failure to meet those expectations puts an employee's job at risk, be sure they are included in the job description.*
- *Be consistent in how you treat employees.* Don't insist that some employees work a rigid schedule while others are allowed flexibility, for example. If you do make exceptions, be sure the exceptions are based on business needs and not favoritism.

Real-Life Example

An executive once told this story about one of his employees. From the day he was hired, the employee made it a habit of meeting with his boss first thing in the morning. Dependably, he would spot the boss coming through the front door and then follow him to his office. Then, while the boss took off his coat and turned on the computer, the employee would start asking questions, updating the boss on progress, and so on. The employee was smart, reliable, and productive—the sort of employee we all hope to have, but he was driving his boss crazy.

The boss had always cherished the first hours of his morning. When he arrived at work, he used that time to enjoy his coffee and plan the day. He saw it as valuable thinking time, and the employee had ruined it. Eventually, the boss began to dread the morning and resent the employee.

When he couldn't take it anymore, the executive shared his frustration. The employee, of course, was surprised, and wondered why nothing had been said before. Together, they devised a new rule: the boss was to be left undisturbed each morning until nine o'clock. After that, the employee, who valued face time with the boss, was in the boss's office each day precisely at nine. Still, it was a solution they could both live with.

Do at Least the Minimum

Be sure employees' expectations are clear about the issues most likely to impinge on their personal time: overtime, vacations, and business travel.

Manage Up

Find out what behavior your boss expects from you, and do your best to meet those expectations.

Get More Information

> *Managers as Mentors: Building Partnerships for Learning,* Chip R. Bell, Berrett-Koehler, 2002.
>
> *The Workforce Scorecard: Managing Human Capital to Execute Strategy,* Mark A. Huselid, Brian E. Becker, and Richard W. Beatty, Harvard Business School Press, 2005.

THE HANDBOOK: HOW TO USE THE RULES TO YOUR ADVANTAGE

Know the Issue

In the beginning, there were the 10 Commandments. All 10 of them include just 179 words, and they seem pretty all-inclusive. But that hasn't stopped people from coming up with more rules. Take something enormously complicated, such as peanut butter. What percentage of peanut butter should be peanuts: 87.5 percent? 90 percent? Transcripts of federal hearings on the debate between those two options run 7,736 pages.

If a 2.5 percent discrepancy in peanut content warrants a debate that runs nearly twice the length of the entire Harry Potter series, how many pages does it take to define the rules in our companies? It depends on our corporate culture. For many years the employee handbook at Nordstrom was printed on an eight-by-five-inch card and ran just 75 words. Even at that, there was room for some niceties ("We're glad to have you with our company") around the real meat of the handbook: "Rule #1: Use your good judgment in all situations. There will be no additional rules." (The realities of employment law have since prompted even Nordstrom to offer a more complete handbook.)

Most companies are a bit more loquacious. At Continental Airlines the handbook became so unwieldy that management launched a turnaround by torching it at a bonfire and replacing it with a slimmer, trimmer version.

On your grumpy days you may have been tempted to burn your own handbook. The rules can seem overbearing, arbitrary, silly, or even counterproductive. But don't do it. Whether brief or voluminous, elegant or imperfect, the handbook is your friend. It enables you to be consistent, to treat people equitably, to avoid managing on a whim, and to keep out of court.

Take Action

- *Know the handbook*. Read the handbook. Then read it again. Know it as close to word-for-word as possible. The handbook is a communication tool that spells out the relationship between the company and its employees. That's a relationship you should understand. And you can bet if your employee wants a particular outcome and the existing handbook supports his position, he'll be able to quote it chapter and verse.

- *Understand the rationale*. Some statements in the handbook may seem arbitrary, but they probably aren't. If you don't understand the reason for a policy, go to HR or the CEO and find out. It's important to be able to enforce the spirit as well as the letter of the rules.

Stay Out of Jail

Comply with the handbook—even if you don't agree with everything in it. Disgruntled employees have won many lawsuits because the policies outlined in the handbook weren't followed. A handbook is a communication tool and a reference guide, but it's also a legal document. This means that ignoring it is about as risky as drinking and driving. Ignorance of the manual is no excuse; if you aren't sure what it says, look it up.

Manage Up

If you spot things in the handbook that are inaccurate, outdated, or not being enforced, bring them to your boss's attention—nicely.

Get More Information

> *Topgrading: How Leading Companies Win by Hiring, Coaching and Keeping the Best People,* Bradford D. Smart, Portfolio, 2005.

INFORMAL RECOGNITION: HOW TO KEEP EMPLOYEES MOTIVATED

Know the Issue

It starts with the gold star on a kindergarten drawing. As we grow older, there are Twinkies passed between friends at recess, notes written in yearbooks, and boosts onto the team's shoulders after scoring the winning touchdown. We are endlessly inventive at finding ways to recognize each other.

Except, it seems, at work. In researching this book, we heard hundreds of stories—good and bad—about what really happens on the job. It's telling that recognition was the issue that came up most often. People feel their work is largely unrecognized, or that it's recognized in ways that actually do more harm than good.

That's disappointing for many reasons, not least of which is that recognition is one of the easiest, cleanest, and least expensive things a manager can do. Almost nothing offers as much bang for the buck, yet we parcel out praise as if we had a very limited supply.

Break the mold. Dole out recognition with the fervor of a preschool teacher, not the parsimony of Ebenezer Scrooge. Find reasons to recognize people, not reasons not to. Get creative like a kid with the big box of Crayolas. Then watch your employees surpass your greatest expectations.

Take Action

- *Decide what you want to encourage.* Any recognition you offer sends a message to employees, so be sure you're sending the right message. In her book, *Management Would Be Easy . . . If It Weren't for the People*, Patricia Addesso talks about a software firm that recognized employees who eliminated bugs from a program. It was a great idea until employees started putting bugs into programs just so they could get rewarded for taking them out. It would have made more sense if the company had offered to reward employees who created bug-free programs in the first place.

- *Think small.* We're all ready to recognize the employee who cures cancer or puts a man on Mars, but those career-making events happen about as often as the Cubs win the

World Series. Recognize the incremental step, the deadline beaten by days, the customer kudo, or the embarrassing error caught in time. The recognition needn't be much; a simple "Thank you" or a chocolate bar on someone's desk makes a big difference.

- *Be relentless.* Saying thanks once or twice a year is nice, but it won't have a big impact on your group's culture. Make recognition a habit. *Keep your personal feelings out of it.* Be careful not to recognize only those employees who are most vocal or whom you like best. Recognize people strictly for their work performance.

- *Make it personal.* Any recognition means more if it's personal and therefore special. If you know something about an employee's hobbies or interests, try to tie what you do to those interests. You might give a can of tennis balls to a tennis nut, or movie passes to someone who wouldn't dream of missing the Oscars. One boss had an employee who collected postcards, and made a point of sending her one whenever he traveled, each one praising her for something she'd done.

  Be sensitive in your choices. Don't give a big box of candy to someone on a diet, for example.

- *Be prompt.* To make the most of recognition, offer it as close to the accomplishment as possible. Make it seem spontaneous. Belabored recognition offered weeks or months after the fact isn't as meaningful. (But yes, late is better than never.)

- *Remember the team.* Sometimes it's tough to single out just one person. When that happens, recognize everyone. Send the group to lunch or bring them all breakfast. Let people know you recognize a group effort.

- *Don't get in a rut.* Vary the recognition you offer to keep it fresh. Create a bank of ideas and then use them all. Recognition that becomes rote isn't too motivating.
- *Be creative.* Recognition is one big opportunity to have fun. Let your imagination run rampant and use all the tools at your disposal:
  - *Time.* Can you let people off early? Give them a longer lunch hour? Let them sleep in? Offer a day off?
  - *Money.* Cash is nice, of course, but so are gift certificates, movie passes, frequent-flyer miles, and so on.
  - *Food.* Everyone has to eat. Consider lunch out or bringing lunch in. Bring in a gourmet coffee bar or have ice cream sundaes one afternoon. There are also the old reliable doughnuts, popcorn, cookies, and Thanksgiving turkeys.
  - *Gifts.* The number of small gifts you can offer is limited only by the number of catalogs and Internet shopping sites you can find.
  - *Presentation.* Say thanks in a handwritten note or with a card. If your employees speak English as a second language, have notes translated into their native language occasionally. Recognize people with balloons or flowers. And don't get your head stuck in the office; surprise a star salesperson by having champagne waiting in her room the next time she hits the road.
- *Offer at least some recognition privately.* Business analyst Louis Ratcliffe points out that if you recognize people in staff meetings, but always take someone into your office to chew them out, then everyone knows what's happening anyway: it might as well be a public reprimand. If you praise privately,

nobody knows what's being said and the dignity of the people receiving reprimands is saved.

- *Remember that not all accomplishments are equal.* Some achievements are a big deal, and the recognition you offer should also be a big deal. (See "Formal Recognition" later in the chapter.)

- *Accept that you'll screw up.* Eventually you'll overlook someone who felt he deserved recognition. It happens. Apologize and move on. Employees will forgive you if you make a consistent effort. If most employees feel recognized most of the time, consider your efforts successful.

Stay Out of Jail

Keep your recognition work-related.

Real-Life Examples

- With numerous drive-in restaurants to oversee, Rick Perkal, vice president of Operations for Austin Sonic, realized he wasn't praising managers enough. "I got caught up in the doing," he says. And he realized that the impact of the praise he did offer was often muted when he shared negatives or opportunities to improve in the same conversation. In response, he developed what he calls praising tours. Twice a month he visits each location for a praising stop. While there, he spots what's right and offers praise. And then he leaves. Any negative observations are saved for another time. He describes the impact of the tours as "profound," noting that people have a desire to please and appreciate the positive feedback. Because the feedback is so direct, Perkal has seen that the praising tours result in greater (and better sustained) improvement than before.

The praising tours are only one tool Perkal uses. He's a believer in standards that he describes as "clear, measurable, and specific," and in measuring against those standards. He also believes that people perform better when those measurements are used in a way that's competitive and fun. One way he does that is a quarterly ranking of supervisors. The company leases a car (such as a Corvette or Cadillac) for the top-ranked supervisor to drive for the next quarter. If they keep their top ranking, they also get to keep the car another quarter. But if someone else earns the top ranking, there's a very public ceremony in which the car keys are handed over. Because everyone wants the keys—and no one wants to surrender them—the competition is a very effective incentive.

- "Although programming was my primary responsibility, there were times I helped the documentation team by writing the more technical sections of manuals," says Catherine, a software engineer. "I considered it just part of my job, and even when the writing team won a national award for one of the manuals, it didn't cross my mind that I deserved any recognition. My manager, however, thought otherwise and gave me an American Express Gift Check in a large denomination! I was overwhelmed by his thoughtfulness and his desire to make sure I was also rewarded."

- Priscilla Ware is a boss who likes to break up the routine. She and another manager stage monthly "unexpected" days. They dress in goofy clothes (cheerleader outfits or feather boas, for example) and have a related treat to hand employees during the day. On Mardi Gras Day they passed out beads all day and had Cajun food brought in for lunch. "Our employees can't wait to see what we'll do next," Ware says. "The laughter breaks up an otherwise boring job."

- Employees had been working for months to solve a problem that jeopardized the company's biggest contract. Nothing had worked, and it looked like the company wouldn't meet its commitment and would pay stiff penalties. One evening an exhausted employee took a break and went to a movie. During the movie, he had a brainstorm and rushed back to the office. He shared his idea, and employees who were still there offered to help him test it. The test worked, and his idea saved the contract. Soon after, the employee was called into the CEO's office. He thought he would hear "Thank you," but instead was reprimanded for working overtime without authorization and for distracting people from their assigned duties. Today, the employee is sharing his brilliant ideas with another employer.

Do at Least the Minimum

Say "Thank you" for a job well done. And say it like you mean it.

Get More Information

Love 'Em or Lose 'Em: Getting Good People to Stay, Beverly Kaye and Sharon Jordan-Evans, Berrett-Koehler, 1999.

Management Would Be Easy . . . If It Weren't for the People, Patricia Addesso, Amacom Books, 1996.

1001 Ways To Reward Employees, 2nd ed., Bob Nelson, Workman Publishing Co., 2005.

FORMAL RECOGNITION: HOW TO CELEBRATE MILESTONES

Know the Issue

Sally Field will never live it down. Accepting her second Oscar, she blurted, "You like me! You really like me!" She's been teased and parodied ever since, but it was an unguarded response to a moment she had worked her whole life to achieve: the acclaim of her peers before family, friends, colleagues, and a billion strangers. (And a chance to wear a cool dress, too.)

Few of us get moments quite like that, but that doesn't mean we don't long for and deserve public recognition. True, you don't want to throw a party every time one of your employees straightens up his desk or even does a good job, but your company, your department, your teams, and your individual employees all achieve milestones worthy of star-studded recognition:

- New product or service launches
- New patents
- Personal development (earning a graduate degree, for example)
- Opening an overseas market or office
- Meeting earnings or profit goals that were a stretch
- An IPO
- Promotions
- Outside recognition (winning a national award, for instance)
- Maintaining a safety record for an extended period
- Meeting specific long-term business goals (increasing the percentage of flights to arrive on time, for example)
- Retirements

Take advantage of these milestones to create formal recognition ceremonies. These ceremonies can recognize individuals, teams, or entire departments. They can be lavish, whole-company affairs or small staff-meeting presentations. The important thing is to make the recognition sincere, appropriate, and public.

Take Action

- *Make the reward reflect the winner.* Recognize personal milestones with trophies, plaques, or merchandise. (Cash is usually a poor choice because it is quickly spent or banked, and therefore has a short afterlife. Trophies, on the other hand, are kept, and remind employees of their accomplishments.) It's okay to reward individuals during other events, such as staff meetings. When recognizing teams or groups of employees, create events that allow the team to celebrate together (such as a chili cook-off or a party).

- *Tell employees how to win.* Although informal recognition is actually enhanced if it's a surprise, formal recognition is another matter. If something in your company is important enough to merit formal recognition, employees need to know ahead of time what that thing is and what they have to do to earn it. Create and share a structure for achieving the recognition:

  - What must one do to be recognized?
  - Who decides who gets recognized?
  - When will the recognition be made?
  - What are the rules? (For example, are employees on disciplinary probation eligible?)

- What form will the recognition take? (A trophy? Money? A new car?)
- Is it a onetime event, or will it be annual?

Make sure the recognition is fair and objective; don't play favorites.

- *Remember, presentation counts.* One employee was startled to see his award slid under the stall partition in the men's room because that's where he happened to be when his boss decided it was time to present it. Somehow, the presentation undercut the impact of the award.

  Employees should feel that the recognition is something special, not an afterthought. You can't always bust the budget with a lobster dinner for 500, but do what you can to make the occasion memorable. Even cheap trimmings (balloons and streamers) can turn a presentation at a staff meeting into a ceremony. If you can afford more, do it. (One CEO flew his entire staff and their families to the Caribbean for a week.)

  As you plan, keep your efforts in scale. Don't make an event to honor a single employee splashier than the ceremony recognizing the companywide milestone.

- *Reflect your culture.* Events work best when they mirror the prevailing culture. If you're in a freewheeling start-up company, a black-tie dinner may not be what gets employees most excited. On the other hand, swing night at the roller rink might not be the best choice for commercial bankers. Events should feel like a natural (albeit special) extension of the workplace. If you're unsure what would most appeal to employees, ask.

- *Don't attach strings.* One boss complained that employees never thanked her when she recognized them. She likened the recognition to Christmas or birthday gifts and said she expected comparable thank-yous. She decided to solve the problem when she recognized employees who worked on a new product launch. She sent them all notes letting them know they would be recognized at a staff event and instructed them to prepare a thank-you speech. She included a list of elements each speech should include. "I didn't feel like I got an award," one employee said. "I felt like I got punished."

Recognition is not a gift—it's something that's been earned. Recognition is about them, not you.

- *Make it personal.* Occasionally, employees may win an award or otherwise be recognized outside the company (by a national trade association in your industry, for example). That kind of recognition is priceless, but employees want to know that it mattered to you, too. Send them flowers or a gift certificate to express your congratulations.

Stay Out of Jail

- *Tie any recognition to the work.* Don't play favorites.
- *Make sure recognition is warranted; don't do it just to make people feel better.* If an employee claims unlawful discipline or discharge, expect to see a trophy as Exhibit One of her worthiness. Did she deserve it?

Real-Life Examples

- Only a handful of employees ever earn one of the highest honors the company bestows. Colleagues nominate recipients for exemplifying the company's values the best. A panel reviews the nominations, and the employees' managers are consulted. Mike was lucky enough to win one, and his coworkers were thrilled; no one deserved it more. But when the day came to present the award, Mike's manager was out. Rather than wait for her to return, the company asked another manager to make the presentation—a manager Mike barely knew. Not only was Mike disappointed, the manager missed her chance to publicly recognize her star employee, his coworkers missed the chance to have a group celebration, and the company missed an opportunity to make a coveted award mean all that it might have.

• Because of changes in the company, the team had had five managers in nine months. Understandably, many things fell through the cracks, including Carla's 10-year pin. Several of her coworkers, who started at the company just weeks earlier than she had, were invited to an elegant luncheon, but Carla missed the cutoff date. The next 10-year luncheon never happened, and so neither did the presentation of her pin. Months had passed by the time someone noticed the oversight. No one offered a luncheon, but they did tell Carla she would get her pin. When the moment came, one of the managers making the presentation looked at the other and said, "Now, what trick should we make her do to get this?" Carla had had enough. "Never mind," she shouted. "Keep your damn pin!"

Get More Information

Love 'Em or Lose 'Em: Getting Good People to Stay, 4th ed., Beverly Kaye and Sharon Jordan-Evans, Berrett-Koehler, 2008.

1001 Ways to Reward Employees, 2nd ed., Bob Nelson, Workman Publishing Co., 2005.

DOCUMENTING PERFORMANCE: HOW TO BE FAIR, COMPLETE, AND LEGAL

Know the Issue

We're good at documenting many things:

- "He leads the league in late-in-the-game stolen bases against left-handed pitchers."
- "That's the fourth-best movie opening ever for a noncomedy in October."
- "The stock closed at its highest price since May 9, 2009, when it was buoyed by a higher earnings projection . . ."

Unfortunately, job performance isn't one of them. If it were, we'd find personnel files with notes like this: "Joan had the sixth-best day of her tenure today when she processed more checks than on any postholiday Tuesday since our merger with GigantiCorp . . ."

Okay, it's a bit much, but it's better than the familiar alternatives, which are inaccurate or incomplete documentation, or no documentation at all.

There is a happy medium: consistent, objective, honest, and thorough documentation of milestones and key conversations. Although that sort of record won't give you the cocktail party cachet of sports stats, it will make for better performance reviews, better management decisions, and a better defense in court.

Take Action

- *Keep track of the big stuff.* You can't document everything, or that's all you'd ever do, but you can and must document key management decisions and the events that influenced them. So, what is the big stuff?

  ○ Counseling and other conversations that could be important in the future regarding discipline, pay, transfer, promotion, demotion, and so forth. Include meetings that you initiate (such as counseling an employee about tardiness) and meetings initiated by the employee (such as conversations in which she expresses interest in a transfer or promotion).

  ○ Discipline, including verbal warnings, written warnings, suspensions, and demotions.

  ○ Evidence of training the employee received.

  ○ Changes in employment (such as raises, promotions, transfers, and commission agreements).

  If there's ever a question about employee performance, you want an accurate record of what was expected, the rewards for meeting those expectations, the consequences for not meeting them, and the training and other support offered to help employees. You also want a record that you will be proud to show to a jury—one that is professional, concise, and based only on work-related issues. You don't want things to degenerate into "he said, she said" finger-pointing with nothing to back you up. If that happens, it will cast doubt on your management ability.

  Most interaction with employees is conversational, so it's lost unless you make a record of it. Document what was said (not word for word, but generally) by both of you. Note the outcome of the conversation. For example: "I pointed out to Julie that she has been tardy six times in the last month on the following dates: August 9, 15, 17, 24, and September 3 and 5. She had no protected reason for the tardiness. This number of absences clearly exceeds what our policies permit. I told Julie that if she's late again during the next 30 days without a valid reason (such as a necessary medical appointment), I will give her a written warning that will go into her file, and that if she's late two or more times in the next 30 days, she could face further discipline, including suspension. Julie explained that she had been having car trouble, but said that she understood and made a commitment to get to work on time."

If a problem gets to the point that a written reprimand is required (see "Discipline: How to Change Problem Behavior" in Chapter 9), then a copy of the reprimand, signed by you and the employee, should be part of your documentation.

- *Be prompt.* No matter how well-intentioned you are, you won't remember the details of your conversations. Notes made weeks or months after the fact aren't as credible as notes made right away. Do your documenting as soon as possible and date whatever you write.

- *Be open.* Give the documentation of the conversation to the employee. Have the employee sign it to acknowledge that he received it. Always allow a place (and sufficient space) for the employee to reply.

- *Keep the documentation.* All documentation should go into the employee's personnel file. That way you can find it when you need it.

- *Limit access to the documentation.* Keeping documentation in the file also keeps it confidential. The only people who should see it are the employee, you, members of the HR staff, and senior management. Even then, no one should see it unless there's a specific management reason to do so.
- *Don't forget informal documentation.* In addition to the formal documentation we've discussed, it's also helpful to keep informal documentation. Many reviews suffer from focusing only on recent events because that's what managers can remember. You can avoid that if you keep notes when employees do something well, or if you notice opportunities for improvement. Because the notes are for you, use any format that works, but keep them brief (for example, "Lillian found a billing error that saved us $10,000") so you aren't discouraged from doing it.

Stay Out of Jail

- *Be absolutely honest.* Don't sugarcoat the truth, or praise employees if you aren't sincere (in hopes of motivating them, for example) or the compliment isn't relevant to their job performance. If a performance problem arises, documentation should prove it, not refute it.
- *Stick to the facts.* Don't speculate. Avoid hearsay and don't express generic opinions. For example, don't just write, "I have lost confidence in this employee's judgment." Explain specifically what happened that caused you to lose faith in his or her judgment.
- *Stick to work-related facts.* Employees' personal lives, beliefs, race, religion, pregnancy status, marital status, and so on are

irrelevant to job performance and therefore have no place in documentation.

- *Verbal discipline isn't worth the paper it isn't written on.* Employees intentionally and unintentionally recall the praise and ignore verbal criticism.

- *Remember that documentation can be a double-edged sword.* Never put anything in writing you would feel uncomfortable having read to a jury slowly, in detail, and while projected on a PowerPoint slide. According to at least one expert, poor, incomplete, dishonest, and inaccurate documentation is the single most common reason that employees file and win employment-related lawsuits.

Real-Life Example

The manager pulled no punches when he called the VP of HR. "I can't stand it anymore," he said. "I have an employee who has a bad attitude, who's chronically late, and who makes a lot of mistakes. She's not doing a good job. She needs to be fired. Preferably today."

The VP of HR agreed that if the employee really had that many performance problems, she should be terminated. He offered to look at the facts in the case and develop a plan.

When he went to the file, however, the VP of HR was stunned: everything in it was positive. There was no mention of a bad attitude, tardiness, or poor work.

He called the manager to ask how long there had been a problem. "Ever since we hired her six years ago," the manager said.

"But there's nothing in the file except reviews saying she's been doing a good job," the VP said.

"Well," the manager snapped, "everyone knows this employee is a problem."

Everyone, apparently, except the employee herself. The VP of HR explained that there was no way to fire the employee without risking a wrongful-termination suit, and even if it were possible, it wouldn't be fair.

Instead of firing the poor performer and hiring the young star he had lined up to replace her, the manager began the long and painful process of documenting all the problems "everyone" knew about. The process was made longer and more painful because of the years of running away from the problem instead of doing the employee and the company the favor of addressing and possibly changing her behavior.

Get More Information

> *Dealing With Problem Employees: A Legal Guide,* Amy DelPo and Lisa Guerin, Nolo, 2003.

PERFORMANCE REVIEWS: HOW TO KEEP EMPLOYEES ON TRACK

Know the Issue

There are all those needles: for blood tests, flu shots, and some of unknown purpose. There are urine samples, cold stethoscopes, and lots of time to catch up on old (really old) magazines while sick people cough all around you. Fun, isn't it? No wonder that despite the fact that annual physicals have proven health benefits, many of us avoid them.

There are proven benefits to annual performance reviews, too. Yet as many or more of us avoid them as well. It requires all that paperwork. Employees argue about what's written or, worse, cry. You're unlikely to get any rewards from your own boss for doing reviews, let alone doing them well. No wonder they're one of the least popular responsibilities managers have.

Although reviews often settle at the bottom of a manager's to-do list, almost nothing bugs employees more than reviews that are late, inaccurate, or never happen. Employees are right—reviews are necessary. You may believe that employees "know how they're doing," but in fact they often don't know. Even if they do know, they want their perceptions validated. Without objective reviews, many of your decisions about raises, promotions, and so on may seem (or even be) arbitrary and unfair.

There is no magic to make reviews stress-free, but you can take certain steps to make them valuable development tools, to enhance your credibility as a manager, help keep you out of court, and help you and your company if one of your decisions is tested by a lawsuit.

Take Action

- *Make reviews a priority.* Block out time on your calendar to write them and to meet with employees. (Share the date with employees so you have an incentive to do the review. Then hold to the date unless you have a really good reason not to.) If need be, take time out of the office to focus on writing the review. If doing reviews is right up there with filing a tax return on your list of favorite tasks, reward yourself for getting them done on time with a nice lunch, a spa visit, or a round of golf.

- *Tie reviews to something.* Some business gurus now argue that reviews should be detached from raises, promotions, or other rewards. The theory is that if the two are linked, employees pay attention only to the amount of the raise and ignore the feedback about their performance. We disagree. We see just the opposite: reviews measure progress against goals and expectations. If the goals are met, employees should be rewarded. (The reward doesn't have to be a raise — it might be a chance to work on a really cool new project, or other perk.) What sort of work would students produce if they had no idea whether their efforts would earn an "A," a "D," or no grade at all?

   Having said that, you may want to detach cost-of-living increases from reviews. Such increases are generally given to all employees to keep pace with inflation. They aren't tied to performance, but people may believe they are if they're discussed during the review. (It's a mistake to give any discretionary raise to an employee at risk of being terminated for poor performance.) Although detaching cost-of-living raises from reviews may mean that people get smaller boosts, they may get raises more often. (For example, Dorothy may get a 3-percent cost-of-living raise in April when the company's fiscal year begins and a 2-percent merit increase in September on her employment anniversary, rather than a 5-percent increase all at once.)

- *Be consistent.* Reviews are not an improvisational art form. They demand a consistent format, especially for all employees in the same job. Your company may have forms that you can or must use. If not, you can buy standard forms or software from management supply firms. You also can create your own form and then use it consistently. There is no "right" format, but be sure you're reviewing behavior and skills related to the position.

- *Be thorough.* Most review forms use a scale, such as "excellent, good, fair, poor" or "far exceeds expectations, exceeds expectations, meets expectations, does not meet expectations," or a numerical scale. Whatever format you use, use the scale as a means and not an end. How does the employee exceed expectations? Existing forms likely rely on very general performance issues, such as decision making or judgment. Those are certainly good things to consider, but go back to the job description and expectations you drafted, and be sure that the review addresses every key responsibility and task. Be specific, and use objective data whenever possible. If you were reviewing a teacher, for example, you could refer to test scores, parent comments, and the percentage of students promoted to the next grade. Offer examples of behavior you'd like to see more of or that needs improvement.

  Also be sure that the review includes examples from throughout the review period. Many reviews inadvertently focus only on the 90 days or so preceding the review, because that's what managers remember. Don't deprive people of credit for great work done during the early part of the review period, or overlook major problems during that time.

  If you're creating your own form, consider the following:
  - Attendance
  - Cooperation and teamwork

○ Communication skills

○ Compliance with safety requirements

○ Compliance with company or department policies

Your mission is not to write *War and Peace*, but a review is an important document, and it shouldn't fit on a cocktail napkin either.

- *Don't play games.* Some reviewers withhold top ratings on the theory that "no one is perfect" or "if I give the top rating, then there is nowhere for the employee to go." Bad idea! Unless you can offer concrete ways in which an employee can do better in a given area, she should get the top rating. Anything less discredits the whole process and your skills. Likewise, never rate an employee higher than he merits to avoid hurting the employee's feelings, having a confrontation, or discouraging him. Our rule for reviews: be totally honest and professional.

- *Don't spring surprises.* Reviews should summarize and validate; they should not shock. Don't wait until the review to let an employee know he's at risk of being fired. Serious performance issues should be addressed promptly, but employees also shouldn't get good news (such as a promotion) during a review unless you've discussed the possibility in advance and they understand that a decision is pending. Reviews should be just one of many conversations you have about performance.

- *Consider other opinions.* There seems to be an unwritten commandment: "Thou shalt apply no imagination to a performance review." Consequently, most reviews consist of one manager assessing one employee. In most cases, that's appropriate, but when an employee has many constituencies, getting other perspectives may be helpful.

For example, suppose you're managing managers. A manager may be well respected by her employees, but not by managers of other departments she must work with (or vice versa). Or a key employee may be an expert at managing up (keeping you happy) while alienating everyone else. One way to get at that information is through multirater feedback, sometimes known as 360-degree feedback, which we have already mentioned.

Multirater feedback is becoming increasingly popular because it can yield richer, more accurate feedback. Of course, no system is perfect, and critics claim that multirater feedback opens the door to hearsay and politicking. To mitigate those risks, consider doing the following:

○ *Include at least five people in the rating.* With any fewer, it's too easy to figure out who said what, which discourages people from being candid. There also are fewer benefits to expanded feedback from such a small pool.

○ *Seek to include raters from all levels.* Limiting feedback to an employee's peers misses the intent of multirater feedback, which is to get a complete picture of an employee's performance.

○ *Keep the feedback anonymous.* If names are attached to ratings, people won't be candid. You also run the risk that the people being rated will retaliate against people who say less than positive things.

- ○ *Be consistent.* If you use multirater feedback for one employee, use it for all employees in the same job.
- ○ *Look for patterns.* Focus on areas where many raters agree. This limits the number of issues the employee must address and minimizes the impact of feedback given with a personal bias.

  Using multirater feedback is a complex process. If you plan to use it, partner with your HR department or contact a professional firm that specializes in such reviews.

- *Get employee input.* A review is an opportunity for dialogue, not a one-sided information dump. Encourage employees to rate their own performance. Most will be honest, and they may raise issues that surprise you. (See the sidebar "Self-Reviews: 12 Questions" later in the chapter for conversation starters.)

  Always leave space on the review form for employees to respond to their reviews.

- *Set a course for the future.* A good review is almost as much about the future as it is about the past. It should give an employee a good idea of what's next. How can he earn another raise? Is training available that the employee needs or can opt for? Are there deficiencies the employee must address? Are there problems that can result in discipline or termination? What opportunities exist for promotion, and how are they earned? What goals do you have for the employee in the coming year? If you don't foresee any significant changes in the employee's job, she deserves to know that, too.

- *Meet with the employee.* A review is an opportunity for discussion, so just handing an employee his review isn't enough.

Sit down with the employee and talk through the year's accomplishments and the next year's goals. These meetings work best if you do the following:

- Set aside at least 30 minutes for a meeting.
- Make an appointment.
- Give the employee a copy of the review during your meeting so he or she can ask questions or comment.
- Get a copy of the employee's comments so you can review them.
- Meet in private and deflect interruptions.
- Meet in a neutral place (such as a conference room).
- Spend at least as much time listening as talking.

- *Review the job description.* If an employee's job has changed enough that her job description is no longer current, now is a great time to update it and review it with her.

Stay Out of Jail

- *Focus on job performance.* Reviews should be fair and objective, so your personal feelings about the employee are irrelevant. Everything in the review should relate directly to job issues. Don't comment on an employee's religion, politics, marital status, or other characteristics. Don't guess at the motivation for behavior.

- *Stick to the facts.* Include objective data whenever possible. When the review is subjective, draw conclusions yourself and base them on specific work-related incidents or behavior. Don't rely on hearsay or gossip.

- *Be honest.* Tell it like it is. If the employee is excelling, say so, but if there's a problem, be candid. Document the problem and outline the steps you expect the employee to take to improve. Don't rate an employee higher than she merits to "encourage" her, reward good intentions, "help" her through a tough personal time, or because you like the employee. Remember, a review could end up in court. It should be the truth.

- *Keep the review.* Copies should go in the employee's file. Have him sign the review to indicate that he received it and understands it. (Include a space for his comments, if any.)

- *Keep it confidential.* The contents of a review should be between you and the employee (and in some cases the Human Resources department). Don't share the contents of a review with anyone else—even if it is positive.

- *Avoid common mistakes.* The road to a good review is studded with land mines. Here are ways to avoid them:
  - Measure an employee's performance against the standards for the job, not against the performance of other people in the job.
  - If no one is performing well, then everyone is falling short of expectations. Poor performance is still poor performance, not average or acceptable performance.
  - Don't let your review of one employee affect your review of others. For example, don't let a superstar or poor performer raise or lower your standards when reviewing the next employee.
  - Don't mistake kindness, favors to you, or loyalty to you for good performance.

- Don't write reviews at 10 P.M. or when you're out of town. Be awake.
- Don't spend less than 30 minutes on any one review, don't do all your reviews in one sitting, and don't set a goal to do a set number of reviews at any one time.
- Go over and proofread your review at least one day after you write it, and don't check reviews in the same order in which you wrote them.

Real-Life Examples

- Dave's review was months late, but his manager assured him he would "get to it." Then, as the six-month mark approached, the manager gave notice that he was leaving. Still, there was no review. Finally, on the manager's last day, he asked Dave for a ride home. As they pulled into the manager's driveway, Dave finally got his review: three lines scribbled on the back of scratch paper.
- Jane ran into her boss in the ladies' room. They said hello, and as Jane entered the stall, her boss told her (over the sound of running water while she washed her hands), "Oh, Jane, by the way, you got the promotion!" Jane, who was by now sitting down, didn't know what to say. When she was first hired she had been told she'd be promoted from an administrative support role to a specialist position after one year. She was now well past the one-year mark, wondering if she'd ever get that promotion. She should have been very relieved and happy, but to be told while sitting in a stall in the ladies' room? Somehow, that scenario had never occurred to her.

- The HR department acknowledged John's five years with the company by giving him his five-year pin, but he didn't get a review. Weeks passed, then months, then his anniversary date. When he finally got his review, along with another five-year pin, it was more than a year late. No one mentioned the entire sixth year he had also worked. "Either I worked my fifth year twice," John said, "or the sixth year doesn't count."

- Madeline had been with her company for more than three years, and it was time for her annual review. It was, as always, positive. Then there it was, in the last sentence on the last page: promotion to manager of her department. Surprise! No one had ever asked Madeline whether she wanted to be a manager. No one had told her that she was being considered for the job, or shared what the job entailed. No one had in any way prepared her for the responsibility she had just been handed.

- Her supervisor put off doing Mary's review because she wanted to identify all the work-related problems she was having with Mary and develop a performance plan to correct them. Months went by and the problems persisted. Then Mary announced that she was pregnant. Two weeks later Mary made another mistake like those her boss had intended to discuss during the review. Feeling that the mistake was the last straw, the boss went to HR with her decision to fire Mary. But HR was surprised that the boss didn't see how her decision seemed to be based on Mary's pregnancy. After all, there was no review to suggest that Mary had performance problems — and certainly not ongoing ones. Mary stayed.

Do at Least the Minimum

- *Do reviews on time.*
- *Put your comments in writing.*
- *Be accurate and honest.*
- *Meet with employees to discuss the review.*

Get More Information

Avoid Employee Lawsuits: Commonsense Tips for Responsible Management, Barbara Kate Repa, Nolo, 1999.

The Essential Guide to Federal Employment Laws, Lisa Guerin and Amy DelPo, Nolo, 2006.

Self-Reviews: 12 Questions

An employee's insight into his or her own performance can be invaluable. Use these questions to jump-start the conversation.

1. Of all the things you've done during the past year, what's the one accomplishment you're most satisfied with? Why?
2. Of all the things you've done during the past year, what's the one accomplishment you're least satisfied with? Why?
3. Based on what you've experienced during the past year, what's a situation you'll handle differently when you encounter it again? How is this new approach better?
4. What have you learned about your job that you didn't know 12 months ago?
5. What have you learned about yourself that you didn't know 12 months ago?

continued

6. When it's time for your next review, what's one thing you would like to have accomplished? Why?

7. In working toward that goal, what resources do you feel are available to you? That is, what here will help you meet your goal?

8. In working toward that goal, are there any obstacles (for example, time, money, lack of expertise) that you feel you face? If so, how can you overcome them?

9. How can I, as your manager, help you meet that goal?

10. What has been your biggest job-related frustration during the past 12 months?

11. What ideas do you have for alleviating the frustrations?

12. How are you more valuable to the organization than you were 12 months ago?

PERSONNEL FILES: HOW TO KEEP YOUR RECORDS USEFUL AND LEGAL

Know the Issue

The story goes that when L. Frank Baum was wondering what to call the setting of the children's book he was writing, he looked up at his file cabinet—specifically at the drawer labeled O–Z.

Your files may not provide such inspiration, but they should provide the first line of defense against miscommunication, misunderstandings, and legal complaints. Of course, this assumes that the files have been kept current and the right material has been kept in them.

Take Action

- *Start at the very beginning.* Begin a personnel file for each employee as soon as he or she is hired. From the outset, the file should include the following:
  - The employee's completed application
  - The employee's résumé and, if applicable, cover letter
  - Material used in deciding to hire the employee, such as assignments, test results, or material provided by an employment agency
  - The offer letter, signed by the employee
  - A signed statement that the employee received and understands the policy manual
- *Keep the file current.* Files should reflect an employee's complete work history, including raises, promotions, transfers, and discipline. Things to include are the following:
  - All documentation (see "Documenting Performance" earlier in the chapter)
  - Performance reviews
  - Evidence of training completed
  - Development plans (if you use them)
- *Don't put just anything in the file.* Some things are not appropriate for a personnel file. They include the following:
  - Information relating to an employee's medical condition or disability (keep that in a separate, secure, confidential medical file)
  - Letters to or from the company attorney

○ Legal claims (such as workers' compensation claims, overtime claims, and grievances)

You may omit other material depending on which state you're in. California law, for example, says that letters of reference and records relating to criminal investigations need not be kept in the employee's personal file. An attorney can tell you the specifics of your state's laws.

- *Keep files in a secure place.* Personnel files should not be readily accessible. Ideally, they should be kept locked.

- *Limit access to the files.* Even with the files locked, people who have no business looking at a file may try to do so. Access should be limited to these people:

  ○ Managers, provided they have a legitimate management reason to review the file

  ○ Members of the HR staff

  ○ The employee him- or herself (under certain circumstances; see "Stay Out of Jail")

Ideally, files should never leave the room in which they're kept. If anyone must take the file (including you), it should be "signed out." You never want a file to be missing or to inexplicably turn up in your living quarters months after it couldn't be found.

- *Don't keep a "shadow" file.* You may be tempted to keep files at your desk on the people who report to you. It may seem convenient, or a good way to keep notes private, but don't do it. Anything worth putting into writing should be kept in the personnel file; otherwise, it looks like you're trying to hide something (which, in effect, you are). Nothing you keep is truly private; your "shadow" files can be subpoenaed in a legal dispute.

Stay Out of Jail

- *Don't put anything in the file you wouldn't want read in court.*
- *Allow employees to see their own files.* Employees have many reasons for wanting to see their files, and in broad terms the courts have said they should be allowed to. The courts also have ruled that access shouldn't be a free-for-all, and that employers should be allowed some limits, such as these:
  - Requiring employees to submit a written request
  - Allowing employees to see their file only by appointment
  - Allowing employees to see their file only during regular business hours
  - Allowing inspection only on the employee's own time
  - Requiring that a representative of the employer (such as you or someone from HR) be present
  - Limiting the frequency of inspections

Virtually every state has laws regulating personnel files. (The Connecticut law, for example, affects both public and private sector employers, defines which records should be included and excluded from files, establishes access rights, states the procedure for correcting information, defines the requirements for disclosure to third parties, and so on.) Check with an attorney about what's required in your state.

Get More Information

> *The Essential Guide to Federal Employment Laws,* Lisa Guerin
> and Amy DelPo, Nolo, 2006.

OVERTIME/COMP TIME: HOW TO PAY PEOPLE

Know the Issue

You've seen the shell game: someone puts a small object (a walnut, perhaps) under one of three identical shells or cups and quickly rearranges them. The challenge is to watch carefully enough so you can identify which shell is hiding the object. Unless the person performing the trick cheats, nothing disappears—it may just appear to.

Paying employees is sometimes like that shell game. Employers start with a basic 40-hour workweek and they shuffle the hours (using alternate schedules, comp time, and other tactics) to avoid paying overtime. But as in the shell game, the hours beyond 40 are still there, and although employees or the law may be temporarily confused, the truth is that employees must be paid for that time. Anything less, no matter what euphemism you use, is cheating and ultimately results in penalties.

Take Action

- *Understand overtime law.* Federal law and the laws of most states base overtime requirements on individual workweeks. The rule is quite simple: nonexempt employees must be paid overtime (1.5 times the regular rate under federal law and most state laws) if they work more than 40 hours in a single week.

Some states also stipulate a daily overtime rule. In such cases, employees must be paid overtime for working more than eight hours in a single 24-hour period. (Note: in at least one state, if an employee asks to make up time lost in the same work week, he can do so without accruing daily overtime, provided that the employee requests the makeup time in writing, without solicitation or encouragement from management.)

- *Don't take overtime lightly.* In a tough economy, many companies watch overtime carefully. But the rest of the time (and sometimes even when times are tough) companies treat overtime as the norm. If you are truly asking employees to work overtime most of the time, then you don't have enough staff. And although there are some employees who welcome overtime because of the extra pay (a trap in itself if they become accustomed to that extra and protest if you cut back), most employees resent the intrusion into their personal lives. Some overtime is inevitable, but don't let it become a crutch.

- *Forget about comp time.* Although the concept of comp time (in which employees are given time off in exchange for, or as a reward for, working overtime) is popular, in reality, there's no such thing. The law doesn't allow this exchange unless it's done in the same week as the overtime was worked. If that happens, there's no reason to call it "comp time" because the employees' time cards will show they didn't work overtime that week. If the requirement isn't met, and employees are given the time off in another week, you may think, erroneously, that you don't have to pay for the overtime actually worked.

The situation is further complicated in states with daily overtime requirements. In California, for example, to even the hours in the workweek, employees must be given 1.5 hours off in the same workweek for every daily overtime hour worked. (In addition, in California, if the time off will be taken in a different week, employers and employees must agree to it in writing. Even that could run afoul of federal law if the employee worked more than 40 hours in the workweek.)

Comp time also exposes you to the risk that how you classify employees will be challenged. Remember that exempt employees aren't eligible for overtime, but if you give them time off and call it comp time, you may imply that they should be eligible for overtime and therefore they are not actually exempt.

Finally, managing comp time can be a nightmare. How much time and money will you spend tracking time that's only being moved from one column to another?

- *Use time off as a reward.* You can still grant time off to reward effort or time worked. Using your discretion lets you reward exempt employees, and you may improve productivity and morale.

Stay Out of Jail

- *Don't cheat.* During tough times, when there is pressure to do more with less, you may be tempted to look the other way about overtime law. You may even be pressured to do so by senior management. Don't. It's immoral, it's illegal, and sooner or later it will come back to haunt you.

- *Pay nonexempt employees overtime for any time exceeding 40 hours in a single week, and as otherwise required by state law.*

Get More Information

The Essential Guide to Federal Employment Laws, Lisa Guerin and Amy DelPo, Nolo, 2006.

NEGLIGENT SUPERVISION: HOW WHAT YOU DON'T DO CAN COST YOU

Know the Issue

As kids we learn there are two ways to get in trouble. We get in hot water for doing the stuff that we shouldn't do: putting crayons in the dryer with Daddy's nice shirts, giving a haircut to the dog, or filling the beanbag chair with milk to see how much it will hold. But we also face the music for not doing stuff we should do: not feeding the dog, not finishing our homework, or not brushing our teeth before bed.

As managers we sometimes forget that we can get into substantial trouble for not doing something. We spend so much energy focused on what we are doing that we overlook the consequences of what we're not doing. Unfortunately, those consequences can be serious. Suppose you send an untrained employee to make a minor repair and he electrocutes himself. Or an employee threatens a coworker, but you decide you'll deal with it when you have time. How will you explain yourself if the employee makes good on her threat before you found the time to deal with it?

These situations are examples of negligent supervision: the failure to meet accepted standards of care, resulting in harm to employees or the public. The law recognizes that supervision is serious business—lives may be at stake. Consequently, you and your firm can be held liable for damage that occurs because of negligent supervision. If you are held liable, the penalties can be substantial, but they're nothing compared to living with the knowledge that you could have prevented a tragedy.

Understand the risks. Be vigilant, and take action.

Take Action

- *Understand your exposure.* It's an exaggeration to say that anything you do (or don't do) might be seen as negligent, but several situations demand particular care:
  - Hiring
  - Training
  - Permitting an employee to use a company vehicle
  - Permitting an employee to be alone with other employees or members of the public
  - Promoting an employee
  - Certifying an employee
  - Failing to fire or discipline an employee
  - Firing an employee without doing an effective investigation
- *Don't make any assumptions about employees.* Just as you shouldn't accept at face value the accuracy of a résumé, don't make assumptions after the hire. Employees may volunteer for additional responsibilities out of boredom, a wish to please,

or to earn a higher wage. It doesn't mean they can actually do the work. Investigate their claims.

- *Don't ignore or minimize problems, actions, statements, or signs that an employee is a potential danger to himself or others.* After the tragic shootings at Columbine High School, the media was filled with evidence of the boys' troubling behavior. The nation wondered: Why didn't anyone notice? Why didn't anyone do something?

- *If something seems amiss, it may be amiss.* It's better to be safe than sorry.

- *Investigate, inquire, and consult with experts—including the police.* Respect employees' privacy rights (see "Privacy: How to Balance the Rights of Employees and Your Company" in Chapter 5), but don't ignore potential problems.

- *Request training on workplace violence.* Learn the warning signs and how to respond.

Stay Out of Jail

- *Be sure employees receive all necessary training before being put in a situation that requires it.* If appropriate, verify that the employee has mastered the necessary skills. For example, as a society we don't accept completion of a driver's education course as evidence that someone can drive; we make them demonstrate their skills to get a license. If an employee has been trained to do a task that involves some risk (making an electrical repair, for example), have the employee demonstrate in a simulation that he can do it before sending him out to do the work.

- *Follow up on all allegations.* Suppose you hear of these behaviors:
  - Proclivity to violence
  - Threats of violence
  - Dishonesty
  - Lack of skills
  - Lack of knowledge
  - Inappropriate behavior from a coworker, vendor, customer, former employer, or even an employee's family member

  Always take such allegations seriously. Your exposure to liability of negligent supervision is greatest if you know of a situation and do nothing. Investigate the accusation immediately, and keep records of your investigation.

  During the investigation, minimize the risk. If an employee tells you that a coworker isn't following safety protocols, for example, pull the employee off the job while you investigate.

- *Take action.* If your investigation confirms a problem, do something. Exercise effective discipline, including termination, where necessary to protect others. For guidance, turn to your employee handbook, consult with human resources, or contact an attorney.

Real-Life Example

Mona was in a no-win situation. A coworker was stalking an employee. The employee was understandably terrified, and the stalker was unresponsive to discipline and even to a restraining order. Mona believed that she needed to fire the stalker and reassign his victim, but the stalker was a diagnosed schizophrenic and therefore protected by the Americans with Disabilities Act. Mona knew that if she fired him, she could expose the company to a wrongful termination suit.

Despite that risk, Mona fired him (and also reassigned the employee). "I was at risk either way," she said. "But I decided that I'd rather go to court than to a funeral."

Get More Information

> *The Essential Guide to Federal Employment Laws,* Lisa Guerin and Amy DelPo, Nolo, 2006.

TRAINING: HOW TO KEEP PEOPLE LEARNING AND GROWING

Know the Issue

Remember the inevitable dinnertime question? "What did you learn in school today?" When was the last time anyone asked, "What did you learn at work today?"

Somehow we get it into our heads that school is a place to learn, and work is a place to use what we've learned. As a result, there's almost no focus on learning in the workplace.

That's unfortunate. If employees are really our greatest assets, it only makes sense to invest in them. Training improves employee contributions. It creates better teams.

It is also a tremendous retention tool. Employees want training, so much so that many cite lack of training as the reason for leaving their jobs. They want the challenge and pride of learning new skills. In today's fluid marketplace, they want the tools to compete in the job market if they have to. (Yes, there's the possibility that an ambitious employee will move on after you've invested in training and someone else will reap the rewards, but what's the alternative—to have someone with minimal skills stay on?)

What kind of training do employees want? All kinds. Some you can provide yourself (teaching an employee to file an expense report, for example), but most training demands subject expertise (sexual harassment training, for instance). It may also demand expertise in adult learning, curriculum design, evaluation, and presentation skills. Training (though sometimes seen as a part of HR) is a profession with its own standards, certification, and associations. Rely on that expertise, whether you find it in your company's own training department, you contract with an outside expert, or you partner with a local community college.

Whatever expertise you rely on, put training at the top of your to-do list. The rewards are limitless.

Take Action

- *Make an inventory.* Before you offer to teach anybody anything, find out what they already know. That doesn't mean you need to put together a complicated formal inventory. Just create a simple form that asks employees to identify the following:
  - *Computer skills* (What software do they know? Are they Internet savvy? Do they have specialized skills, such as familiarity with local area networks?)
  - *Language skills* (Which job-related or computer languages are they fluent in? Consider writing and reading skills as well as speaking and understanding.)

○ *Equipment skills* (Can they operate all the equipment in your office, such as the telephone system, copier, fax machine?)

Ask employees to note whether they have any job-related certifications (such as being certified by the American Red Cross in first aid). Also ask them to list any training courses they remember taking in their current or previous jobs.

The goal is not to note every skill of every employee, but to get a sense of the general skill level of employees and to identify people who may be able to coach their coworkers.

• *Identify training needs.* Before you contract for training or develop a training plan, determine specifically what you'd like employees to be able to do. A lot of training fails because it isn't measurable or applicable; it's a generalized knowledge dump. Suppose you think employees need better computer skills, for example. What do you envision? Do you want them to be able to open a word processing program, write a letter and save it, print the letter, and use a mail-merge function to print an address label? Or do you want them to be able to open a spreadsheet program, create a spreadsheet to use as an expense-report form, enter the expenses of an actual trip, and save and print the report? Develop specific, measurable training goals that will serve as learning objectives. Trainers can use these goals to design the training, and employees will understand what they're expected to learn and whether they've learned it.

Employees may also have ideas of training they'd like. Solicit those ideas at staff meetings, during performance reviews, or through informal surveys. Don't feel compelled to find a way to honor every request, though. Even if you wanted to, you couldn't. There aren't enough hours in the day or dollars in your budget. And you shouldn't. Training should never be offered for training's sake; it always should support a business goal.

If you think an employee's request has merit, ask him to justify the training. The idea isn't to intimidate or discourage people, but to have them think in business terms. What's the value of the training? Do they need enhanced skills to do better in their current job? Or do they feel they need the skills to be promoted to the next job? Employees should be as specific as you are about what they'll be able to do after the training. Although training can be a retention tool for your top performers, you should never offer it to people just to placate them.

- *Look for cross-training opportunities.* The receptionist is out sick, and within minutes the awful truth is apparent: no one else knows how to use the phone system. Or you lay awake at night in terror that your system administrator, the person everyone turns to when they have computer problems, will resign.

  No one wants to be in those situations, and training can help you avoid them. Take time to make a list of all the skills your department needs to keep functioning. Beside each one, identify who has the skill. If only one name is beside any skill, it's time for cross training. Have employees teach each other. Then ask the employee who has just learned the skill to teach you. Teaching is often the best way to learn, so employees will reinforce the skills they just gained, and you'll learn, too.

- *Offer training before you have a problem.* Don't wait until you're fighting a crisis.

- *Find out what training is readily available.* If you have an internal training department (or an HR department that offers training), become familiar with what it offers. Are there courses your staff needs? Encourage employees to sign up. If you have a handful of people who need training, but not enough to justify a whole class, find out if another department is being trained; perhaps your staff can sit in on that training. In addition to teaching courses themselves, a training department may be able to recommend off-the-shelf training products or may have licensed certain training programs for company use.

  If nothing currently exists internally to meet your needs, see if HR or the training department will work with you to develop and test a program.

- *Investigate outside resources.* If internal training isn't feasible, pursue outside resources. If the training you need is fairly generic and widely needed (computer training, for example), you may be able to contract with a local community college. Many colleges work with businesses, and rates are usually inexpensive. For training that is highly technical or specialized, or training you'd like customized, you'll probably have to use a professional training firm. Such training can be expensive, but expertise usually is.

- *Choose a training package carefully.* The most affordable way to use a professional firm is to choose an off-the-shelf training package. Such packages, written by the training company, provide instructional materials (to train the trainer), a training script, workbooks, and other support material. Most often, no one from the firm actually does the training.

How do you choose a training package? Find out which training programs are available by checking out *Training* or *T+D* magazines. You can see many of the products available and talk to training company representatives at the American Society for Training and Development's annual conference.

- ○ *Ask for preview materials.* Most training firms make material (such as videos or workbooks) available for preview. The preview period is usually limited, and some charge a preview fee. (When they do, the fee may be applied to the purchase if you decide to use the program.) Study the materials. Did you learn anything? Are the learning objectives clear? Is the tone appropriate? Does the amount of information seem appropriate?

- ○ *Ask for references and call them.*

- ○ *Ask about the development of the material.* What are the author's credentials? Was the training pilot-tested? If so, who was the sample audience? How old is the program? Is it current?

- ○ *Clarify costs.* Are you buying the program outright to use as you like? Or are you licensing the program for a specified number of uses? Are ongoing fees paid per trainee or for materials? Are you entitled to any updates or revisions to the program?

- ○ *If your staff is large enough for it to make sense, do a pilot.* Use the program to train a group and get their feedback. Did they learn anything? What did they think worked or didn't work?

- • *Choose a training firm carefully.* Packages aren't always the best solution. If you need training that is technical or customized, a training firm can work with you to develop a program, and then teach people in your company to deliver the training. Or choose a firm to design and deliver the training on a contract basis. How do you choose a firm?

○ *Review their promotional literature or visit their Internet site.* What sort of work do they do?

○ *Ask for references and call them.* Ask how well the training worked, but also ask about the client's culture. You may wish to be very involved in developing a program, for example, whereas someone else may have wanted no involvement. Or the training company's laid-back style may have worked well in the client's Silicon Valley work site, but might raise eyebrows in your buttoned-down corporate headquarters. Try to find references with a culture similar to yours.

○ *Ask for a preview.* See if you can attend a training session at another client, or ask if the firm will do a preview session for you and other stakeholders. Get a sense of the trainer's style and how he presents material.

○ *Find out who you'll be working with.* Large training firms are like consulting firms and have many employees. Don't assume you'll be working with the first person with whom you meet.

○ *Find out how the firm develops curriculum.* What are the principal's credentials? What resources do they use? How customized to your needs will the training be?

○ *Explore the firm's approach to training.* Will trainers lecture, or will the training be interactive? What technique does the firm use to engage people who have different learning styles?

○ *Ask how the firm will evaluate the training.* How will they know whether the training has been effective?

○ *Clarify pricing.* Are you paying a flat fee to develop the program or a sliding scale? What control do you have over the final cost? Once the program is complete, who owns it—the training firm or your company? For the training itself, do you pay a set fee per session or is it priced per trainee? Who will pay to produce any necessary training materials?

○ *Get outside the box.* Most corporate training is methodical, highly structured, and even a bit, well, boring. It doesn't have to be. Training can be fun if you let your imagination run wild. Ken Adelman teaches management lessons by having trainees act out scenes from Shakespeare. Dick Eaton, founder of the training firm Leapfrog Innovations Inc., has asked trainees to design and construct holes for a miniature golf course. Other trainers have taught management skills using clips from classic films and by having trainees organize an assembly line to make peanut butter and jelly sandwiches.

• *Put the training in context.* Once you've chosen a course of action, explain it to employees. Tell them why you've decided to offer the training, why you selected the program or trainer you chose, and what you expect them to get out of it. Without that, employees can easily dismiss the training as the flavor of the day.

• *Apply the training.* People won't remember the training any longer than they remember a fast-food meal if they don't use what they've learned. Structure activities that give employees the chance to use their new skills. Suppose employees just received sexual harassment training, for example. Take time at a staff meeting to discuss incidents in the news or on popular television shows.

- *Evaluate the training.* Don't ask employees how the training went and accept "Fine" as a definitive answer. Write formal evaluations of any training programs. Look for commonality in the observations. Were some parts of the training confusing or especially helpful? Do people still have questions that haven't been answered?

  If you're teaching difficult skills (such as computer skills), consider a post-training test to measure whether employees met the learning objectives.

- *Accept that training isn't always the answer.* Despite training's complexity, it's often seen as an easy fix when there are productivity problems. Suppose, for example, that the handoff from one group to another is always difficult. Each group says the other isn't meeting its commitments. Product specs differ, deadlines are missed, and tempers are short. One solution is to offer training on communication skills or project planning.

  Even if employees learn something, the training may not improve the situation at all. Perhaps communication is fine but the groups feel their priorities are unclear. What if the groups consistently get supplies too late? Or if the sales department changes the order mid-project? What if the production schedule is simply unworkable?

  Before you offer training, talk to employees. Ask what they think the problem is. Observe the situation yourself. Do you see a skills gap? What do employees need to be able to do that they aren't doing? If you have an HR or training function, they can be a great resource at this stage.

- *Be serious about training.* Procedures and technical skills (such as creating a spreadsheet) can usually be learned quickly. But significant adult learning—the kind that results in behavior change or expertise—takes time. Don't try to teach something complex in two hours and hope that it sticks. Invest in follow-up training or coaching to reinforce the learning. Give employees time to practice and use what they've learned, and reward their successes. Anything less will be much less effective, and perhaps little more than a waste of time and money. Don't squander an opportunity for genuine change.

Stay Out of Jail

- *Document all training performed, including who received the training, and keep records of employee training in the appropriate personnel files.*
- *Offer training based on need.* Don't offer training only to employees you like. Be particularly careful not to single out gender, racial, or other demographic groups either to receive training or not to receive it.
- *Understand that you can be held liable for negligent training if you don't offer employees the training they need to perform their jobs safely.* For example, if you put a truck driver on the road without the training to keep him from being a hazard, you could be liable if he caused an accident. Similarly,

an employee could file a claim if he were injured because a coworker hadn't been trained to properly use equipment. Believe it or not, an employee can even claim he can't be terminated because the reason he caused $10 million in damage by forgetting to set the fire alarm at night was that he was not properly trained to do so.

Get More Information

The American Society for Training and Development, 1640 King Street, Box 1443, Alexandria, VA 22313–2043, 703/683–8100, www.astd.org.

The ASTD Handbook of Training Design and Delivery, 2nd ed., George M. Piskurich, Peter Beckschi, and Brandon Hall, editors, McGraw-Hill, 1999.

Structured On-the-Job Training: Unleashing Employee Expertise in the Workplace, 2nd ed., Ronald L. Jacobs, Berrett-Koehler, 2003.

The Trainer's Handbook: The AMA Guide to Effective Training, Garry Mitchell, Amacom, 1997.

MEETINGS: HOW TO GET THINGS DONE (WITHOUT WASTING TIME)

Know the Issue

Imagine what would happen if operations in an air traffic control tower were like the average corporate meeting: people speaking over one another and interrupting, random outbursts that have nothing to do with the topic at hand, some participants texting while others sleep, no clear assignment of responsibility, and no follow-up. Scary, isn't it?

The sad truth is that most meetings are pretty scary, too. Meetings are the topic of countless office jokes, widely seen as black holes that absorb huge amounts of time and accomplish very little (if anything). That sort of waste is never a good idea, but in tough times when fewer people are trying to do more, it's simply untenable.

It's tempting to solve this problem by just not meeting. After all, people who were there don't remember that Walt Disney *ever* called a meeting during the year or so that it took to design and build Disneyland—he just gave people responsibilities and expected them to work together to get it done. There's a concept. Realistically, though, we can't really eliminate meetings from today's consensus-building cultures. But just because there aren't jumbo jets full of passengers at stake doesn't mean we can't still run meetings with the efficiency of an air traffic control operation. After all, meetings *should* be an orderly exchange of information to achieve desired results. And they can be.

Take Action

- *Know your purpose.* An excuse to eat doughnuts is *not* a good reason to call a meeting. When you consider that meetings are expensive (the direct cost to the company is the hourly rate of every person in the room multiplied by the length of the meeting), you should only call one when you can justify the cost. What are those justifications?
  - *Effective communication.* Sometimes, a memo just won't cut it. When you need people to really understand something (a change in the company's strategic direction, a new

threat from your competition, a reorganization) and get on board, a meeting is the most effective option. You can make sure everyone hears the same thing at the same time, and you can better judge the response when you can see people. You may also give people the chance to weigh in or ask questions.

○ *Shared expertise.* Except in Congress, two heads (or more) are generally better than one. So when you face especially daunting challenges, getting people with different expertise and perspectives together to address the problem is a smart use of resources.

○ *Consensus.* Like many things in business today, the search for consensus has been overdone. The pace of progress can slow to that of molasses in January as we struggle to get everyone in the building to agree on what should be done next. But while you really don't need consensus on what kind of paper to put in the copier, you may want it on whether to launch a new product. If so, a meeting can be the most efficient way to get there.

○ *Productivity.* Sometimes, even the best-laid plans go awry. When you hit a roadblock, you can mimic most companies and let all work come to a halt to allow for a lot of finger-pointing and hand-wringing. Or you can bring people together to identify the problems and figure out how to get past them.

Whichever of these is your goal, know and communicate that to everyone involved. And do yourself (and everyone's rear end) a favor and don't try to accomplish all these things in the same meeting.

- *Develop an agenda.* Too many people confuse an agenda with a grocery list. They list everything that everyone wants, usually in whatever order it occurs to them. But an agenda is a tool to ensure that a meeting is effective. An agenda should:

  ○ *Include the time, location, and duration of the meeting.*

  ○ *List topics to be discussed in order of importance.* How many meetings have you been to in which the most important subject was given short shrift at the end after time was wasted on trivia? It happens because people convince themselves that getting the small stuff out of the way is more efficient. It isn't. Start with the most pressing matter and proceed in order of diminishing importance.

  ○ *Point people in the right direction.* Sometimes you want to pick people's brains or weigh the pros and cons of a decision; sometimes you want something done. Labeling agenda items "For Discussion" or "Action Item" helps people understand what's expected and keeps them on track.

  ○ *Allocate time for each agenda item.* People who chronically run overlong meetings would do well to serve penance writing a prime-time soap opera, such as *Desperate Housewives.* That's because the writers of such shows are forced to figure out how to move the story along and incorporate all the characters within a finite time frame. They decide what's most important each week and then pace the episode accordingly. You can do the same. If you distribute an agenda showing that 40 minutes of a 60-minute meeting will be devoted to a single topic, people will know what to expect and how to focus their energy.

○ *Assign prework.* Meetings become time wasters when the assembled group doesn't have the information it needs. Review your agenda. If there's information you need at the meeting—financial data, status reports, sales histories—assign someone the responsibility of bringing that information to the meeting (and doing any work that might be required to get it *in advance*). Making such assignments public on the agenda boosts the peer pressure to get the work done; that's a good thing.

○ *List desired outcomes.* What do you want to happen at the end of the meeting? If you don't know, you're not ready to have the meeting. When you do know, include it in the agenda. Everyone in the room should understand what you're trying to accomplish.

• *Run the meeting.* All your smart prep work will only pay off if you actually run the meeting effectively. That means you can't sit back and just watch, as if you've ordered soldiers to march in formation. Running a meeting is more like herding cats. To do it well:

○ *Start on time.* If you start late, you've wasted time before a word has been uttered. And it's rude. If the posted start time is two o'clock, start at two o'clock. Or maybe 2:03, but *not* 2:20. One manager we know actually locks the door at the start time—if you're late, you lose out on the information being shared and get no voice in the decisions being made. We're not advocating for such an extreme tactic, but trust us: start punctually a couple of times and chronic latecomers will suddenly reform.

○ *Take minutes.* You don't want the proceedings of the meeting to turn into tin-can telephone, so be sure there are official minutes. It's best if you don't take minutes yourself, because it's too difficult to take good minutes and run the meeting at the same time. There's usually someone in the group eager to take notes, but it can be more effective to rotate the assignment.

○ *Stick to the agenda.* If you don't follow the agenda, there's no point in having one. Stick to the items on the agenda and to the timeline you've identified. If people veer off topic, gently pull them back to the topic at hand. If they keep veering, get less gentle. (One manager has people stand throughout meetings, on the theory they are less likely to roam off point if they aren't too comfortable. Again, we're not necessarily recommending this tactic.) If someone raises a legitimate issue that truly warrants further discussion, either table the issue to a subsequent meeting or bump something else on your agenda to make room for it. Do *not* just extend the meeting.

○ *Encourage participation.* Although it may seem that all your meetings are like an episode of *The View*—in which everyone talks at the same time and you can't get people to listen to what others have to say—in truth you are probably dealing with two extremes: those who dominate meetings and those who barely say a word. Neither extreme is helpful, since the whole point of a meeting is to hear from several perspectives. Work toward better balance by taking an active role in the conversation. Encourage participation from those who are typically quiet by assigning tasks in advance (so they can prepare something and have a specific part to play) or by asking them directly for their opinions. Thank those who tend to dominate for their participation, but remind them that time is limited and you want to be sure everyone has a chance to speak. (You'll have to remind them of this more than once.)

○ *Respect a diversity of opinion.* If everyone in the room spends the meeting nodding in agreement, then you probably aren't having a good meeting. The goal should be to hear a variety of perspectives, so let naysayers have their say. Yes, you ultimately want consensus (or at least to agree to disagree), but it's best to let all objections and counterpoint to surface early in the process. Make sure that all perspectives are treated respectfully; this is a business meeting, not talk radio.

○ *Determine next steps.* The work of the meeting should not end when participants walk out the door. If you've reached the outcomes identified in the agenda, talk about next steps. If you haven't, identify what needs to happen so you can reach those outcomes. Assign tasks and responsibilities, and set deadlines for the work. People should leave the meeting knowing what to do next.

○ *End on time.* People feel disrespected when meetings are allowed to run longer than their allotted time. Wrap things up and let people get back to the rest of their work.

• *Follow up.* No matter how focused and energized participants are when they leave the meeting, you can't count on it lasting. It's only natural for people to be distracted by phone calls, e-mail, and job tasks. It will fall to you to keep things moving. To do that:

- *Distribute the minutes.* Review the minutes for accuracy and then distribute them to all participants. Be sure to get them out promptly; the longer you wait, the less likely people are to pay attention. Highlight any assignments and deadlines that were set during the meeting.

- *Follow up with individuals.* There may be loose ends when people leave a meeting—people you don't feel are fully on board, questions that weren't answered, concerns that need addressing, assignments that weren't done. Whatever the issue, don't just let it drop. Take time to meet with people one on one to talk it through—*before* the next meeting.

- *Monitor milestones.* Although it would be great to just assume everything that is supposed to get done will be done, life rarely works that way. Set milestones and then make sure things are on track. For example, suppose that someone is assigned to develop a budget before the next meeting. Don't wait until that meeting (or the night before) to find out whether the budget is done. Check in a few days earlier, so there is still time to get it done (and for you to offer help if needed).

Get More Information

Death by Meeting: A Leadership Fable ... About Solving the Most Painful Problems in Business, Patrick Lencioni, Jossey-Bass, 2004.

You Don't Have to Do It Alone: How to Involve Others to Get Things Done, Richard H. Axelrod, et al., Berrett-Koehler, 2004.

WORKING WITH HR: HOW HUMAN RESOURCES CAN HELP YOU GET THE MOST OUT OF YOUR TEAM

Know the Issue

Using a popularity scale of 1 to 10, with 10 being wildly popular (Mickey Mouse, a free lunch, and after-Christmas sales) and 1 being wildly unpopular (telemarketers, the IRS, and rush-hour gridlock), where would you place human resources?

Many people would rate HR a 2—right in there with the Wall Street power suits who flew to Washington in their private jets to ask for a federal bailout. And, honestly, there are some people in HR who deserve that reputation: the paper-pushing, picnic-planning, policy police who are relics of the *Mad Men* era of three-martini lunches and secretaries "named" Honey.

Fortunately, most HR professionals today are more enlightened and more effective. They jump in to help solve problems and they work as partners, not opponents. How do you know whether your HR department is friend or foe? There are two simple tests.

The first is to look at where HR reports. If HR reports directly to the CEO, then the department is more likely to be a true business partner, looking at employees as assets to be developed and working to help employees reach their potential. On the other hand, if HR reports to the CFO, then the department is likely to see employees as a cost center to be controlled, and you're far less likely to find a true partner.

The second test is to consider how well the people at HR understand your part of the business. If no one can tell you your department's turnover rate, how long it takes (on average) to fill a job in your department, how much your department contributes to the bottom line, or what your best performers actually do all day, then

HR is probably a foe. In such cases, we encourage you to ignore these people—except when it comes to legal matters, or if you think you have a chance to turn them into a friend.

Today's best HR pros are business-focused. They help engineer ways to make the business better, and to do this they have to understand the business and all its components. This means that someone in HR can offer you much more than just accurate information about the vacation plan. She could help you redesign jobs, create an incentive plan to drive up profits, or find an assessment tool to improve your hiring success. If someone from HR asks about your business, is willing to hear about your business, or (best of all) works alongside you in your part of the business, you've just found a valuable partner.

The trick is then getting the most out of that partnership. As with any successful relationship, it demands give and take. But if you invest in a partnership with HR (assuming you have an HR function where you work), you're more likely to rate HR an 8 on the 1 to 10 scale, or better.

Take Action

- *Show your respect.* It will be difficult—if not impossible—to have a good working relationship with HR if you have no idea what HR does, if you only contact HR to whine or complain, or if you expect HR to clean up your messes.

- *Identify your resources.* Start by figuring out how HR is structured. In some cases, a central HR function serves the entire organization. The department has specialists in each discipline of HR, such as staffing, compensation, and benefits. In other organizations, each business unit or department has its own HR function; they are usually staffed by HR generalists who have broad knowledge in all areas of HR. Some large companies have a hybrid of these two models.

None of these is the "right" approach. The only thing that matters is that you know who to go to for help. The ideal is to bond with an HR generalist who can either work with you directly or connect you with the appropriate specialist. That person can also advocate for you within HR. If you can't identify a single person with whom to work, find a handful of specialists and build relationships with them.

- *Teach a crash course.* For anyone in HR to really help, they need to understand your part of the business and understand it almost as well as you do. Offer to take your HR contact to lunch once a week and spend the time teaching. Be willing to invest some serious time because your course needs to be thorough:
    - What do you see as the primary purpose of your department?
    - How is your department's success measured?
    - Where is your department excelling and where is it failing? Why?
    - Who are your star performers? What sets them apart?
    - Who are your poorest performers? What sets them apart?
    - What are your biggest frustrations and challenges?
    - What do you see as your key strengths?
    - Where would you like the department to be in a year? Why? How do you plan to get there?

○ What happens in your department every day? What are your production schedules, budgets, deadlines, productivity goals, and so forth?

Be honest. Painting an artificially rosy picture won't get you the help you need.

- *Take a crash course.* Invest some time learning about HR, too. Listen to what your contact tells you about his job. And if you don't know, ask the following questions:

  ○ How does HR function every day? How are priorities set?

  ○ What expertise does HR have to offer?

  ○ Who do they see as HR's key customers?

  ○ What makes them say yes or no?

  ○ How is HR's performance measured? How does it win or lose?

  ○ Which HR programs or initiatives do they think are working best? Why?

  ○ What challenges does HR face? (Budgetary? Staffing HR? Time?)

  ○ How do HR initiatives in your company (pay rates, benefits, employee development) compare to those of your competitors? How do they compare to the average company in your area?

- *Put your cards on the table.* This relationship—like any other—demands honesty. Share how you really feel about HR, pro and con. Explain where those feelings come from. Are they based on bad experiences, successes, or hearsay? Talk about what you appreciate about HR and what drives you crazy. Bring up HR efforts in other companies that you've heard about and like or don't like. Then ask HR for the same feedback about you and your department.

- *Keep HR in the loop.* Once HR has a solid understanding of your department, they need to stay current. The more they know, the better, and the more they can observe firsthand, the better. There are lots of ways to do that:
  - ○ Invite your contact to shadow you for a day or parts of days — let them watch you and your department in action.
  - ○ Invite HR to sit in on your staff meetings.
  - ○ Send HR copies of key memos, status reports, and other information tied to department milestones.
  - ○ Plan regular lunches or meetings with your HR contact.

- *Choose your battles.* Don't drop 15 problems in HR's lap and expect equal attention to them all. Other departments need help, too! Identify your top concern and work with HR to resolve it. Getting one thing done will give you a sense of accomplishment and boost everyone's credibility.

- *Don't jump to conclusions.* It's great to go to HR with ideas, but don't get too invested in a single course of action. Your HR partner may see other options. Managers often request a training program, for example, when they face a challenge. But changes in hiring practices or even job design may ultimately be the better solution. Respect HR's expertise.

- *Be willing to be a guinea pig.* Perhaps you read about a cool HR effort in the *Wall Street Journal*. Or perhaps you had a great idea yourself. If you find yourself wondering, "Why don't we . . ." then consider volunteering to pilot a program. You can team up with HR to develop a program, and then test it in your department. Together you can work out the kinks. If it works, you'll get the benefits and you can enjoy the acclaim as the program is rolled out through the rest of the company.

Stay Out of Jail

- *If you have an HR function, you should always consult with them about the following:*
  - Hiring
  - Discipline
  - Termination
  - Employee leave
  - Workers' compensation
  - Employee complaints (such as sexual harassment and discrimination)

  Check with HR before you take action.

- *No matter how great your partnership is, HR will sometimes say no.* It doesn't mean they don't like you. Remember that one of HR's greatest responsibilities is to protect the company from lawsuits. (As one HR executive observed, "The better we do our job, the less visible we become.") Employment law is complex; trust HR's counsel.

Real-Life Examples

How would you like to have a binder on your desk that walked you through every stage of employee development for every employee you manage? A binder that includes job descriptions, required competencies, aptitude tests, specific interview questions, tailored performance appraisal forms, and more? A binder that gave you enough information so you could focus on day-to-day operations and help employees solve problems?

If you worked at Valspar Corporation, you'd have one. That's because HR has created those binders for every one of the company's more than 3,800 jobs. The effort started as a small-scale attempt to identify core competencies in the manufacturing department, and it spread from there.

Salespeople at Buckman Laboratories International, Inc. make big sales pitches—pitches in which million of dollars in revenue are at stake. But how can a salesperson in Thailand get the information she needs to close a sale if the home office is closed?

At Buckman, the salesperson can get the information anytime, from anywhere in the world. That's because HR has worked with managers to promote knowledge sharing. The idea is to take the axiom "two heads are better than one" and turbocharge it with technology. Thanks to online forums, connected knowledge bases, electronic bulletin boards, and virtual conference rooms, employees can tap into each other's knowledge and experience like nowhere else.

At one time Continental Airlines was the laughingstock of the airline industry. The carrier had been through two bankruptcies and there was a revolving door in the executive suite. Passengers could expect poor service, late arrivals, and lost bags. No wonder employees tore the company patches off their uniforms at the end of the day; they didn't want anyone to know where they worked.

Then management teamed up with HR and took the airline from worst to first. An incentive pay program, streamlined policies (to replace the policy manual that management publicly burned), and aggressive communication improved every area of performance. Today, employees keep the patches on their uniforms and share in the airline's newfound profits.

Employee teams setting goals and measurements for themselves? Employees teams managing themselves while managers act as coaches? Believe it. It's a profit-driving reality at GE Fanuc Automation of North America, Inc. More than 40 work teams are proving it can be done, and the best coaches are the managers earning the greatest rewards. It works because HR partners with managers in the coaching process; an HR staffer is part of every department.

Get More Information

> *The Essential HR Handbook: A Quick and Handy Resource for Any Manager or HR Professional,* Sharon Armstrong and Barbara Mitchell, Career Press, 2008.
>
> *Human Resource Champions: The Next Agenda for Adding Value and Delivering Results,* Dave Ulrich, Harvard Business School Press, 1997.
>
> *Human Resources Kit for Dummies,* 2nd ed., Max Messmer, IDG Books Worldwide, 2006.
>
> www.shrm.org
>
> www.workforce.com

5

And Then There's Real Life

The best-laid plans . . .

You know the rest: things don't always pan out the way we had hoped. That can be true of everything from a dinner party to a presidential campaign, so it shouldn't be any surprise that it's true at work, too.

You can hire the best people, establish the best policies, manage in the most enlightened way, and real life will, alas, still intrude. People will do things they aren't supposed to do; they will make mistakes; they will get sick.

It's fruitless to lose sleep worrying that something will happen, and pointless to beat yourself up when it does. What you *can* do is take steps to respond in ways that are effective, compassionate, and minimize the risk of getting into legal trouble.

CONFLICT MANAGEMENT: HOW TO RESOLVE DISAGREEMENTS (WITHOUT BLOODSHED)

Know the Issue

Please allow us to oversimplify. There are two kinds of problems in the world: the right kind and the wrong kind. At work, you can burn up a lot of time and effort seeking a problem-free workplace, but in our combined 60 years of consulting, speaking, and writing about work, we've stumbled across very few of those. (Okay, truthfully, none of those. But that doesn't mean there isn't one out there somewhere.)

The right kind of problems push an organization toward new possibilities. The wrong kind of problems paralyze and distract. What does this have to do with conflict? Everything. Because some conflict is inevitable at work. It's often the result of bright and driven people who believe they are doing the right thing, encountering other bright and driven people who also believe they are doing the right thing—just not the *same* right thing. Until these bright people can agree on how to resolve the conflict, it's a problem. But odds are high that the conflict will eventually result in something better than the bright, driven people had so far put forward.

Then there are the wrong kind of problems, in which people are standing behind these two groups of bright, driven people taking potshots at them from the rear. Or doing their own personal imitation of a speed bump. Or worse.

So this section is about conflict management, not conflict avoidance. We've listed some questions that you should ask when you come across a conflict at work.

Take Action

- *Share responsibility (rather than just blaming the other party).* Smart moms never let you off the hook when you blame your friends for your arguments; you are just as much at fault. So try starting with a simple apology for everything you've contributed to the mess.
- *Look to the future (and let go of the past).* Conducting an autopsy of your past problems will only endanger your current precarious truce. Instead, ask, "What do we each have to do from now on to preserve our working relationship?"
- *Focus on what you need (rather than what you want).* As Mick said, you can't always get what you want, but if you try sometimes, you just may find, you get what you need. Forget your wish list; focus instead on your bottom line.
- *Be flexible.* In disputes, flexibility always seems to be the first casualty. Can you both make the commitment to be more flexible in the future?
- *Focus on what's best for everyone.* Sometimes helping the combatants take a step away can give them much needed perspective.
- *Accept differences in style.* Has someone suggested a great idea that you would never have thought of in a million years? Chances are that their brain is wired differently than yours, or they've had different experiences or their strengths are different from yours. Whatever their origin, differences in style are something that should be appreciated and embraced, not resisted.

- *Stop being selfish.* Aside from Mother Teresa, most of us have our selfish moments. If you're the one acting selfishly, try to stop. If the other person is the selfish one, rather than focusing on one selfish act, remember all the people who've let you back in their good graces after you've done something negative. Return the favor by being more charitable now.

- *Find out what's going on.* Believe it or not, people usually have a reason for believing what they believe. Taking the time to ask your coworker about her perspective could provide you with a new idea, could give you insight into how she arrived at a position different than yours, or could finally prove that she is totally crazy. Simply asking her about her position increases the odds that you can find common ground.

Real-Life Example

A boss wrote to Workplace911.com to share his strategy for resolving conflict. He has a standing offer to any two employees engaged in a conflict: he'll buy them lunch to work out their problems. The catch? They have to come back and tell him how they've resolved their differences. He calls it "the cheapest problem-solving tool ever."

Get More Information

The Coward's Guide to Conflict: Empowering Solutions for Those Who Would Rather Run than Fight, Tim Ursiny, Sourcebooks, Inc., 2003.

The Fifth Discipline Fieldbook, Peter Senge, Broadway Business, 1994.

How to Mediate Your Dispute, Peter Lovenheim, Nolo Press, 1996.

FEAR AND MISTRUST: HOW TO OVERCOME NEGATIVE EMOTIONS THAT INFECT THE WORKPLACE

Know the Issue

We all love a good scare: the big drop on the roller coaster, the icky chills in a Halloween haunted house, the unexpected lunge in a suspense flick. That fear is a quick adrenaline rush, usually followed by the release of a good laugh.

Yes, we love a good scare—but not at work. The fear that infects the workplace isn't quick, and there's no rush to it. Instead, it lingers in the workplace, sapping energy and morale, undermining productivity and brewing suspicion.

That sort of crippling fear can infect the workplace even in good times, but we are especially susceptible when times are tough. And once fear invades, it's very hard to displace. Remember how your grandparents or parents talked about the Great Depression—as if it had just happened yesterday? Our recent travails—layoffs, foreclosures, corporate collapse, shrinking 401(k)s—won't leave the public consciousness quickly. Even as the economy picks up, people will hold onto their desks with white knuckles for a while. Losing your livelihood and hope can do that to you.

Of course, you can't control Wall Street excess, H1N1 flu, or other triggers of widespread fear. But you have a strong influence over the atmosphere you work in. What you do can help mitigate the fear or add to it. Need proof? Lynn Taylor Consulting conducted a national poll in which 76 percent of workers said they become fearful when their boss closes his or her door. Not when their boss announces a layoff. Not when their boss conducts a disciplinary hearing. No, 76 percent of people become afraid when their boss closes the door.

If closing a door can have that kind of effect, imagine what kind of fear other activities may stoke. As amazing as it may seem, some bosses actually work to *create* fear. For some, it's just one facet of a power trip; others believe that a little fear motivates people. It doesn't. The sooner you can eliminate that kind of negativity from your workplace, the better.

Take Action

- *Teach, don't punish.* Do you yell first and ask questions second? When employees make mistakes, do you tend to reprimand before you have all the data? If you reprimand first, you discourage the kind of employee experimentation that raises morale and promotes progress, and you instill fear. Turn fear into respect by using mistakes as growth opportunities.

- *Cut the sarcasm.* Is there a lot of sarcasm in your workplace? Where there's sarcasm, there's usually fear, because sarcasm makes people the butt of the joke. You can eliminate that source of fear by working to eliminate all sarcastic jokes and comments from your workplace. Start with your own repertoire, then make it clear you won't tolerate sarcasm from others either.

- *Discuss the undiscussables.* What are the "undiscussables" in your workplace? Every place has them: employees who get favored treatment, policies that aren't followed, managers who inspire fear. But as they say in politics, sunlight is the best disinfectant. Ask your employees about the undiscussables and then listen intently to what they say. They won't confide in you immediately, but if you gently keep at it, don't retaliate, and instead take constructive action, you can build their trust. That goes a long way toward reducing fear.

- *Play dumb.* Instead of blowing in like a hurricane and blasting people with directions and information, *ask lots of questions.* That can be one of your best methods for "lightening up." You'll be amazed at what people already know. And your employees will appreciate your respect and deference to their knowledge.

  Model the behavior you'd like to see. Workplace911.com got an e-mail from someone who worked in an office where everyone left early and was constantly goofing off—everyone except Mary. Believe it or not, Mary gradually changed everyone else's behavior simply by modeling what everyone knew they should be doing. Leading by example does work.

- *Use humor.* Humor is a great way to both disarm people and to get them to remember what you're saying. So don't leave your humor at home—it's a great release valve for fear. Just remember not to make fun of others. And you don't need to; you'll be surprised how far self-deprecation will get you.

Get More Information

Driving Fear Out of the Workplace: Creating the High-Trust, High-Performance Organization, Kathleen D. Ryan and Daniel K. Oestrich, Jossey-Bass, 1998.

The Power of Indirect Influence, Judith Tingley, Amacom, 2000.

SEXUAL HARASSMENT: HOW TO RECOGNIZE AND PREVENT INAPPROPRIATE BEHAVIOR

Know the Issue

Which of the following true incidents do you believe are sexual harassment?

- A coworker keeps his wife's picture on his desk. The picture was taken on their Hawaiian honeymoon, and she's wearing a bikini. The picture is visible to anyone who enters his office.

- An older man in the office refers to the younger women in the office as "the girls." When addressing them, he calls them "honey" or "sweetheart." Sometimes he puts an arm around a shoulder, and tells the woman that "pretty girls keep this old guy going."

- As they walked out of a restaurant following a business lunch, the boss dropped a handful of M&Ms into his secretary's breast pocket and squeezed her breast.

- A newly hired employee leaves his wife and two children at home when he accepts a job on an offshore oil rig. On the rig, he's taunted by other employees and supervisors. One day a coworker holds him in a shower stall while another coworker shoves a bar of soap between his buttocks and threatens to rape him.

    Perhaps you find all these incidents offensive; or perhaps you find the photo harmless, the older man lacking in judgment, and the M&Ms and soap incidents repugnant. Therein is the challenge of sexual harassment—what's hostile or offensive is, to a large extent, in the eye of the beholder, which makes it hard to define.

Officially, the Equal Employment Opportunity Commission (EEOC) says that sexual harassment includes "unwelcome sexual advances, requests for sexual favors, and other verbal or physical conduct of a sexual nature." Specifically, such requests, advances, or sexual conduct constitute harassment when

- Submission to such conduct is made a term or condition of employment, or submission to or rejection of such conduct is used as a basis for employment decisions affecting the individual (these are often referred to as quid pro quo or economic harassment).

- Such conduct has the purpose or effect of unreasonably interfering with an employee's work performance or creating an intimidating, hostile, or offensive working environment (commonly known as hostile work environment or environmental harassment).

This polite legalese covers—if you'll pardon the phrase—a multitude of sins: pressure for sex, touching, groping, suggestive behavior, provocative clothing, sexual humor, sexually explicit or suggestive photos, Internet porn, a *Sports Illustrated* swimsuit issue, a Victoria's Secret catalog, and much more.

Are all those examples of sexual harassment under any circumstances? No. The courts have generally determined that something is harassment by using the standard of a "reasonable person." (Some courts have held that if the alleged victim is a woman, then the standard is what a reasonable woman—not "person"—considers unwelcome and sexual.) That legalese certainly sounds, well, reasonable, but it hasn't kept sexual harassment from becoming the most controversial, divisive issue in the workplace.

That's because it's proven surprisingly difficult to reach a consensus about what's "reasonable." Cultural changes—including the greater prevalence of sexual images, language, and discussion throughout society, a backlash against ideas seen by some as "politically correct," the use of false allegations of sexual harassment to retaliate, and an increase in workplace dating—have complicated the picture.

So what's a boss to do? Look the other way and hope for the best? Or clamp down on workplace behavior with more rules and policies to make sure no one is ever offended? Both approaches have been tried without much success. Ignoring the issue can lead to class-action suits and multimillion dollar judgments, as Flushing Hospital in Queens, New York, discovered in early 2009 when a jury awarded a nurse $15 million after supervisors ignored her complaints that she was being harassed by a physician. More policies led down an Orwellian path to "love contracts," in which employers require dating colleagues to sign a document stating they wouldn't claim sexual harassment if the relationship goes sour. (Don't misunderstand: we agree such a contract may be legally desirable under certain circumstances.)

The prudent approach is to take the middle road. State clearly that you take sexual harassment seriously and that you'll investigate all complaints promptly. Then follow these guidelines. The guidelines won't guarantee that no one will ever be offended. Indeed, sexual harassment law is so complex that we can't help you through every possible scenario, but the guidelines can help you through most situations.

Take Action

- *Foster a climate of respect.* Sexual harassment is usually not about sex; it is about power. Harassment reflects a misguided sense of superiority (particularly over the person being harassed), and it's therefore more likely to happen when disrespect of any kind is tolerated. Don't allow employees to post sexually explicit photos, even in locker rooms or restrooms. Don't tolerate inappropriate humor, language, or familiarity at work. For example, don't permit jokes or cartoons based on racial, ethnic, or gender stereotypes to circulate. Don't allow employees to use profanity. Be sure that employees refer to one another by name, rather than using nicknames or terms of endearment ("sweetheart," for instance).

- *Look for warning signs.* If you create a positive environment, employees usually step forward when a problem arises, but this is not always the case. It helps to be aware of the signs that may indicate a problem. Parallax Education, a Santa Monica, California-based firm that specializes in sexual harassment issues, suggests watching for:

  ○ A noticeable change in the behavior of an employee, including, but not limited to, tardiness, absenteeism, and mood swings

  ○ An employee who avoids another employee or shrinks from another employee's physical proximity

  ○ Openly sexual behavior between employees, even if it seems welcome (for example, one employee sitting in another's lap)

○ Frequent after-work partying or heavy drinking

○ Unprofessional behavior during business trips or conventions

If you observe any of this behavior, don't assume there's a sexual harassment problem. You should, however, counsel employees not to engage in any openly sexual behavior at work, and remind them to act professionally when they represent the company, even if it's outside the office. If individual employees seem troubled, don't ask if they're being harassed, but do ask if you can help with anything.

- *Take seven steps to fight harassment.* In a 1998 ruling on sexual harassment, the Supreme Court said that employers may be able to avoid liability or limit damages if they can establish the following:

  ○ They exercised reasonable care to prevent and promptly correct any harassing behavior.

  ○ An employee unreasonably failed to take advantage of any preventive or corrective opportunities provided by the employer, or he or she otherwise failed to take reasonable steps to avoid harm.

  There are steps you can take to demonstrate a good-faith effort in preventing and correcting the problem, and encouraging employees to step forward if a problem arises (see "Stay Out of Jail" later in the chapter).

- *Take all complaints seriously, but don't assume guilt.* Any charge of sexual harassment should be taken seriously and investigated promptly (see "Stay Out of Jail" for more information), but don't assume that all accusations have merit. Employees may charge they've been harassed if a consensual relationship ends to settle a score or to express anger. (One employee, for example, filed a sexual harassment complaint within hours of being disciplined for excessive absenteeism.) In each case, look at the evidence presented by the witnesses and do your best to reach an impartial conclusion. (The disciplined employee, for example, provided a list of witnesses to the alleged harassment, but in the investigation, none of them corroborated the incidents.)

- *Be sure you don't take action without sufficient grounds to do so.* In an effort to stop sexual harassment immediately, some supervisors have stepped in to solve problems that didn't exist. It's possible, for example, to overhear a conversation or to hear something out of context and assume that sexual harassment has occurred, when the employee in question views the situation differently. But always investigate if you have reason to believe harassment has occurred or a complaint is filed, and take action when it is warranted.

- *Keep sexual harassment complaints and investigations confidential.* You won't accomplish anything good by letting the whole office know about a sexual harassment investigation, and you could do a lot of damage. For example, if an employee is accused of harassment and later found innocent, the employee could argue that he was defamed if word of the charges is spread. Generally, limit any conversation to the following:

  ○ The employee who claims to have been harassed

  ○ The person accused of the harassment

  ○ Representatives in your HR department

○ An attorney representing your employer in the case

○ Any people who are witnesses or possible witnesses to the alleged harassment or similar conduct by the alleged harasser or witnesses who the alleged harasser says will support his denial

Caution everyone involved to respect an employee's confidentiality and not to talk about the situation or the investigation.

- *Come to a conclusion.* The investigation's purpose is to determine whether sexual harassment occurred, and if it did, to swiftly punish the conduct so it doesn't happen again. If you fail to take swift and effective action to prevent sexual harassment, you stand to lose all credibility in the eyes of your employees, the EEOC, and the courts. It can also result in punitive damages. Remember, whether you took effective action to prevent sexual harassment will probably be judged in hindsight and be based, at least in part, on whether sexual harassment occurs again under your watch.

- *Track complaints.* Keep confidential records of all harassment complaints. Without records, you could be unaware of a pattern of harassment by the same person. Such a pattern could be relevant in determining someone's credibility or in disciplining an employee.

- *Don't ignore the aftermath.* Sexual harassment investigations are painful, especially if the allegations prove true. Even when the investigation is complete and you've taken action, it will take time for the wounds to heal. Take these steps:

  ○ Do not answer questions about the case from other employees; the details should be confidential. You can answer questions about the company's policy on harassment or about how claims are addressed.

○ Put a copy of the conclusion reached following the investigation in both employees' personnel file.

○ An employee who's been harassed may feel uncomfortable continuing to work alongside the harasser. If the employee who was harassed asks to be separated from the harasser, consider honoring the request by moving the harasser. Doing this shows good faith on your part. It isn't always reasonable to honor such requests. It is generally a bad idea, however, even to consider reassigning an employee who was harassed; if she is unhappy with the new assignment, you may face complaints that you made the assignment in retaliation for the harassment claim.

○ If you have an employee assistance program (EAP), remind the employee who was harassed about the program. If you don't have an EAP, consider paying for a limited number of sessions with a professional therapist. Counseling is the compassionate thing to do and can help the employee be more productive at work.

Stay Out of Jail

• *Understand the legal landscape of harassment.* Sexual harassment takes many forms. It can happen at work or off-site. It may involve employees, customers, or vendors. Very few people are truly experts on harassment law, but you should know the basics.

• *Follow these steps to fight harassment.*

1. *Make sure your company has a written (and legally satisfactory) antiharassment policy.* Work with an expert, such as an attorney, to develop a policy on sexual harassment. The policy should be easy to understand. Be sure it includes specifics about the procedures for making a complaint. The procedure should give employees options for making a complaint to more than one person.

2. *Distribute the policy.* Having a policy in a three-ring binder somewhere is not enough. Make sure all employees have a copy. Review it with them and have them sign a statement that they received it and understand it.

3. *Conduct training.* All managers and supervisors (yes, that means you) should have training on sexual harassment regularly (we recommend annually). One of the best ways to prevent harassment is to teach all employees about specific prohibited behavior and tell them they will be held accountable for such behavior.

4. *Audit employment decisions.* Be sure that all employment decisions (such as promotions or terminations) are handled appropriately and consistently, and that no decisions are made outside the system. Otherwise, for example, employees might be unfairly punished for resisting a supervisor's advances. If you work in a large organization, ask HR for help.

5. *Conduct prompt and thorough investigations.* Take every complaint seriously and investigate promptly. If your firm has an HR department, work with HR to conduct the investigation. If you don't have an HR department, consider bringing in an outside expert (such as an attorney or a consultant with expertise in sexual harassment). That's

because a thorough investigation is critical, and an incomplete, inaccurate, or biased investigation can make the situation worse. The investigation should include the following:

- Interviews of the employee making the complaint
- Interviews of the person charged with the complaint
- Interviews with witnesses (usually identified by the employee who was harassed or by the person charged with the harassment)
- Review of any evidence presented by either side (such as notes, e-mail, voice mail messages, photographs, and so on)
- Documents outlining each step of the process and any findings

6. *Take prompt and effective remedial action.* If you conclude that harassment has occurred, take swift action to stop it and prevent its recurrence. Depending on the situation, that action might include the following:

- Oral or written warning or reprimand.
- Transfer or reassignment.
- Demotion.
- Reduction of wages.
- Suspension.
- Discharge.
- Training or counseling of harasser to ensure that he or she understands why the conduct violated the employer's antiharassment policy.
- Monitoring the harasser to ensure that harassment stops. Ascertain what the complainant believes would be

appropriate discipline. Although it's important to consider the complainant's opinion, keep in kind that her suggestions may be too punitive or too lenient. The discipline meted out should reflect the seriousness of the offense. If the harassment was minor, such as a few crude remarks by someone with no history of misconduct, then counseling and an oral warning may be all that's needed. If the harassment was severe or persistent, however, suspension or discharge may be necessary.

7. *Remember, it's up to you to take swift and effective action to prevent a recurrence.*

8. *In most cases, it may also be necessary for the company to rectify the consequences suffered by an employee who was harassed.* This may include:

- Restoring leave taken because of the harassment
- Expunging negative evaluation(s) in an employee's personnel file that arose because of the harassment
- Reinstating a fired employee
- Asking the harasser to apologize
- Monitoring treatment of the employee to ensure that he or she is not subjected to retaliation by the harasser or others in the workplace because of the complaint
- Correcting any monetary harm caused by the harassment (for example, compensation for losses, including emotional distress and lost wages or salary)

9. *Follow up on remedial measures.* Check back with the employee who made the complaint to be sure your action

has been effective. Document any follow-up interviews, including the employee's comments.

Real-Life Examples

- Rena Weeks was employed as a secretary by the legal firm of Baker & McKenzie for just 70 days. During that time, she was assigned to work with attorney Martin Greenstein for less than a month. But shortly after leaving the firm, Weeks filed suit, claiming that Greenstein had sexually harassed her. Her claim resulted in a judgment against the firm of $3.5 million in punitive damages and $50,000 in compensatory damages. Greenstein personally was ordered to pay $225,000 in punitive damages.

  This case underscores how seriously you should take sexual harassment because those judgments were rendered despite the facts that Weeks worked in the firm such a short time and worked for Greenstein an even shorter time. Beyond that, the incidents Weeks defined as harassment happened over a two-week period and, compared to many incidents of harassment, were relatively tame. Weeks accused Greenstein of:
  - Dropping a handful of M&Ms into her breast pocket and squeezing her breast following a business lunch.
  - Lunging toward her with cupped hands and saying, "What's wrong? Are you afraid I'm going to grab you?"
  - Repeatedly asking her during lunch, "What's the wildest thing you've ever done?"
  - Grabbing her buttocks as they were packing items into a van.

But Weeks didn't win her case alone. The jury heard testimony from seven other women who claimed that Greenstein also harassed them, and decided that the firm had not made sufficient effort to stop the harassment. The jury initially awarded damages of $6.9 million, but the judge later reduced this figure.

- The doctor felt an immediate affinity for the new lab technician, and as they talked, he learned that they had a lot in common. He was particularly struck by how similar their backgrounds were: Both had been born in Africa and raised in France before immigrating to the United States. Consequently, they shared many cultural values and perspectives.

  The doctor made a point of saying hello to the technician, and eventually began asking for her by name. He tried to arrange it so she could do the lab work he required.

  One day the technician mentioned the doctor's visits to her supervisor and shared some of his comments. Days later she was called into the supervisor's office. There, she was greeted by her supervisor and by the officer for medical affairs. They wanted details about the sexual harassment she had experienced from the doctor. They talked to her at some length about what had happened and assured her that the matter would be resolved.

  The following day, the technician called the medical affairs officer from her home. She said that she had been surprised and upset by the meeting. She didn't feel the doctor had harassed her and didn't want his reputation to suffer. She said that she hadn't complained to the supervisor and didn't understand how the situation had spiraled out of control.

Ultimately, the investigation was dropped and the supervisor was coached by HR for taking aggressive steps without a complaint or any evidence that there was a problem.

Do at Least the Minimum

- *Insist that employees treat each other with respect.*
- *There are no shortcuts when it comes to sexual harassment.* Follow the multistep plan outlined above. Investigate complaints promptly, confidentially, and thoroughly every time.

Get More Information

The First Line of Defense: A Guide to Preventing Sexual Harassment, Wanda Dobrich and Steven Dranoff, Wiley, 2000.

The Manager's Pocket Guide to Preventing Sexual Harassment, Terry Fitzwater, Human Resource Development Press, 1999.

What Every Manager Needs to Know About Sexual Harassment, Darlene Orlov and Michael T. Roumell, Amacom, 2005.

PRIVACY: HOW TO BALANCE THE RIGHTS OF EMPLOYEES AND YOUR COMPANY

Know the Issue

While doing the laundry, you find a note in your son's pocket that suggests he may be using drugs. Do you ignore it? Do you ask him about it when he gets home? Or do you rush to his room and search for evidence? What if instead of a note you find a permit to buy a gun?

The answers aren't easy. If you ignore the evidence, someone could get hurt, or worse. Your son's grades, reputation, and health are at risk. On the other hand, if you search his room, you risk shattering his trust in you and undercutting any willingness he might have to discuss difficult topics with you. Unfortunately, these are dilemmas faced by parents every day.

Managers face them, too. On the one hand you have a responsibility to protect employees and company property, including equipment, data, and money. But getting results demands communication, and employees are less likely to talk with someone they don't trust.

The issue is further complicated by the fact that the workplace privacy issue is far from crystal clear. All of us struggle with where the right to privacy begins and where it ends because there is no single authority on the topic. There isn't a single word in the U.S. Constitution about privacy, yet the Supreme Court has ruled that there is a "penumbra" of rights that address the issue. Yet because the Constitution restricts government action, decisions on privacy rights in the workplace involving the Constitution apply mostly to federal employees. That hasn't stopped many states (including California) from including guarantees to privacy in their constitutions that apply to private employers. Privacy standards have been shaped by state and federal statutes and regulations and by court decisions.

By now that may sound like enough to send you running from the room, but stay with us; there are ways to balance employees' right to privacy with your right to protect people and your company's assets.

Take Action

- *Establish expectations.* Ironically, the less your employees expect privacy, the less likely you are to have a problem.

Practically speaking, low expectations mean employees are not disappointed or surprised by their employer's actions. Low expectations also provide the legal defense often needed if there is a lawsuit. Employee handbooks, job application forms, written policies, and contracts should all carefully set forth your right to inspect, search, test, and check for illegal substances and objects, illegal activity, and the improper use of company equipment (including computers, telephones, desks, lockers, locks, and e-mail) consistent with applicable laws.

- *Focus on business reasons.* Just because you can search an employee's desk doesn't make it a good idea. If employees believe their privacy is invaded, they may feel distrusted and angry, and morale may suffer.

  Therefore, don't even think about conducting a search unless you have evidence or a strong, verifiable reason to believe the following:

  ○ An employee is stealing.

  ○ An employee is using company equipment improperly.

  ○ An employee is engaged in illegal activity (such as selling or possessing illegal drugs).

  ○ An employee's safety may be at risk.

  Don't mistake suspicion for a reason based on objective fact. You should always have a compelling reason based on objective fact to jeopardize an environment of trust.

- *Consider doing a search only as a last resort.* First, try old-fashioned detective work and simple questioning of employees; that's often enough to "crack the case."

- *Stay out of employees' private lives.* Don't ask employees about their marital status, the health of their personal relationships, or other issues unrelated to work performance.

  In addition, it's usually best not to try to regulate employees' off-duty activities. Some employers, for example, have tried to dissuade employees from parachuting or bungee jumping (for fear of injury and therefore expensive medical claims). Others have sought to keep employees from moonlighting or from participating in events that the employer feels may cast the company in a negative light (marching in a political protest, for example). But 28 states now limit such restrictions, and four (California, Colorado, New York, and North Dakota) ban any employer restrictions on lawful activities after hours.

Stay Out of Jail

- *Because so many jurisdictions govern privacy law, be sure you know and understand the law that applies to you.* Consult with your HR department or with an attorney. A misstep can result in a lawsuit involving emotional distress damages and punitive damages, as well as poor public relations. Jurors take privacy issues seriously. You should, too.

- *Be very careful about searching anything that isn't company property*, such as purses, briefcases, or pockets. Such action should always be discussed with an attorney first, should never be done without an objective reason for suspecting an individual, and should be supported by "airtight" language (such as in your handbook).

- *Consult your policies and follow them.* Don't make up the rules as you go along.

- *If an employee does not voluntarily open her purse or desk, or otherwise doesn't cooperate with an investigation, the last thing you should do is touch the employee.* Do not physically detain, push, grab, grab at, or move an employee or her purse or other belongings. Assuming the employee was obligated to assist in the search, it's better to consider the employee's evasion as an implied admission of guilt and try to get the information some other way.

- *Never conduct a search or inspection with respect to an employee because he or she is a member of a group* (for example, a minority or a political group).

- *Don't overreact or react emotionally.* Drugs in the workplace, pornography, and illegal gambling are serious offenses and you can't ignore them. But whatever you do should reflect reality. The fact that there may be (or is) a problem on the manufacturing floor does not mean that employees' rights may be ignored.

- *If an employee shares personal information with you, keep it to yourself.*

Do at Least the Minimum

- *Be sure your employee handbook and other key documents accurately clarify expectations of privacy consistent with the applicable law.*

- *Do not conduct a search or investigation without having a compelling business reason.*

Get More Information

Privacy Rights Clearinghouse

www.privacyrights.org/workplace.htm

MEDICAL PROBLEMS AND THE FMLA: HOW TO HELP AN EMPLOYEE THROUGH A PERSONAL OR FAMILY MEDICAL CRISIS

Know the Issue

A star athlete pulls a hamstring and there's no question: he goes out on the disabled list, he gets the best treatment, and, unless the injury is exceptionally severe, he comes back. No one—coaches, fans, teammates, or sports writers—questions any of it.

What a contrast to what sometimes happens when the average employee gets sick or injured. She begs for time off to get treatment. She gets demoted to lesser jobs. Behind closed doors managers wonder, "How do we get rid of her?" To her face they make it clear that her illness better not get in the way of her job performance.

Why this ugly disparity? It's simple: sports teams understand that players are their greatest assets; the focus is on getting the player back because losing him or her is expensive and painful. Many employers don't understand that employees are their greatest assets, so they believe it's easier and cheaper to replace someone than to face lost productivity or take a hit on their medical insurance premiums. They are wrong on both counts.

Because of this mistaken thinking, the problems faced by sick and injured employees have become so prevalent that Congress has taken action to protect them. The 1993 Family and Medical Leave

Act (FMLA) gives about 70 percent of the workforce basic protections when they or their loved ones face a serious medical problem.

However, the law is so complex that many people—employers and employees alike—don't understand it; therefore, it's often used incorrectly or not at all. Almost a third of the workforce isn't covered by the FMLA. Many aspects of managing an ill or injured employee aren't addressed by the law.

Employees will get sick and injured, so this isn't an issue to ignore. Understanding the basics of the FMLA helps (and, if you're in a company with 50 or more employees, it's a necessity), but it isn't enough. Go beyond the FMLA and imagine that all your employees are star players and the Super Bowl is approaching. Think about how you can help them get well and come back.

Take Action

- *Encourage employees to stay healthy.* There's no magic wand to keep employees from getting sick, but encouraging healthful behavior can significantly reduce the risk. If you work for a large company that has a wellness program, encourage employees to use it. If you don't have that resource, think about other things you can do, such as:
  - Brown-bag lunch programs or training on nutrition, exercise, CPR, first aid, prenatal care, HIV, and even defensive driving
  - Smoking cessation programs
  - Partial or total reimbursement of gym memberships
  - Encouraging before- or after-work walking programs

These efforts needn't be expensive. Classes are available from many nonprofit organizations that charge nominal fees. Even training by professionals is less expensive than paying a claim after something happens.

- *Don't encourage people to work when they're sick.* Do you see every cough, sniffle, and wrenched back as a personal affront or a sign of weakness? Do you make employees feel guilty for taking time off? If so, you prolong symptoms, impair productivity, and spread germs throughout the office. You also send a signal that employees are only cogs in the machine, not people.

  Keeping top people is easier if you let them take care of themselves. If your company has a sick or personal leave policy, encourage employees to use it. If your firm doesn't have a policy, advocate for one. If people come to work a hacking, sneezing mess, encourage them to go home, and then deploy other resources to make sure the work gets done. If you're sick, do everyone a favor—model the right behavior and stay home.

- *Keep medical information confidential.* The nature of an employee's illness isn't anyone's business—not even yours. You need to know only two things: that an employee is too ill to come to work, and that he or she is well enough to return. You don't need to know why, and you don't want to know. If you have medical information about an employee, you run the risk of a discrimination charge if you take any action the employee feels is negative, even if you know your action is unrelated. You also carry the burden of protecting the employee's privacy. If you don't know, you can't tell.

Many companies have a policy requiring a doctor's note for an employee to return after an absence of a specified period (more than two days, for example). The policy is reasonable, but advise employees that the doctor needn't put a diagnosis on the note.

Any medical information about employees should be kept in a confidential file separate from their personnel file.

- *Respect employees' wishes.* Employees may choose to share medical information with you. (Studies have shown that when people are diagnosed with a serious illness, someone at work is often the first person they choose to tell.) If that happens
  - Ask why the employee is telling you. (Does she simply need someone to listen? Is she requesting an FMLA leave? Does she need a reasonable accommodation? Is the employee offering an explanation for what she may feel is diminished performance?)
  - Find out what the employee would like you to say, if anything.

  Some employees may want to keep the diagnosis private; others may want to share it with coworkers; still others may want coworkers to know, but want you to tell them. If the employee asks for privacy, do not talk to others. If the employee asks you to share the news, ask her to make the request in writing and keep a copy in her medical file.

- *Be sure employees understand their benefits.* Employees often don't think about their benefits until they are ill and need them. However, they don't always think clearly under stress. If you have an HR department, set up an appointment for the employee to meet with someone who can explain his coverage. If you don't have an HR function, contact the insurance carrier and ask for someone who can help the employee understand the plan. Employees need to understand their coverage, their rights, and their responsibilities.

- *Understand the Americans with Disabilities Act (ADA).* Some illnesses and injuries are serious enough that employees become disabled. If that happens, they may be protected by the ADA and entitled to reasonable accommodation. (See "Disabilities: How to Help Employees Give Their Best" in Chapter 7.)

- *Understand the Family and Medical Leave Act (FMLA).* Depending on the severity of an illness or injury, employees may need time off to recover. If you're in an organization with 50 or more employees, your company is subject to the FMLA. If you have fewer than 50 employees, you may still choose to follow FMLA guidelines. Doing so is good for morale and retention (and may be required by a state law). Just be consistent; don't pick and choose who can take leave on any basis other than a legitimate business reason.

- *Don't discriminate based on pregnancy.* Until fairly recently it was common for companies to refuse to hire pregnant women, to fire women during their pregnancies, or to refuse to allow a woman to return to work after giving birth. All of these practices are illegal. A woman's pregnancy tells you nothing about her ability to do the job, so assume it's not relevant in any hiring, promotion, work assignment, or termination decision. Beyond that, do the following:

- View a disability caused by pregnancy or a related condition just as you would any temporary, physical disability. (In California, leaves may have to be more generous than those provided for other temporary disabilities.)
- Don't attempt to practice medicine; rely on actual medical observation and opinion.
- Recognize that employees aren't the only ones who get sick or injured. Employees may face a crisis at home if a spouse, child, parent, or partner is ill or injured. They may even need time off to be a caregiver. The FMLA provides for employees to take leave as a caregiver for a spouse, parent, or child in certain situations. Some companies also give leave to employees who must care for a domestic partner.

Stay Out of Jail

- *Don't make decisions about hiring, promotions, work assignments, termination, or other work activities based on an employee's actual or perceived illness, injury, or other medical condition.* (The exception to the rule is when an employee brings medical evidence justifying, for example, a transfer.)
- *Don't permit jokes, remarks, comments, or inappropriate statements relating to any employee's illness, injury, pregnancy, or related conditions.*
- *Don't decide yourself when an employee's condition merits a leave or transfer.* Rely on a doctor's opinion.

Real-Life Examples

- The manager's secretary was diagnosed with a serious illness and needed to take time off. Because the manager liked the woman, and in fact found her indispensable, he told her that she should take whatever time she needed and that her job would always be there. A few weeks later another employee needed a medical leave. This time the manager gave the employee notice that she was being put on a 12-week FMLA leave and gave her paperwork explaining her rights.

  Ultimately, one of the employees sued the company. Which one? The first employee to go out on leave. While she was out, her manager left the company. Without him, no record of the arrangement was made and the company terminated her employment. She claimed, unsuccessfully, that a promise had been broken.

- An employee was a young mother fighting a rare kind of cancer. Traditional therapies didn't work, and doctors wanted to try experimental treatment. The treatment would require her to spend a day every two months as a hospital outpatient, and would leave her weak and tired. Nonetheless, she wanted to keep working, and she didn't want anyone's pity.

  With her manager's approval, she decided to use her personal days for treatment. Together, they shuffled deadlines and work schedules so her absences wouldn't coincide with crunch times. The employee also offered cross training to some of her colleagues so they could help if need be when she was out.

The employee was thrilled. "I got the treatment I needed and I didn't have to talk about being sick all the time," she said. "We just talked about how to get the work done. That's what was right for me."

- The star employee hadn't been himself, and then he started calling in sick. The CEO asked the HR director what was wrong, but she refused to tell him. One Friday he cornered her, threatening her job if she wouldn't tell. Reluctantly, she acknowledged that the employee had AIDS. She made the CEO promise not to tell anyone else.

The next morning the employee did his usual weekend errands at the post office, the cleaners, and the grocery. Everywhere he went he was treated differently than he'd been treated before, and not in a way that made him feel loved. He had told only one person his diagnosis, so on Monday he went to the HR director. She admitted telling the CEO and apologized. After the employee left, she went to the CEO. "You promised not to tell anyone," she said.

"I only told my wife," the CEO said, but his wife had decided that people in town "needed to know, to protect themselves." Several weeks later the man resigned his job and left town, his life in ruins. The company began fighting an expensive lawsuit that it was destined to lose.

Get More Information

The Essential Guide to Federal Employment Laws, Lisa Guerin and Amy DelPo, Nolo, 2006.

DRUG AND ALCOHOL ABUSE: HOW TO CONFRONT THE ADDICTED EMPLOYEE

Know the Issue

When the *Exxon Valdez* ran aground and spilled millions of gallons of oil into Alaska's pristine offshore waters, it was an ecological disaster. It was also a high-profile example of what can happen when employees abuse drugs or alcohol on the job. Exxon spent years slogging through the aftermath.

Drug abuse is a serious problem. That's why many employers carefully screen applicants to help keep users of illegal drugs off their payrolls. (See the sidebar "Types of Drug Tests" in Chapter 8.)

But what if drug users slip through the screening and get hired? Or existing employees begin using illegal drugs? You can still take steps to protect your employees and your business.

Take Action

- *Know your organization's policy.* Review your employee handbook. Most organizations have a stated policy about drug testing and illegal drug use. Whatever the policy, follow it. Don't be the only manager to require drug tests unless, for example, you manage the only department in which employees directly affect public safety.

- *Don't keep the policy a secret.* If your policy requires employees to pass drug tests as a condition of employment, remind them of that. You might post notices of the policy in work areas, for example.

- *If no company policy exists, develop one for your department.* Don't do drug testing using the whim system. Determine why and when you'll test for drug use. When hiring, focus your attention on employees whose jobs involve safety or security. Once employees are hired, you also want to be able to test if you have a reasonable suspicion or evidence of drug use. The policy also should expressly prohibit the sale or possession of illegal drugs. Make sure the legal department or an attorney approves it.

- *Know the law or consult with someone who does.* Drug testing, like many employment issues, pits two competing sets of rights squarely against one another: the employee's right to privacy, and the employer's right to a safe, productive work environment. Given this conflict, it isn't surprising that federal and state legislatures and courts have enacted laws or expressed opinions on the subject. Your options must be evaluated within the limitations of the states and court decisions that apply to you and your company's employees.

- *Know your options for testing.* You can't discipline an employee for drug use merely on the suspicion of drug use. You need to have evidence of drug use, which is why testing is so important. (Of course, you can discipline an employee for poor performance, violation of company rules, insubordination, and so forth whether the infractions are drug-related or not.) You have options for testing, and there are appropriate uses for each:
  - Periodic testing is conducted, as the name suggests, periodically; in conjunction with an annual physical, for example.

But periodic testing also may include unannounced tests for a group of employees (such as people in jobs in which safety or security are at issue) when random testing is impractical because of the number of employees involved. Periodic testing can be controversial because it is unrelated to any suspicion or evidence of drug use and therefore unlawful in some states. Controversy is mitigated if the physicals are job-related and consistent with business necessity, if employees are told before being hired that they'll be tested, and if employees are told they're subject to discipline if they fail the test or refuse to take it.

○ Reasonable suspicion testing may be done if you have direct, specific, and immediate observations of behavior, appearance, odors, and/or speech that suggest drug use or if you have evidence that your substance abuse prevention policy has been violated. (Symptoms of drug withdrawal also may be grounds for testing.) It's best to have another member of management confirm your observations.

○ Postaccident testing assesses employees who have had an on-the-job accident that caused a fatality, a serious injury, or significant property damage. Such testing may also be done after near-accidents, as when an employee loses control of a vehicle but manages to stop without hitting anything. Unfortunately, in many states the fact that an accident occurred is not sufficient grounds for creating the suspicion that drugs or alcohol were involved. Check with an attorney about the laws in your state.

○ Random drug testing refers to selecting employees for testing at random and without notice. It may also refer to testing the entire workforce on a date selected at random and not announced. (Note: employers in some industries—including trucking, shipping, airline, and nuclear power—are required to do random testing of some employees.) As a legal matter, this is the most risky type of drug testing you can require. There are fewer justifications for it, and employees are not warned. Random testing is illegal in Rhode Island, Vermont, and other states.

○ Return-to-work testing is used after an employee has tested positive for drug use or otherwise violated a company's drug policy, after rehabilitation and before returning to work. Follow-up testing is designed to encourage recovering addicts to stay clean. Testing is done after rehabilitation at predetermined regular intervals. Before doing either of these kinds of testing, check the law. It's also a good idea to draft a written contract that addresses the terms and conditions for return-to-work and follow-up testing.

• *Choose a methodology.* There are several methods of drug testing. The accuracy, legality, and expense of the tests vary, so review your options and choose what's best for your company. (See "Types of Drug Tests" in Chapter 8.)

• *Choose a vendor.* If your HR department already has identified a testing vendor, use that one. If not, be sure to select a reputable and reliable vendor (see "Types of Drug Tests" in Chapter 8).

• *Encourage employees to seek treatment.* Even if you are not required by law to give employees leave to seek treatment (see "Stay Out of Jail"), consider allowing such leaves if employees request them. (Usually, policies allow employees to take leaves without disciplinary consequences if employees volunteer for them before employers find they have violated policies.) There are good reasons to do so:

○ Drug-abuse prevention programs that include employee assistance or rehabilitation are most effective at achieving drug-free workplaces.

○ Employees have incentive to seek treatment earlier.

Stay Out of Jail

- *Know the law in your state or seek legal advice before taking action.*

- *Don't subject an employee to a drug test merely because he associates with another employee known to use drugs. Base your decision to test strictly on observable job-related behavior.*

- *Be consistent in asking employees to be tested for drug use. Be careful, for example, that you are not singling out only employees of a particular racial or ethnic background.*

- *The Americans with Disabilities Act (ADA) is complex legislation that has some implications for drug testing* (see "Disabilities: How to Help Employees Give Their Best" in Chapter 7):

○ Current use of an illegal drug is not protected by the ADA.

○ Addicts who are participating in or have completed a supervised drug rehabilitation program and are no longer "current users" are protected.

- ○ Those wrongly perceived as using illegal drugs are protected.
- ○ Employees taking drugs under a physician's care are protected. Therefore, give employees who test positive for drugs the chance to provide medical documentation to explain the results. Do not require employees to reveal prescription drugs they are taking.
- ○ Current users of alcohol may be disabled under terms of the ADA even though current drug users are not. However, even a current user of alcohol is not covered if the alcohol is affecting the employee's job performance or conduct.
- *Keep the results of drug tests confidential.* Keep the results in medical files separate from an employee's standard personnel file.
- *The Family and Medical Leave Act (FMLA) is another federal law with provisions that relate to drug and alcohol use.* If your firm is subject to the FMLA, you must allow qualifying employees to take leave for treatment of drug addiction or alcoholism.
- *Where practical, use the same lab to assure uniformity of testing.*
- *Employees who test positive for illegal drugs may claim they are not users. In such cases, they may ask for another test to confirm the results.* (Normal protocols for testing stipulate that labs test only one-third of the sample provided. That means they can conduct another test without getting another sample.) You are not obligated to pay for the second test.

However, false positives are possible. Many employers choose to pay for the second test as a matter both of fairness and precaution.

Get More Information

National Institute of Drug Abuse Workplace Help Line, (800) 843–4971 or www.nida.nih.gov

6

It's Not Your Father's Workplace

When *Mad Men* debuted, people were shocked by the world of 1960s corporate New York that it portrayed: three-martini lunches and drinking during meetings; groping of secretaries (usually called Honey or Sweetheart)—and secretaries actively covering up their bosses' dalliances; a glass ceiling for women that was about six inches off the floor; blatant racism; anti-Semitism; and homophobia. Men wore *suits* to work. It all seemed as alien as Regency France.

To quote an ad campaign popular at the time, we've come a long way, baby. That the characters in *Mad Men* wouldn't recognize a modern workplace is entirely a good thing. Today's environments are more egalitarian, more creative, and offer better opportunities for everyone.

They also present some challenges that dwarf such petty concerns as where to let the drunk people sleep after an office party. Today's managers must contend with everything from Internet porn and Crack- (er, Black-) Berry addiction, to employees working from home—or halfway around the world.

But it's also a time of unparalleled innovation and opportunity, a time in which a manager can make a real difference. And that beats a three-martini lunch.

INNOVATION: HOW TO GET CREATIVE IN TOUGH TIMES

Know the Issue

Chico Marx, of the famous Marx Brothers comedy team, was once asked if he loved his brother, Harpo. "No, but I'm used to him," he replied. Does that remind you of the way your company does much of what it does? Not necessarily because anyone loves it, but because everyone is used to doing it that way?

Unfortunately, it doesn't stop there. Organizations are remarkably effective at squashing innovation. As we discussed in the opening chapter, the Corporate Immune System in most organizations is remarkably capable of squeezing the life force out of any new idea or initiative.

That's especially true, unfortunately, when times are tough. Instead of looking for new ideas (and thus adapting to a new reality), many companies assume a bunker mentality and become more entrenched than ever, as if they are waiting out a long winter. A hibernating bear isn't likely to blaze new trails.

But you can. Lead the charge of being innovation-friendly by following the strategies below. Your company's future just may be at stake.

Take Action

- *Learn how and why things are currently being done the way they are.* The status quo is there for a darn good reason—it often works. It just might not be the best way, the most efficient way, or the smartest way to operate. But before you throw the baby out with the bathwater, find out everything you can about the current approach and why it's being used.

- *Seek advice from unconventional sources.* The corporate tradition is to round up the usual suspects when you want to improve how things are being done. You're better off rounding up the *un*usual suspects: vendors, other departments, customers, and even company troublemakers.

- *Accept that some things should stay just as they are.* Again, chances are good that some parts of the existing operation are actually working. So don't just toss away things for the sake of change. Keeping some constants in the organization will also provide necessary stability for people who are struggling to adjust.

- *Understand how innovation happens.* Harvard Business School psychologist Dr. Teresa Amabile identified four key stages of the creative process. In simplest terms, they are:

  1. *Preparation.* The creative person first becomes immersed in the problem.
  2. *Incubation.* The mind is at work, even if the problem seems to be neglected.
  3. *Illumination.* The ah-ha moment comes.
  4. *Execution.* The creator takes action on the idea.

As the boss, it's imperative to understand and support these stages. For example, pushing people to go from preparation to execution isn't realistic. You can be most helpful during the fourth stage, because implementing an idea requires determination, effort, and courage. Helping to gather resources and remove obstacles is vital to the process.

- *Put star innovators in a bubble.* You know who your most creative people are. Do your best to protect them from the red tape, noise, and process that slow creativity.

- *Celebrate the small innovations.* Not every new idea is a barn burner. But if you celebrate the small innovations, then you foster a culture that supports the big innovations.

- *Look to change the metrics.* There are many rules in business that no longer apply. For example, the best way to make more money is to raise prices. The airlines learned that by lowering fares they actually made more money by increasing market share. What notions do you have about your business that are outdated?

- *Get involved.* If you have creative employees who are innovating, that's great. But innovation is not a spectator sport. Get in there and get your hands dirty—work at being innovative yourself, and be an active partner in nurturing new thinking. Your active participation is vital to sustaining an innovative culture.

- *Stay curious.* Keep your mind actively processing new information. You can do that by deliberately shaking things up: Force yourself to find a new route to work, for example. Try unfamiliar food. Read a book you wouldn't otherwise read.

Visit an art exhibit that doesn't interest you (it likely doesn't interest you because you don't know anything about it; now is a great time to learn). You never know where (or how) inspiration will strike.

- *Have a contingency plan for overcoming the Corporate Immune System.* Develop contingency plans for dealing with the immune system and for getting from point A to point B when the shortest route is blocked.

- *Commit to seeing the best ideas through to completion.* Nothing will kill innovation faster than if people see you give up on a good idea too soon. True innovation is a long process that demands stamina and patience, but the rewards are worth it. Show people you can go the distance.

- *Accept that there will be resistance.* Resistance to change is the norm. That's why it's so important to plan for it by getting potential resisters involved in the planning process. People tend to resist less when their fingerprints are all over the change.

Real-Life Example

Sara Blakely's story is proof positive that inspiration can strike from anywhere—and that determination will make a good idea a successful one. Sara's story began by trying to find a way to wear white pants without unsightly panty lines. Then she had the lightbulb moment: cut the feet off panty hose. That worked perfectly. Soon, Sara was working hard to sell her idea.

Predictably, no one took her seriously. She needed mill owners to make her product, but they all said it would never sell. (She finally found her mill when the owner's daughters thought she was on to something.) She sought lawyers to help with her patent and they laughed at her. ("They later admitted they thought I had been sent by *Candid Camera,*" Sara says on her Web site.) So she did the application herself. And so it went. When she finally had a prototype, she asked the buyer at Neiman-Marcus for 10 minutes and then flew to Dallas on her own dime to make her pitch. "During the meeting, I had no shame," Sara recalls. She asked the buyer to follow her into the ladies' room, where she proceeded to demonstrate the before and after value of her product. Three weeks later the product was on the shelves at Neiman-Marcus.

The rest, as they say, is history. She's now well on her way to being sole proprietor of a $30 million company (Spanx)—and she's been on *Oprah.*

Get More Information

> *The Goal*, Eliyahu M. Goldratt and Jeff Cox, North River Press, 1992.
>
> *Intrapreneuring in Action: A Handbook for Business Innovation*, Gifford Pinchot and Ron Pellman, Berrett-Koehler, 1999.

ORGANIZATIONAL CULTURE: HOW TO MANAGE IN SYNC WITH YOUR COMPANY'S VALUES

Know the Issue

Close your eyes and imagine going to work for Tiffany & Co. How are you interacting with people? What's the office environment like? What are you wearing? Now close your eyes and imagine going to work for Jamba Juice. Ask yourself the same questions. Are the answers the same? What if the two organizations were Memorial Sloan-Kettering Cancer Center and Cirque du Soleil? Or the Department of Homeland Security and Victoria's Secret?

It's not necessary to have worked at any of these places to know that working there offers very different experiences. So why do so many people assume that a manager's job is a manager's job is a manager's job? The truth is that management jobs are very different from one company to another. Your success or failure will be measured in terms of your work within the context of your organization's culture. An action that earned you a bonus at one company could get you fired from another.

So before you start setting goals and coaching employees, take a hard look at how decisions are made and what behavior is rewarded. The more familiar you are with your organization's culture, the better the odds that you'll triumph.

Take Action

- *Look at the big picture.* Defining the myriad elements of your company's culture will help you know how to succeed.
  - ○ *Success.* How is success defined in your organization? It may be measured only by revenue or profit, but it may also be measured by meeting goals, learning, maintaining certain standards, customer rankings, or other measures. How does your company define winning? Also take a look at the recent initiatives that people describe as successful. Did the people behind those initiatives follow the rules or did they forge a new path?

- *Time.* Is your organization focused on the next quarter or the next five years? If you fail next quarter but win over the long term is that all right? How much time is given for an effort to succeed before the plug is pulled? What is the organization's attention span?

- *Mistakes.* We all make mistakes. How are they handled? Are people who err punished or celebrated? Do people rally to fix a mistake or step back and point fingers? Does the company learn from its mistakes or make the same ones repeatedly?

- *Decisions.* How are decisions made? Are they made at the top and work their way down, or is consensus important? Are decisions respected or second-guessed? Is rethinking a decision in light of new information encouraged or frowned upon? Are decisions explained or defended?

- *Risk.* How is risk tolerated? Is the organization prone to bet the farm (as Boeing did on the 747 and Disney did on Disneyland) or are bets hedged? If you climb out on a limb, will people stand below with a net or saw off the limb?

- *Ethics.* How important are ethics in making decisions? Does the company volunteer the truth or wait to be asked? Does the company's public relations department deal with crises head-on (as Johnson & Johnson did after some doses of Tylenol were tampered with), or resort to denial and euphemisms (as the Peanut Corporation of America did after E. coli was discovered in peanut butter made at one of its manufacturing plants)? Does the company consider human rights or environmental issues when making business decisions?

- ○ *Trust.* Do employees trust each other or are you advised to watch your back? Do people trust what they hear from management?

- ○ *Formality.* Do employees interact with top management directly? Do meetings follow Robert's Rules of Order or are they free-flowing? Do you have casual dress or is everyone in a blue suit? Does every office space look unique, or does the place look like a spread in *Office Beautiful*?

- ○ *Employees.* Does the company really believe that employees are its greatest asset or are they seen as an expense? Do managers fight for employees or against them? Does management treat employees with respect until they do something to lose that respect, or does management disrespect employees until they "earn" respect?

There are no right or wrong cultures, but every culture has right and wrong ways of doing things.

- • *Listen.* If you've worked for your company for any time, you probably can answer the above questions easily and cite examples to make your case. If you're new, you can learn over time and possibly make job-ending mistakes along the way, or you can ask questions—lots of questions.

  This doesn't mean you should don a fedora and move through the office like Sam Spade, supersleuth. But it does mean you should ask people questions during meetings, over lunch, and at the water cooler. Pose the questions as a request for advice ("This project I'm working on could go like gangbusters or really tank. What do you think?") as opposed to a challenge ("Why doesn't anyone around here seem to care about employees?"). Listen without judging, and take in the information. Is the feedback that you're hearing consistent, or does everyone seem to have a different take?

- *Observe*. Pay attention to how things are done. Does everyone seem to be using the same playbook, or are they running into each other in a frantic attempt to control the ball? Are words and actions consistent, or do people say one thing and do another? Pay particular attention to how people behave under stress. Let's say you've been told that employees are the company's greatest asset. When numbers are down, do you spend time at a meeting talking about how to downsize or does the idea never come up?

- *Create a matrix for yourself*. Most cultures are not clearly articulated. To make it easy for you to see the culture in which you're working, spend 10 or 15 minutes creating a grid for yourself. In one column, list the areas we discussed above. Then add the following in columns beside each area:
  - Use a few words to describe the prevailing culture ("encourages taking risks").
  - List examples.
  - Note people in the company who are known to have these qualities and are admired for them.

  When you're done, you should have a good idea of your environment, and a handy cheat sheet to review when you make decisions. (You'll have people to go to for advice and a precedent you can follow.)

- *Embrace the culture or leave*. Once you've identified the culture, live by it or get out. Any culture is bigger than you are, and you won't be able to change it. Remember, you can't teach a pig to sing; it will frustrate you and annoy the pig.

A proviso: if the culture isn't clear (it has no consensus) or it's schizophrenic (the culture values learning but discourages taking risks), it's hard to win. The best companies have strong cultures that give you clear parameters for making decisions.

Stay Out of Jail

If you choose to work in a company that doesn't value employees, beware! Subverting the law, cutting corners on documentation, discriminating against employees in any group, and other tactics designed to show employees "who's boss" will get you in legal trouble—it's just a matter of time. Even if you act with the tacit or overt approval of the company, understand that you could spend a lot of time in court defending your actions. You may find it difficult to find another job if you're seen as playing fast and loose with common sense. And you could even end up charged in a lawsuit yourself.

Manage Up

When you're sizing up the culture, pay particular attention to what your boss says and does. Don't get caught in the cross fire of a culture war.

Get More Information

> *The End of Bureaucracy and the Rise of the Intelligent Organization*, Gifford and Elizabeth Pinchot, Berrett-Koehler, 1993.

Gray Matters: The Workplace Survival Guide, Bob Rosner, Allan Halcrow, and John Lavin, Wiley, 2004.

E-MAIL: HOW TO MANAGE ELECTRONIC COMMUNICATION (AND NOT LET IT MANAGE YOU)

Know the Issue

There's a reason people have started calling it e-jail. What started out as a speedier version of typing a letter and putting it in an envelope has become a 24/7 black hole of spam, jokes, love letters, advertising, special offers, reminders, updates, appointments, and bills—all of it demanding attention and a response *now*.

Still, it's e-mail. It's not a sentient being or alien life force. It can only control us if we let it. So let's not.

Take Action

- *Don't hide behind e-mail.* Using e-mail for all communication makes about as much sense as hoping your doctor can make a diagnosis without ever seeing you. Unless you're the Usain Bolts of typing, e-mail is too time-consuming. E-mail is more easily misinterpreted because it doesn't allow for give-and-take discussion and people aren't guided by facial expressions and vocal intonations. And the more dependent you are on e-mail, the more mysterious you become. Even the Wizard of Oz learned that being the man behind the curtain only gets you so far. Go down the hall, hang out in the lunchroom, or pick up the phone at least some of the time.

- *Use e-mail intelligently.* Just because you can use e-mail doesn't mean you should. Limit your use to concise messages:
  - Request, confirm, or change appointments.
  - Remind people of deadlines.
  - Make announcements (such as which days the office will be closed for holidays).
  - Let people know when you'll be out of the office (and how to reach you).

  You can also use e-mail to forward documents that you expect people to file electronically for further reference, such as meeting minutes or budget reports.

  Do *not* use e-mail to:
  - Ruminate on strategy
  - Announce changes in strategy
  - Announce major changes (such as mergers, acquisitions, reorganizations, or downsizing)
  - Announce major policy changes (such as vacation time or benefits coverage)
  - Send information likely to generate questions

  Now that we've said the rule is never, remember that rules are made to be broken. You can use e-mail occasionally for more complex communication, but don't let it become a crutch.

- *Don't let e-mail become a tennis match.* We've all known e-mail debates that have volleyed back and forth more times than a tennis ball at Wimbledon. If an e-mail goes back and forth more than three times, and especially if the distribution list gets bigger, that's a sure sign that the discussion is bigger than e-mail. Call a halt and bring people together to resolve the issue.

- *Think twice before you click Send.* E-mail will not protect you from yourself. Be careful that you are sending what you intended to send, and that you are sending it to the right person. One employee read a general e-mail from the boss and found it insulting. In the heat of the moment, she typed an angry comment to her colleague that ended, "Does she think we're stupid?" Imagine her red face when she received another e-mail from the boss that said simply, "Yes, I do." If you can't e-mail something nice . . .

- *Use e-mail controls.* Most e-mail programs, including Microsoft Outlook, include sophisticated control tools. Invest the time to use those tools and set up a system to manage your mail. For example, you can set up distribution groups (to make communicating with your whole team easier) or direct all e-mail from specific senders into a preset folder. Not only does it make it easier to find what you need, it also makes it easier to screen out the junk.

- *Avoid Reply all.* Of all there is to hate about e-mail, the "Reply all" function is the one we hear the most complaining about. Although it is (very) occasionally useful, it is ridiculously overused. Don't use it just CYA, or for politicking (so that the known universe knows you share in congratulating someone on her promotion), or out of laziness or carelessness.

- *Focus on your own e-mail.* Snooping through other people's e-mail is a risky activity. (For more information, see

"Privacy: How to Balance the Rights of Employees and Your Company" in Chapter 5.)

- *Keep it all business.* Don't use your business e-mail for personal stuff. And don't use your business e-mail to forward jokes, cartoons, YouTube links, or anything else that isn't directly business related. When you receive such material, delete, delete, delete.

- *Establish an e-mail policy.* Without guidelines, every member of your team is likely to use e-mail differently, and some people may use it inappropriately. If your organization doesn't have an e-mail policy, draft one. To get started, see the discussion in the next section, "The Internet: How to Keep an Asset from Becoming a Liability (or a Lawsuit)."

Stay Out of Jail

- *Don't put anything in e-mail that you don't want to see in the newspaper or hear in court.* Now that organizations as diverse as Microsoft and the White House have found their internal e-mail printed in newspapers and read in court, you know that even "private" e-mail is not really private. Nor can it be easily deleted. Don't put anything confidential in e-mail. That includes:
  - Salaries
  - Comments about employee performance or discipline
  - Information about job candidates, and the reasons they are or aren't hired
  - Personal opinions about employees
  - Proprietary information (such as passwords)

○ Anything that may be construed as interfering with union business or union organizing activities

Remember, e-mail is a document, and not even a note on scrap paper that might get lost or destroyed. Look at everything you write with the idea that it could be found and used against you. That includes personal e-mail sent or received at work. More than one couple involved in an office romance has found their most intimate thoughts broadcast to the entire company.

- *Be careful about humor.* Just because you think something is funny doesn't mean that others will. Although e-mail has become almost as popular a source of humor as late night TV, sending jokes at the office is risky, especially if the humor is based on race, ethnicity, gender, age, or sexual orientation. Something you thought was hilarious could end up being used as evidence in a sexual harassment or discrimination suit. Chevron, for example, was forced to pay $2.2 million to settle a harassment case based in part on e-mails with such titles as, "Why beer is better than women." If in doubt, don't send it.

- *Counsel employees.* If you receive any e-mail from an employee that is inappropriate (or might be perceived as inappropriate), do *not* just ignore it. Make sure the employee understands he should not be using business e-mail for such purposes. Document the warning.

- *Keep e-mail that may be evidence of employee performance problems.* Hang onto e-mail that shows an employee is stealing, engaging in unethical behavior, underperforming, harassing employees or customers, or otherwise violating company policy or standards. Ideally, print it and keep the hard copy. Yes, experts can often retrieve e-mail, even if it's been "deleted," but it's easier to find if you've kept it.

Real-Life Example

Employees from all over the company were inquiring about exactly how much time they had accrued for personal use, such as vacation or sick leave. The HR department charged with answering the questions spent so much time on it that it was becoming a productivity drain. Finally, someone decided to send an e-mail broadcast to employees so that everyone would have current information.

It's easy to see why the idea seemed a good one, but it all went terribly wrong when the person sending the e-mail didn't notice that salary information was being sent along with the leave data. Within moments everyone in the company knew exactly how much everyone else was making, and within weeks 20 percent of the workforce was gone. The HR employee who sent the e-mail was probably among them.

Manage Up

Be as smart about using e-mail to your boss as you are to your employees. Keep e-mail brief, focused, and professional. Keep it clean and don't send confidential information.

For More Information

Send: The Essential Guide to E-mail for Office and Home, David Shipley and Will Schwalbe, Knopf, 2007.

THE INTERNET: HOW TO KEEP AN ASSET FROM BECOMING A LIABILITY (OR A LAWSUIT)

Know the Issue

If only Pandora had never opened the box the gods gave her. But curiosity got the better of her, and she lifted the lid enough to release a swarm of all things evil. Poor Pandora slammed the lid shut, but it was too late. We've had to live with evil ever since, a state mitigated only by the gods' foresight to place hope among the dark contents of the box.

Today's employees face similar temptation. The technogods have given them a box that also contains all things evil, and they have been asked not to open it. But many "Pandoras" have opened it, and used the Internet at work to view pornography, gamble, buy illegal drugs, and harass one another. That lid can't be closed again; the Internet is here to stay.

Although Pandora had only hope to offset the evil, the techno-gods have given us much more. The benefits unleashed—communication, learning, research, shopping—are so plentiful that we don't want to close the lid. We simply want to control what we allow to escape.

Gaining that control is not simple, popular, or perfect, but it is necessary. Rely on a combination of software, rules, and diligence.

Take Action

- *Know the risks.* Internet porn gets all the press, and it's ugly. It's also only the tip of the iceberg. Employees have found more ways to misuse the Internet than Baskin-Robbins has flavors. You need to know what you're up against:

○ *Harassment and cyberstalking.* Under a cloak of presumed anonymity, employees can send each other sexual propositions, racial epithets, attacks on religion, and threats of violence ("I have a gun and I know where you are"). E-mail messages, postings on message boards, and discussions in Internet chat rooms can all be used. If the messages persist, it becomes stalking. The stalking extends beyond the virtual. One stalker posed as his victim and used the Internet to post "her" fantasies of being raped; six men showed up at her home.

○ *Cyberlibel.* Disgruntled employees vent their anger by making false and harmful statements about their employers and disseminate them using the Internet. A former CFO was accused of posting messages that his employer's future was "uncertain and unstable" on an investment message board. An Internet post falsely claimed that electronic greeting cards made by Blue Mountain Arts contain a virus that destroys the recipient's computer system when they're opened.

○ *Possible trademark infringement.* Employees can use your company's name in ways you wish they wouldn't. Most commonly, this takes the form of Internet sites created as gathering spots for employees and customers to diss you; U-Hell and netscapesucks.com are examples. These sites are never fun, but they become even less fun when they're used for blackmail. An ex-employee might agree to shut down a complaint site in exchange for a more lucrative settlement to a lawsuit, for example.

○ *Posting personal information.* An angry consumer posted the home addresses, phone numbers, Social Security numbers, and other data of several employees at a collection agency that he felt had wronged him.

○ *E-mail abuse.* E-mail is a cheap method of mass distribution. A former employee sent regular mass e-mails to thousands of current employees warning them of pending layoffs and urging them to distrust management.

○ *Disclosure of trade secrets.* Employees can wittingly or unwittingly reveal trade secrets while chatting online or posting to message boards.

○ *Fraud and misrepresentation.* Employees and applicants can use the Internet to transmit false documents because their authenticity is harder to discern. Applicants may supply false transcripts, for example, during the hiring process.

○ *Excessive Internet use.* Employees may spend 80 percent of their day (or more) surfing the Internet. Psychiatrists assert that addiction to the Internet is a serious problem; they label the disorder Internetomania, computer addiction, Internet addictive disorder, and cyberaddiction. Internet addiction is most often associated with pornography sites, but that's hardly where it ends. Gambling sites, cyber games, online auctions, social networking sites, blogs, and other destinations can also eat up employee time.

○ *Train employees to use the Internet.* Employees are routinely offered training in how to use various software programs, but rarely get training on Web surfing. If you're currently offering computer training, add an

Internet component. If not, offer stand-alone training. Be sure to present your Internet policy (see "Stay Out of Jail") at the training, and demonstrate how to navigate the Internet to reach specific sites and to avoid others.

○ *Block access to inappropriate sites.* Software is available that blocks access to sexually explicit and other inappropriate sites; use it.

○ *Monitor use.* Work with your Information Systems (IS) department or an independent consultant to be sure you can track Internet use. Do random checks of how much time employees spend on the Web and where they go. Employees should be on notice that such checks will occur.

○ *Help employees separate business from personal.* With many employees traveling for business and working overtime, it's tempting for them to check their personal e-mail at work. Discourage employees from doing so. They may not realize that when they use the company computer to check e-mail, it gets stored on the company server and becomes company property. Beyond that, it makes it more likely that inappropriate or personal information (such as a medical diagnosis or bank account information) may be seen by someone else.

○ *Discourage employees from sending or forwarding jokes or other forms of humor.* What one person finds humorous another may find offensive. People should exchange such e-mails from home, on their own computer on their own time.

○ *Set a good example.* Monitor your own Internet use at work. Limit the time you spend online, and don't visit inappropriate sites.

Stay Out of Jail

- *Have an Internet policy.* Be sure the policy is thorough:
  ○ Warn employees that e-mail and messages posted on the Internet are formal communication. Remind them that e-mail messages are not easily deleted and may be retrieved.
  ○ Outline acceptable uses of the Internet, such as for research, communication, or ordering supplies.
  ○ Delineate unacceptable uses, including using the Internet for personal gain or to advance individual views; soliciting for any noncompany business; sending e-mail anonymously or under an alias; using another employee's password; and sending, saving, or viewing offensive material.
  ○ Advise employees that the company has the right to review employees' Internet use, including any information, e-mail, or files transmitted or stored through the company's computer. (That includes laptop computers, if the company pays for them and they are used for company business.)
  ○ Remind employees that e-mail and Internet access are not entirely secure.
  ○ Counsel employees not to copy or distribute copyrighted material.

  Also remind employees that activities otherwise prohibited (such as harassing a coworker) are prohibited online as well.

Tell employees that violating the rules will result in disciplinary action, including possible termination.

- *Have an attorney review the policy.*

- *Distribute the policy to all employees.* Have them sign a document stating that they received the policy, understand it, and agree to abide by it.

- *Enforce the policy consistently.* Take steps to monitor Internet use and discipline employees if need be. Don't neglect disciplining an employee because you like him or because an employee's Internet use doesn't appear to interfere with his work. Match the punishment to the crime: a verbal warning may be enough if an employee simply spends too much time online, but more is called for if an employee is harassing others or circulating offensive material.

Real-Life Example

An employee complained to HR that a coworker was sending her sexually explicit images using the company's e-mail system. HR investigated her complaint and was stunned to discover thousands of pornographic images stored on the company's intranet. The pictures had been downloaded from Web sites by dozens of employees, who in turn circulated them among themselves and with employees of other companies.

Working with the IS department, HR monitored Internet use for several days and cataloged the images as evidence. Before the dust settled, dozens of employees were terminated and others disciplined. HR was particularly shocked to find that some managers had been participating.

"I thought it wasn't right," one employee told HR when he was fired. "But when my manager did it, I was confused."

Get More Information

> *The E-Policy Handbook: Designing and Implementing Effective E-Mail, Internet and Software Policies,* Nancy Flynn, Amacom, 2009.

TEXTS, TWEETS, AND THE NEXT NEW TECHNOLOGY: HOW TO STAY CONNECTED (WITHOUT LOSING YOUR MIND)

Know the Issue

Star Trek is set hundreds of years in the future, but we've already surpassed the crew's communication tools: Captain Kirk can't use his communicator as a GPS or to access the computer. Yet we continue to make communication ever faster and, depending on your point of view, either easier or more complicated.

For those who consider e-mail too laborious and slow, we now have texting. And for those who can get the job done in 140 characters (and who love a mass audience), we have tweeting. And who knows what new tools are on the horizon. These are indeed the best of times and the worst of times, depending on how much of an early adopter you are.

Texting is common knowledge to most of us, the process of sending written messages directly from one mobile device to another in real time. It's similar to e-mail, while bypassing a server and e-mail provider. Texting is one-to-one communication and discrete. Its strength is that it's immediate, going instantly and directly to someone, whether or not they're at their desk. Depending on your phone plan, texting can either be your lifeblood (if you have an unlimited plan) or an expensive pain (if you pay per text message).

Tweeting can be one-to-a-few or, if you decide to go public, one-to-many communication using the proprietary Web service Twitter. Officially, Twitter defines itself as "a real-time short messaging service that works over multiple networks and devices." This means users can send messages of a finite length to other users of the Twitter service—potentially thousands of such users. Tweeting has some great uses: alerting people to an event, making last-minute changes, and soliciting feedback. It is a tool that allows you to have your finger on the pulse of your company and product at all times. But it can also be a tool for you to lose credibility by being heavy-handed or trying to control your message or image.

Both forms are both reviled and adored, and like all new technology, using them has pros and cons—especially in the workplace. But both are here to stay, so we encourage you to make friends (or at least peace) with them.

If there is one thing we're sure of, new tools will be created in this space in the coming months and years. So don't get too comfortable once you master texting and tweeting, because there will be new lessons to learn and things to accomplish.

Take Action

- *Allow new technology to change the way you view and do business.* Business has long been comprised of research, marketing, sales, support, and development. But using today's latest technology instead we can instead listen, talk, energize, support, and embrace with our customers, vendors, and employees, all in real time. It's easy to see IM, text, Twitter, Facebook, LinkedIn, etc., as a pain. But you can also see it as an ongoing focus group, resource, R&D lab, sales tool, and so on. In short, a vital part of staying connected to your key constituencies.

- *Allow your people to embrace new technology.* Tony Hsieh, the CEO of Zappos Shoes (which he recently sold for close to $1 billion), not only encourages his people to tweet, he threw down the gauntlet to all organizations. "If you don't trust your employees to tweet freely, it's an employee or leadership issue, not an employee Twitter policy issue."

- *Participate with new media.* From a Computer World Canada story: "A recent job posting on Best Buy Co. Inc.'s Web site for a Senior Manager—Emerging Media Marketing position based out of the company's corporate headquarters in Richfield, Minn.," listed two preferred job qualifications: a graduate degree and 250-plus followers on Twitter. Basic qualifications for the position include a bachelor's degree, "two plus years of mobile or social media marketing experience" at the director or strategist level, "four plus years people or resource leadership experience" and "one plus years of active blogging experience." Try new media, it could be the difference between getting hired and not getting hired. Heck, you could also learn something in the process.

- *Prepare to surrender some control.* If you still have a bit of control freak in you, then the new technology will either cure you of this affliction or drive you totally crazy. At the same time you'll now be able to know what your employees and customers are thinking and doing in real time. Welcome to the land of TMI. A place that can seem overwhelming at first, but soon can make you wonder how you ever did business before.

- *Consider your purpose.* If you're stuck on the runway with no access to e-mail, texting is a viable way to get an important message to a colleague or subordinate. But it isn't a good replacement for e-mail for most communication. It's too abbreviated, too informal, and too temporary (or perceived as temporary—more on that later) to be effective.

  Twitter is too much a social tool (and too limited in the message size it allows) to be an effective, ongoing workplace communication tool either. It can be great for recruiting or marketing, however, when you want to get short messages to a large group quickly and/or frequently.

- *Don't count on privacy.* Twitter is intended for a large audience, so it doesn't even make sense to expect tweets to be private. They can be "retweeted" endlessly. Texts are less private than e-mail, too, because they don't go through an e-mail account and can be seen by anyone who picks up a phone or PDA and looks at it.

Stay Out of Jail

Treat texts and tweets as any other document. Contrary to popular belief, text messages and tweets are *not* temporary. They are stored on service provider servers and can be accessed later. Therefore, don't send any text or tweet through a business account (or device owned by your employer) that you wouldn't feel comfortable hearing in court. Do not send any text or tweet with comments about an employee's performance or that includes any derogatory remarks. Be sure your employees have the same understanding.

Real-Life Examples

- On Twitter, a message can easily be retweeted and instantly seen by thousands of people—as one marketing firm executive discovered after posting a job on Twitter: "Within 15 hours, this tweet went from a few thousand to 15,000 people." Twitter may be a great tool for spreading the word about a job, but it can be "unwieldy" for applicants, says *BusinessWeek*'s Rachael King. For example, Twitter users can sign up to follow AT&T's jobs board at @attjobs, but the postings are about every available position at AT&T with no filter based on position or location.

- A lucky job applicant tweeted the following:

  Cisco just offered me a job! Now I have to weigh the util-ity of a fatty paycheck against the daily commute to San Jose and hating the work.

  This tweet caught the attention of a channel partner advocate for Cisco. He responded:

  Who is the hiring manager? I'm sure they would love to know that you will hate the work. We here at Cisco are versed in the Web.

  Ouch! The person who dissed the Cisco offer quickly took her Twitter account private. But Twitter search retained the record.

Get More Information

Groundswell: Winning in a World Transformed by Social Technologies, Charlene Li and Josh Bernoff, Harvard Press, 2008.

VIRTUAL EMPLOYEES: HOW TO MANAGE THE PEOPLE YOU CAN'T SEE

Know the Issue

Out of sight should not be out of mind. Nor should out of sight drive you out of your mind. Yet both scenarios are pretty common when it comes to managing today's virtual workforce.

We're talking about all those people who you don't see regularly but are still making big contributions: employees who work primarily from home, freelancers, contract workers, and outside service providers (such as consultants or trainers). They are an ever-larger proportion of the workforce, and today's managers can't afford to ignore the realities of managing them.

And why would you want to? Sure, it can drive you crazy to supervise people you can't see ("What is he *doing* today?"). It can be tough to give up some of the things you take for granted, like getting a sense of what people are up to just by walking around, and having an impromptu meeting in the break room or elevator. But employees who aren't mired in day-to-day minutiae and politics are also more likely to see things more objectively. Because they're not in the box, they are always thinking outside it, and they can bring fresh perspective and big ideas to the team.

They may be more productive, too. Have you ever noticed that when you get to work early, stay late, or come in on a weekend, you get a lot more done? That's what can happen when you give people room to work on their own. It turns out that the refrigerator and even the TV are less distracting than the normal workplace.

Finally, virtual employees also just make sense, especially in today's climate. Telecommuting is environmentally and family friendly. As the boss, you can have work done when it needs to get done. You can draw on expertise when you need it, but not pay for it when you don't. You can become a better manager by looking at things differently and challenging yourself in new ways.

Take Action

- *Focus on results.* It really shouldn't just be about face time for anyone you supervise, but that's especially true for virtual employees. If they are freelancers or contract employees, you have very little (if any) control over *how* they do the job. Even if they are a regular employees working off-site, you have less control over process. That actually relieves you of worrying about such things and lets you focus on what's really important: *what* they are doing. Be explicit about deliverables and hold people accountable for meeting their commitments.

- *Look for an entrepreneurial spirit.* Although the idea of working in pajamas may appeal to everyone, it doesn't mean that everyone can do it well. Working virtually in any capacity requires being a self-starter who is effective at managing time and not easily distracted. Take time up front to assess how well people can manage themselves. Ask for specific examples of situations in which they've done that before and what the results were. Although you can't abdicate all responsibility for managing a virtual employee, you do want someone who will at least meet you halfway.

- *Trust people.* If you call a virtual employee at home and don't get an answer, you may assume they're at the beach for the day or watching *Oprah*. Don't. People use the restroom, they take breaks, they eat lunch. If they are a freelance employees, they have other clients. It doesn't mean they aren't working or won't get the job done. The truth is, you don't really know what *any* employee is doing every minute. Letting your imagination run wild will only drive you crazy.

- *Communicate, communicate, communicate.* The one area in which virtual employees are a clear additional burden is communication. You'll need to do more of it—a lot more of it. They aren't in the office, so they miss a lot of the communication the rest of us take for granted. We pick up a lot just walking around and overhearing things. People also share things when they run into each other or when they eat lunch. Keep virtual employees in the loop. You don't want to look them in the eye and say, "Didn't anyone tell you? That deadline got changed."

- *Be inclusive.* Just because people aren't full-time employees sitting at a desk within view doesn't mean you should treat them like the unpopular relatives at a family wedding. As we've noted elsewhere, people perform best when they find meaning and community. Both of those are pretty hard to achieve when everything you do makes it clear that they are Not One of Us. Invite them to attend meetings (they can't contribute anything if they aren't there), ask them to join you and the gang for lunch (or dinner) if there's a group activity, keep them apprised of your department's goals and progresses. Help people understand how they fit in.

- *Use technology.* When working with virtual employees, it's a given that they'll use laptops and BlackBerrys or smart phones. Don't overlook other technology that can make it easier, too. That includes using a company intranet or FTP site to post information and shared work, Webinar software to improve virtual meetings, collaboration tools, and even VOIP or video teleconferencing. You'll be surprised how much difference it makes to everyone when they can see— as well as hear—each other.

- *Don't overrely on e-mail.* Yes, technology is a good thing. And it's easy to rely on e-mail because it's fast, easy, and readily available 24/7. But don't let it be a crutch when you (and others) communicate with virtual employees. E-mail is impersonal and makes it harder to build bridges and establish bonds. The informality of e-mail (and, let's face it, the scant attention we usually pay to writing it) also opens the door to misunderstandings about tone and intent. Pick up the phone. Have meetings.

Stay Out of Jail

- *Don't play favorites.* If your virtual employees are actual full-time employees of your company, do not play favorites. For example, don't allow some people to work at home simply because you like them better. Establish clear business-related reasons for deciding who may work at home, and be consistent in using those reasons.
- *Put it in writing.* Any agreement with a freelancer or contract employee should be in writing. Spell out the scope of the project, the deliverables, the timeline, and payment terms. (Most freelancers will present such a contract, but if they don't, then you should.) Do not trust that everyone will remember what the agreement was. You need a document in case there is a dispute.

- *Monitor performance.* Out of sight can't be out of mind. You'll need to maintain the same performance documentation—and do the same regular performance reviews—for full-time virtual employees as for others. (That doesn't apply to independent contractors or freelancers, who technically work for themselves or another firm.)

- *Protect confidential material.* Virtual employees potentially have access to all manner of proprietary information: business plans, marketing strategies, and much more. You don't want them sharing what they know, either carelessly or deliberately. Have them sign a nondisclosure agreement.

- *Consider ergonomics.* Having an employee working at a desk, in a comfortable chair, is one thing. Having him work at a makeshift stack of orange crates, on a stool, is another. The latter opens the door to potential workers' compensation claims. If a virtual employee is a full-time company employee, be sure that he has essentially the same (or equivalent) work space set up as the people in the office. It's also a good idea to occasionally visit the employee's home office (with notice, of course) to make sure that the space isn't a workers' comp claim waiting to happen.

- *Consider overtime.* There aren't many situations in which a nonexempt employee is working virtually. But if it happens, be sure you set parameters for the time they work—and monitor them to make sure they are complying. You don't want to encounter an unforeseen liability for overtime. (Even for exempt employees, setting some parameters is a good idea; it helps prevent burnout.)

Get More Information

> *The Distance Manager: A Hands-On Guide to Managing Off-Site Employees and Virtual Teams,* Kimball Fisher and Mareen Fisher, McGraw-Hill, 2000.

EMOTIONAL INTELLIGENCE: HOW TO RECOGNIZE AND USE THE DATA IN YOUR EMOTIONS

Know the Issue

Suppose you made a decision and things didn't turn out as well as you had hoped. When your boss asks you to explain, you say, "I'm not surprised it didn't go well. After all, I ignored half the data."

That may sound crazy, but in truth many leaders make decisions every day while ignoring a lot of the data available to them. That's because they discount the value of heeding their emotions, under the mistaken belief that "touchy-feely" stuff has no place at work. Wrong! That's because emotions are not messy distractions best left to greeting cards and chick flicks. They are hardwired and essential activities in normal brain function.

If you're skeptical that emotions are data, think of it this way: at the most basic level, an emotion like fear helps prepare our bodies for fight or flight, because the emotion triggers an adrenaline rush and heightened awareness. But emotions help in more complex ways, too. Positive emotions help us expand our thinking, generate new ideas, and encourage us to consider new possibilities. And negative emotions improve our ability to focus clearly, examine details more efficiently, and identify errors.

It's hard to overstate the importance that emotions play in our thinking. A study by Antoine Bechara of the University of Iowa's

Department of Neurology showed that people who suffered damage to the ventromedial sector of the prefrontal cortex (the part of the brain that processes emotional signals) had a marked impairment of their decision-making ability; the quality of their decisions was seriously compromised.

Some people compromise their ability voluntarily by suppressing or ignoring their emotions. No doubt you've seen these people at work—smart, highly skilled people who somehow seem unable to achieve the performance and success expected of them. Maybe you've even seen that person in the mirror each morning as you get ready for work.

Fortunately, our emotional intelligence can be both measured and developed. The better you understand emotional data, the better your own decisions can be—and the more you can help the people who work for you. The payoff for organizations can be substantial; American Express found, for example, that financial advisors trained in emotional intelligence grew their businesses by 18 percent.

Take Action

- *Understand the basics of emotional intelligence.* There are two fundamental ways to think about emotional intelligence. The first is to consider our ability: four key skills (identifying emotions, using emotions, understanding emotions, and managing emotions) describe how our brains respond to emotional data. Although the abilities are universal, some people have developed them much further than others, and few people have developed all four abilities equally well. Someone may be good at identifying emotions ("Boy, is she mad!"), for example, but not as good at understanding emotions ("Why did that upset her?").

The second way to consider emotional intelligence (EI) is to look at our behavior. Let's consider an actual example: A man went out for an after-dinner walk, and came home with a new car. This wasn't a planned purchase; he saw it, he wanted it, he bought it. To say that his wife was surprised is an understatement. In this example, the man's poorly developed abilities to understand emotions ("Why do I want the car? How will I feel if I buy it? How will my wife feel if I buy it?") and manage emotions really cost him (in more ways than one). Behaviorally, he has poorly developed impulse control skills.

Experts have identified 15 such skills, which fall under five broader categories: intrapersonal, interpersonal, adaptability, stress management, and general mood. (See the sidebar "What Is Emotional Intelligence?" later in the chapter.) Understanding these skills will help you see your employees' strengths and weaknesses. You may see them with greater empathy, too. (One employee might easily manage stress levels that would overwhelm another, for example.)

- *Identify which skills are most important for your employees.* Just as no individual is equally skilled in all areas, few jobs require strength in every area. Interpersonal skills are less important for accountants than for salespeople, for example. Problem-solving skills are more crucial for engineers than for valet parking attendants. Decide which abilities are most important for the jobs you supervise.

- *Assess skills.* Once you know which skills are most important for specific jobs, assess employees. Begin informally.

Let's say you're supervising an airline gate agent. The potential for stress in that job is about on par with being Bernie Madoff's PR rep, so it's important that employees in that position can handle stress. How do employees react when flights are delayed or canceled? How do they respond to several passengers talking to them at once? What happens if angry passengers yell? Watching these situations will tell you whether employees need help.

You may also take a more formal approach. There are several assessments of emotional intelligence on the market. Two highly respected examples include the Bar-On Emotional Quotient Inventory, or EQ-i®, and the MSCEIT™ . The EQ-i is a self-reported, multiple-choice assessment that measures behavior by asking people how they typically respond to specific situations. The MSCEIT (the Mayer-Salovey-Caruso Emotional Intelligence Test, named for its creators) is an ability-based assessment that measures EI skill levels. For example, people taking the test look at photos of numerous faces and identify the emotions they see expressed; the answers are then compared to the answers of a wide representation of the population and those of EI experts. Both tools are administered by experts and have been validated.

- *Coach to reinforce the appropriate skills*. Once you've focused on key skills, help employees hone those skills. When you see them effectively use the skills, point it out and praise them. If they miss opportunities, take a moment (privately) to ask them to suggest some other ways they might have handled the situation. If they don't have other ideas, suggest some of your own and discuss whether they'd be comfortable trying other approaches. Don't force the issue; emotional intelligence can be coached, but it can't be imposed.

- *Reward improvement.* Although improving emotional intelligence is possible, it isn't easy. When employees improve, reward their efforts. Rewards can range from a note in their annual review to free movie tickets or even promotion to another job. It all depends on how important the skill is to a job and how much improvement you see. Watch for sustained improvement.

- *Keep emotional intelligence in perspective.* There's a difference between emotional intelligence and personality disorders. For example, being assertive is not the same as being aggressive. Although you might offer coaching to an employee who seems to have a negative attitude, you can't let employees get away with being abusive or disruptive. In those cases, employees need discipline.

Stay Out of Jail

- Don't make hiring, promotion, or work-assignment decisions based on an employee's real or perceived emotional intelligence. Consider it only as one of the tools you have to assess performance and coach for improvement.

- Focus on work-related behavior. Don't ask employees to make generic improvement ("You need to be more flexible"). Instead, explain why being flexible is important in their job, and offer examples of what flexibility looks like when performing their job tasks.

- Be sure any test you use is legal. The test:
  ○ Should not invade privacy (questions in the test should not request information about personal feelings and beliefs that one would generally not want to divulge publicly)
  ○ Should not reveal protected information about someone's mental or physical health
  ○ Should be validated and test what it professes to test (presumably something work-related)
  ○ Should not disproportionately limit the hiring, promotion, or retention of employees in a protected class

  Ask the test publisher to address those concerns. If you still have concerns, ask an attorney.
- *If you formally assess an employee's emotional intelligence, keep his scores confidential.* (In fact, don't expect to see the actual scores yourself. Most certified administrators of the tool give results only to the person assessed. Instead, you might get a summary report showing overall strengths and opportunities for improvement.)
- *If you formally assess individuals or a group, be sure to follow the administration guidelines provided by the instrument's publisher.*

Real-Life Examples

Poor impulse-control skills are one thing when they result in eating too many bowls of Chubby Hubby ice cream or having favorite online shopping sites in your favorites list. But they're another thing entirely when they result in toxic behavior that impacts morale, productivity, and turnover.

Consider the boss described by one former employee as "the boss from hell," a walking time bomb who could explode at any moment for seemingly no reason. Not only did she frequently drop "f-bombs" at virtually everyone around her, she once threw her cell phone across her desk, and another time threw a stack of art boards on the floor and expected the employee to pick them up. "She called me an idiot and other choice words within ear range of other people. She yelled. She screamed. She ranted and raved about me, my work, and anything and everything else," the former employee recalls. "I couldn't sleep. I couldn't concentrate. I couldn't think. I was numb. I began to feel like a complete idiot." Eventually the employee decided that the boss was the idiot and left the organization. It turned out that she was just one in a line of people who couldn't work for the screamer, resulting in high (and costly) turnover.

Here are some other examples of less-than-ideal emotional intelligence skills:

- Every day, employees said "Good morning" or "Hi" as they passed their coworker in the hall or saw her at the coffeepot, and every day they were greeted with silence. No one ever heard "Good morning" in response, or even made eye contact as she strode by, eyes to the floor.

- An employee did as she was asked and decorated the office for Christmas. Several coworkers told her how much they enjoyed the decoration, but the boss said, "They're nice, but the color scheme doesn't match the office. The lights should have been purple and blue, but we've had too many expenses this month so it will do. My Christmas theme at home is white and blue. You should see it; it's so beautiful."

- An employee told her colleague that she was going to be out for a few days, explaining that she was going to get married. "Okay," said her coworker. "You might as well get your first marriage over with."

Manage Up

Have your own emotional intelligence measured. Identify areas in which you could improve. Develop a plan for improvement and share it with your boss. If you think your boss has the skills you're seeking to improve, ask for coaching help.

Get More Information

Emotional Intelligence, Daniel P. Goleman, Bantam Books, 1995.

Emotional Intelligence at Work, Hendrie Weisinger, Ph.D., Jossey-Bass, 2000.

The EQ Edge, Steven J. Stein, Ph.D., and Howard Book, M.D., Stoddart Publishing, 2000.

Working with Emotional Intelligence, Daniel P. Goleman, Bantam Books, 1998.

The Bar-On EQ-i®

MSCEIT™

Multi-Health Systems Inc., 3770 Victoria Park Avenue, Toronto, ON, Canada M2H 3M6; (800) 268–6011; www.mhs.com

What Is Emotional Intelligence?

Psychologists and social scientists began discussing something they called "social intelligence" as far back as the 1920s. In the decades since, the idea has been called "emotional factors" and "personal intelligence," among other things. In 1980, psychologist Reuven Bar-On, who had been studying the idea, coined the phrase "emotional quotient." Finally, in 1990, John Mayer of the University of New Hampshire and Peter Salovey of Yale coined the phrase "emotional intelligence" (EI) and defined it.

It was Daniel Goleman's best-selling book, *Emotional Intelligence,* that popularized the idea. Over time, we've learned more about the complexity of emotional intelligence and, in the process, developed several ways of looking at and assessing it. Mayer and Salovey define emotional intelligence as "the ability to monitor one's own and other's feelings and emotions, to discriminate among them, and to use this information to guide one's thinking and action." Bar-On defines it as "an array of noncognitive capabilities, competencies, and skills that influence one's ability to succeed in coping with environmental demands and pressures."

Mayer and Salovey's ability-based perspective focuses on four skills: identifying emotions, using emotions, understanding emotions, and managing emotions. Identifying emotions, for example, is our ability to recognize the emotional data we receive—how well we can read the emotions in a facial expression, for example. Understanding emotions measures how well we can identify the source of emotions, predict the evolution of emotions (how does one escalate from irritation to rage?), and anticipate how others are likely to respond emotionally ("If I tell her that the dinner isn't very good, it will hurt her feelings."). Although their model explores the four abilities discretely, in truth the abilities are connected (once we identify an emotion, we use it) and we are constantly moving through an ongoing loop of the four abilities as we encounter new information.

In developing the EQ-i, Bar-On captured emotional intelligence in five areas, with 15 subsections or scales:

continued

Intrapersonal

Emotional self-awareness. The ability to recognize and understand one's feelings and emotions, differentiate between them, and know what caused them and why.

Assertiveness. The ability to express feelings, beliefs, and thoughts, and defend one's rights in a nondestructive way.

Self-regard. The ability to look at and understand oneself, respect and accept oneself, accepting one's perceived positive and negative aspects, as well as one's limitations and possibilities.

Self-actualization. The ability to realize one's potential capacities and to strive to do that which one wants to do and enjoys doing.

Independence. The ability to be self-reliant and self-directed in one's thinking and actions, and to be free of emotional dependency; these people may ask for and consider the advice of others, but they rarely depend on others to make important decisions or to do things for them.

Interpersonal

Interpersonal relationships. The ability to establish and maintain mutually satisfying relationships that are characterized by intimacy, and by giving and receiving affection.

Empathy. The ability to be attentive to, to understand, and to appreciate the feelings of others; being able to "emotionally read" other people.

Social responsibility. The ability to demonstrate oneself as a cooperative, contributing, and constructive member of one's social group.

Adaptability

Problem solving. The ability to identify and define problems, as well as to generate and implement potentially effective solutions.

continued

Reality testing. The ability to assess the correspondence between what is experienced (the subjective) and what in reality exists (the objective).

Flexibility. The ability to adjust one's emotions, thoughts, and behavior to changing situations and conditions.

Stress Management

Stress tolerance. The ability to withstand adverse events and stressful situations without falling apart, by actively and confidently coping with stress.

Impulse control. The ability to resist or delay an impulse, drive, or temptation to act.

General Mood

Happiness. The ability to feel satisfied with one's life, to enjoy oneself and others, and to have fun.

Optimism. The ability to look at the brighter side of life and to maintain a positive attitude, even in the face of adversity.

Source: Multi-Health Systems, Toronto.

7

Today's Diverse Workforce

Employees beginning third careers in their 60s, parents working flextime to attend Little League games, domestic partners enrolled in the benefit plan, and 27 languages spoken in a single company cafeteria. No other workforce in history has had such varied experiences and brought them all into the workplace. No wonder there has been so much misunderstanding.

Yet all of this diversity offers us an unparalleled opportunity to solve problems using multiple perspectives, to relate to customers in their native languages and cultures, to improve communication, and to turbocharge creativity. This is "two heads are better than one" at an exponential level.

To move from misunderstanding to productivity, we must stop talking about diversity (especially in terms of villains and victims) and start taking advantage of it.

CULTURAL VALUES: HOW TO GET PAST RACE AND ETHNICITY

Know the Issue

Don't do diversity training! (Well, not the way it's done most often.)

For almost two decades American business has had an obsession with diversity. We've spent millions on diversity training. People have trudged across the country to attend conferences. Books on the subject have flown off bookstore shelves. All of this has been well meaning, but much of it has been misguided. Why? Because too often race, ethnicity, and gender have been shoved front and center, and that's the last place they should be. Instead of examining people's external characteristics (what they look like), we need to explore their underlying values, because the real reward in diversity training is learning to work effectively with people who think differently than we do.

Consider this: native-born Americans generally value directness. We tend to "tell it like it is." As managers we're encouraged to be straightforward and offer constructive criticism. Well, if we're managing people with that same value, this is no problem. But suppose we're managing people who value indirectness. To them, saving face can be very important; straightforward criticism, even politely offered, can be humiliating. It can even undermine your suggested changes. You'd be far more effective if you offered a subtle suggestion: "When Mary tried it this way, she had great success." Perhaps that seems uncomfortably vague, but that's only because you're probably an acculturated American.

Be wary of the stereotypes, however. Consider Latinos who have lived in the United States for a decade. Are their values Latino? American? Or a blend? And what are "American" values anyway?

Any presidential candidate will tell you that the core values of Jews in New York City are not identical to the core values of Louisiana Creoles. Ultimately, each of us has values all our own.

Understanding those values and observing the behavior that reflects them will make you a better manager. The better you can see another person's point of view, the better you can communicate with her. You'll get the results you need, and people will feel respected. What better retention tool could you have?

Take Action

- *Learn the core values.* There are 13 basic, or core, areas in which people's points of view determine much of how they function in the world. Do you feel you have a lot of control over your life, or do you believe that what happens to you is fate? This question has no "right" answer. Most people's view is somewhere between the two extremes. The same is true for each of the 13 core values (described in "The Values Continuum"). Getting familiar with the list will begin to give you insights into yourself and your employees.

- *Learn basic business values.* No articulation of values applies across the board to every member of a group, but in every country there are some generally accepted values. Learn what they are, not because they are absolutes, but because they'll offer a framework for understanding differences.

- *Identify your own values.* Think about what you really believe. Place yourself on the continuum. How does your perspective affect how you manage? Think of ways in which you reflect values without even thinking about it.

- *Identify your employees' values.* Where do your employees fall on the continuum? It's helpful to look at them individually. Are there places in which their values are different from the norm? If you aren't sure about their values, ask. Keep the conversation respectful. Don't make assumptions ("You people don't really care about being on time, do you?") and don't ask employees to speak on behalf of a group ("What do people from your country think about this?").

- *Where appropriate, ask employees to respect the business values.* Employees want to do a good job. If people fall short of your expectations, it may be a reflection of differing values. For example, if an employee is chronically late, she may have a different value about time. Share the American business value of timeliness. Be respectful and make it clear that her values are not "wrong." Ask the employee to respect your values while at work. (These are complex discussions; if employees aren't fluent in English, consider using a translator.)

- *Meet employees halfway.* When it's a matter of policy or business necessity, asking employees to adapt is reasonable, but in other cases, making the effort to respect other values is a gracious thing to do. For example, if an employee's values make it difficult for her to accept praise in public, adjust your style and offer praise privately. Yes, we know—that's not how things used to be. But don't focus on how things have changed—focus on what you need to do to get things done.

- *Offer training.* If you have a large number of employees with different cultural backgrounds, offer training in the underlying values of the prevailing business culture. Make sure all your employees are trained, not just those from different backgrounds.

Stay Out of Jail

Don't make hiring, promotion, or work assignment decisions based exclusively on employees' values. For example, don't assume that someone who values being indirect can't succeed in sales. Explain what the job entails and let people make choices. Then hold them accountable for their performance.

Get More Information

> American Institute for Managing Diversity, 1200 W. Peachtree Street NW, Suite 3, Atlanta, GA 30309; www.aimd.org
>
> *Making Diversity Work: 7 Steps for Defeating Bias in the Workplace,* Sondra Thiederman, Kaplan Publishing, 2008.
>
> *Managing Diversity: Toward a Globally Inclusive Workplace,* Dr. Michalle E. Mor Barak, Sage Publications, Inc., 2005.
>
> *Patterns of American Culture,* Dan Rose, University of Pennsylvania Press, 1991.
>
> *The Values Americans Live By,* L. Robert Kohls, San Francisco State University, San Francisco, 1988.

The Values Continuum

People's views in each of these areas determine much of how they function in the world. Where do you fall on each continuum? Where do your employees fall? Where does your company fall? In most American organizations, the dominant values are those on the left side of the continuum.

I have control over the environment; what happens in my life is up to me.	1 : 2 : 3 : 4 : 5 : 6 : 7 : 8 : 9	What happens in my life is fate; I'm living out my destiny.

continued

Change is progress; it's a good thing.	1 : 2 : 3 : 4 : 5 : 6 : 7 : 8 : 9	Tradition is our strength.
I control my time; being late is rude.	1 : 2 : 3 : 4 : 5 : 6 : 7 : 8 : 9	I don't control time. If I meet a friend on the street, I must stop to honor the relationship; I'll get where I'm going when I get there.
We're all equal, and I try to be fair to everyone.	1 : 2 : 3 : 4 : 5 : 6 : 7 : 8 : 9	I show my respect to people of higher rank or status and I expect respect from those of lower status.
It's every person for him- or herself; I do what's best for me.	1 : 2 : 3 : 4 : 5 : 6 : 7 : 8 : 9	We're all in this together; I do what's best for the group.
If I work hard, I can do anything and get anywhere in life.	1 : 2 : 3 : 4 : 5 : 6 : 7 : 8 : 9	My place in life will reflect my birthright.
I feel good when I win.	1 : 2 : 3 : 4 : 5 : 6 : 7 : 8 : 9	I feel good when I help others.
I'm focused on a better tomorrow.	1 : 2 : 3 : 4 : 5 : 6 : 7 : 8 : 9	I honor the past.
It matters what I do; I need to get things done.	1 : 2 : 3 : 4 : 5 : 6 : 7 : 8 : 9	It matters who I am; I value each day.
I'm informal; it's friendly and democratic.	1 : 2 : 3 : 4 : 5 : 6 : 7 : 8 : 9	I prefer formality; it shows respect.

continued

I tell it like it is; honesty is the best policy.	1 : 2 : 3 : 4 : 5 : 6 : 7 : 8 : 9	I am not direct; it's important to people to save face.
I do what I need to do to get the job done.	1 : 2 : 3 : 4 : 5 : 6 : 7 : 8 : 9	I follow the best proven method for getting a job done.
Success is a big house and a nice car.	1 : 2 : 3 : 4 : 5 : 6 : 7 : 8 : 9	Success is inner peace and contentment.

Source: Adapted from *The Values Americans Live By,* L. Robert Kohls, San Francisco State University, San Francisco, 1988

THE GENERATION GAP: HOW TO HELP EVERYONE GET ALONG (AND GET THINGS DONE)

Know the Issue

People over 30 are inflexible, too formal, intimidated by technology, have a hard time learning new things, and are hopelessly out of touch with the world around them.

People under 30 are undisciplined, disrespectful, value technology more than relationships with other people, have short attention spans, and are oblivious to anything that happened before their time.

How you respond to those generalizations depends a lot on, well, how old you are. No wonder we call it the Generation Gap. But just because people have tripped over that gap for generations doesn't mean we should keep doing so. The truth is that people of every age can be inflexible and out of touch, just as people of every age can be vital and productive.

President Obama's chief speechwriter, Jon Favreau, was 27 when the president was inaugurated; at 83, Angela Lansbury won her fifth Tony award for acting. Both of them excelled because they were judged by what they brought to the table, not by the date on their birth certificates.

Okay, your work environment probably isn't as rarified as the White House or Broadway. But that doesn't mean that you, too, can't have a high-performing workforce of all ages. And for business to succeed we're going to need a productive workforce of all ages. The U.S. Census Bureau reported in 2009 that the median age in the United States was 36.7. More than a quarter of the population (27.6 percent) was younger than 20, while 12.6 percent were 65 or older. Every age group is simply too large to ignore.

The secret to managing such diversity is neither to obsess about the differences between generations nor to ignore those differences. Instead, hold everyone equally accountable for results while understanding and respecting the differences—and insisting that others do the same.

Take Action

- *Value older employees.* No, members of the Silent Generation or Traditional Generation (those born between 1925 and 1945) and the Baby Boomers (people born between 1946 and 1964) don't know everything. But they do know a lot, and we don't just mean the lyrics to the Beatles songbook or large portions of the dialogue in *Casablanca.*

If you doubt whether the Silent Generation is still relevant, consider this: According to Value Options (a Web site devoted to understanding the generations), they hold three-quarters of the nation's wealth and are the executive leaders of some of the most established and influential companies in America. This generation was shaped by the Great Depression and World War II, and was instrumental in shaping the United States as an economic and military power. Although often stereotyped today as stodgy, in fact this was a generation of innovators: they developed the vaccines that wiped out many serious diseases, launched the space program, and laid the foundation for the technology boom.

Value Options notes that Silent Generation attributes include being disciplined, seeing history as a way to plan for the future, disliking conflict, and being detail-oriented. They value conformity, authority and rules, logic, a strong sense of right and wrong, loyalty and respect for authority. At work, they seek consistency and uniformity, technological advancements, and a command-and-control, hierarchical structure.

With increased educational, financial and social opportunities, the Boomer generation is often portrayed as a generation of optimism, exploration, and achievement. Compared to previous generations, more Boomers pursued a college degree or left home and family to pursue their degrees or careers. Boomers came of age during the early days of space exploration, readily available long-distance travel, and general prosperity. Boomers also actively participated in the civil rights movement and the women's liberation movement (among other social changes), and their careers advanced in a more diverse workplace.

Value Options summarizes Boomer attributes as adaptive, goal-oriented, and focused on individual choice. They value individual choice, community involvement, ownership, self-actualization, and health and wellness, and their work style emphasizes team building, group decision making, and conflict avoidance.

To draw on the expertise of older employees, begin by understanding and respecting who they are. Beyond that:

○ *Create mentor programs pairing older workers with younger ones.* Both groups can learn from the other; think of such programs as *Up* without helium balloons and talking dogs.

○ *Don't let people rest on their laurels.* Yes, experience counts, but the question "What have you done for me lately?" is valid, too. A woman over 50 told Workplace911.com that she doesn't hire peers who lack energy, a spark in their eye, and a willingness to take risks. It's reasonable to expect employees over 50 to have passion for their work, too.

○ *Whenever possible, be flexible.* Most employees report that they prefer easing into retirement by cutting back on work hours, rather than going cold turkey. Work within your company's policies to allow productive older workers to scale back gradually. In tough economic times, this may be an effective way to trim payroll costs, too. Just don't assume that all older employees want to work less, and be equitable in making the effort (don't extend the offer only to your favorite employees), and don't burden younger workers in the process.

- *Offer training.* Don't assume that older employees don't want to or can't learn new things. Older employees should be given the same opportunities for training as everyone else.

- *Advocate for benefits.* As a manager, you probably don't have much control over which benefits your company offers, but you can still do two things. First, be sure that all employees understand the benefits they have. Don't assume a correlation between an employee's benefits needs and her age. Many people are raising their grandchildren, for example, and may value dependent-care benefits. Second, advocate that your employer not overlook benefits that may appeal to older employees, such as long-term care insurance and retirement plans.

• *Leverage Gen X energy.* When talking about younger employees, we're actually talking about two different generations: Gen X (defined by Neil Howe and William Strauss, authors of the book *Generations*, as the 57 million people born between 1965 and 1980) and Millennials (or Gen Y), a group less formally defined but usually considered to be those born between 1980 and 2000. Although they share some characteristics, they are also different in some key ways.

Rebecca Ryan, founder of Next Generation Consulting, says that Xers have been unfairly maligned ("More than 75 percent of media coverage about Generation X is negative," she says), and she has plenty of data to back her up. The Bureau of Labor Statistics says that Xers work almost four hours longer per week than the average employee. A Marquette University/University of Michigan study found that Xers are responsible for 70 percent of all start-up firms in the United States. A CNN/*Time* poll found that three out of every five Xers aspire to be their own bosses. All of which probably contributed to *Forbes* magazine branding Gen X as "the most entrepreneurial generation in American history."

As they've matured, Xers have become pragmatic, "Will this work?" types. "In companies that are in transition," Ryan says, "Gen Xers are stepping up and leading, engaging in rigorous debate and ruthless pragmatism to design solutions that will make their organizations competitive for many years to come."

Clearly, viewing Gen Xers as couch-potato scoundrels will only result in a waste of talent.

○ *Earn their trust and respect.* Gen X came of age during Watergate, Iran-Contra, the *Challenger* explosion, and soaring divorce rates. "The result is a generation who don't talk to strangers and rely on themselves," Ryan says. "They are skeptical." But they are not unreasonable. Don't tell them to respect you; give them reasons why they should.

○ *Set clear expectations and then get out of the way.* This is America's first generation of latchkey children; 40 percent of them were raised in single-parent households. They learned to rely on themselves to set the VCR, set the table, and set the agenda for quality time with Mom and Dad. They are adept at thinking for themselves. Let Gen Xers come to you with questions, rather than micromanaging them. Ryan says that one of the most frequent complaints she hears from Gen Xers is that they don't feel they have autonomy. Let them be entrepreneurs within their departments. (Hint: This is pretty good advice for managing most people, not just Gen Xers.)

○ *Give a lot of feedback.* Take a few minutes every day (not once a year at review time) to talk with Gen Xers. To make it easy, Ryan says make it QUIC: QUality (brief, specific), Immediate, and Constructive (for example, say, "This is what you can do better, this is how this project is tied to your longer term goals").

○ *Get to the point.* Xers grew up with hundreds of TV channels, video games, and computers, so they're adept at sifting through data, and more responsive to short e-mails and memos with bullet points than to a treatise.

○ *Offer professional and personal development opportunities.* Xers learn four or five software programs per year; they thrive on stretching themselves. As long as the employee's work doesn't suffer, support professional and personal development for Gen Xers.

• *Take Millennials seriously.* Many people (wrongly) assume that Millennials (born between 1980 and 2000) are like Gen Xers on speed. "Nope," Ryan says. Unlike Gen Xers at the same age, Millennials *love* adults. And at work, you—their boss—are the Adult. How do effective organizations hire, develop, and retain Millennials? Ryan has some advice:

○ *Understand that Millennials and their parents have a close relationship.* Play to that relationship. At some large public accounting and consulting firms, HR professionals invite parents to come with their children to open houses and onboarding receptions. In these situations, parents can talk to the people with whom their child will be working, and get answers to any questions they have. In the words of one recruiter, "If we involve the parents now, it prevents them from calling their child's manager later."

○ *Give Millennials structure.* They want to know what will be expected of them—and what they can expect in return—when they come to work for you. Having a career conversation with them and focusing on the two-, five- and 10-year plan is reassuring to them.

○ *Help Millennials feel that they're a part of something bigger.* They've been volunteering through high school and college and are willing to sacrifice big salaries to make a big difference. Make sure you connect them to the larger purpose your organization serves.

Real-Life Examples

• "I've had some great mentors who trained me to look at each candidate based on his own sense of worth and need for fulfillment," says David Barrett, president of BearCAT Productions in Oakland, California. "In making a case for those applicants over 40, I've found they generally need to share the highlights of their careers in a meaningful way, to pass the baton to the next generation. They have something to teach. I encourage that because it promotes stability and makes for a stimulating culture.

"The average age in our company is the late 40s, and I'm convinced that experience leads to better judgment. And though I want them to teach, I also want them to learn, so I foster an environment that encourages experimenting without worrying about mistakes."

- In a case so notorious that it ended up in an EEOC treatise on age discrimination, a new 30-year-old CEO got into trouble immediately. On his first day, he called everyone over 50 into his office. He told them that he didn't believe that older people have any sense, and added, "You'll have a tough time proving to me that you can fit in with my 21st century philosophy. Time to get some new blood into this stodgy business!"

For the next several months the CEO questioned whether older workers could do the job. During a single meeting, he presented the 55-year-old loading-dock supervisor with a cane and a walker, called another older executive "Methuselah," and suggested an afternoon nap time for all of the "old codgers." The CEO also encouraged younger employees and supervisors to taunt the older workers with remarks about their age. At the end of four months all the workers over 50 had quit, and the prejudiced, insensitive, and overly talkative CEO was the key witness in some costly lawsuits.

Stay Out of Jail

Don't make any hiring, promotion, or work-assignment decisions based on an employee's age. The Age Discrimination in Employment Act prohibits discriminating against employees aged 40 or older.

Get More Information

www.valueoptions.com

Live First, Work Second, Rebecca Ryan, Next Generation Consulting, 2007.

Managing Generation X: How to Bring out the Best in Young Talent, Bruce Tulgan, W.W. Norton & Co., 2000.

Not Everyone Gets a Trophy: How to Manage Generation Y, Bruce Tulgan, Jossey-Bass, 2009.

DISABILITIES: HOW TO HELP EMPLOYEES GIVE THEIR BEST

Know the Issue

What comes to mind when you picture an employee with a disability? Perhaps because of the ubiquitous blue-and-white handicapped symbol, many people see someone using a wheelchair, but in today's workplace that image is far from complete.

To even begin getting the complete picture, you also have to consider vision and hearing impairment, epilepsy, multiple sclerosis, cancer, heart disease, HIV, diabetes, and depression. Then there is chronic psoriasis, Crohn's disease, bowel disorders, and high blood pressure. Some employees have claimed (largely unsuccessfully) that sleep disorders, menopause, fainting, and injuries sustained in car accidents are disabilities. Even all of these disabilities barely scratch the surface.

Of course, people have faced most of these health issues for as long as people have been working. However, the passage of the Americans with Disabilities Act (ADA) in 1990 put the question of what constitutes a disability and how it should be managed at work in an entirely new framework. Now disabilities are as much a legal matter as they are medical and social concerns.

In a nutshell, the ADA defines "disability" as an impairment that limits one or more major life activities. However, the law doesn't specify which activities, so those are being determined in court. Furthermore, one of its key points—that employers should make reasonable accommodations on behalf of employees with disabilities—has been interpreted differently from one job to another. Those facts make managing employees with disabilities perhaps the most complex issue that supervisors face today.

ADA compliance is a full-time job for many attorneys, so there isn't any way we can explore every nuance of the law. But we can offer you some fair, sensible guidelines to handle most situations.

Take Action

- *Review the basics of the law.* Not every ailment or injury is a disability, and not every proposed accommodation is reasonable. Review the basics of the law (see "The ADA: A Primer" later in the chapter) so you're comfortable recognizing situations in which the ADA is probably pertinent.

- *Work to make reasonable accommodations.* Many employers get into legal trouble because they make no effort to accommodate a disability. Yet most accommodations are not difficult or expensive. Peter Blanck at the University of Iowa did a study in which he found that the average cost of an accommodation is less than $50, and that 75 percent of all accommodations cost less than $100. Do everything you can to make a reasonable accommodation. It's the best strategy for keeping good people, too.

- *Focus on the accommodation, not the disability.* Once we hear someone's diagnosis or the nature of his injuries, it's easy to become an amateur doctor and decide what he can or can't do. Don't. A diagnosis or injury report actually tells you nothing, because different people in different situations have different capabilities. Beyond that you're actually better off not knowing an employee's diagnosis because then there's no risk you'll breach his privacy. All you really need to know is whether an employee can perform the core job functions, with or without a reasonable accommodation.

  For example, suppose a doctor says an employee is unable to lift more than 15 pounds. It makes no difference whether the employee is limited because of a lower back injury, arthritis, medication that causes dizziness, or any of 20 other possible reasons. You must decide whether, on behalf of the company, you should ask for a second opinion. If you decide against making that request, then you must decide whether the limitation impacts a core job function, and if so, what reasonable accommodation to make. (You don't have to make the "most" reasonable or "best" accommodation, only a reasonable one.) If you can't make any reasonable accommodation, you don't have to retain the employee. (Just remember that you can't fire an employee because of a limitation that doesn't affect a core job function, whether you can make an accommodation or not.) Remember this mantra: ask what employees can do, not why.

- *Educate employees to focus on accommodation, not the disability.* Some employees value their privacy and won't even admit that anything is wrong. Others want to share every detail of their doctor visit. Neither extreme is helpful. If you've been told that an employee's performance of a core job function is limited by an ADA-covered disability, what you need to do is have a good-faith conversation to decide whether you can make an accommodation, and if so, what it will be.

Explain to employees that you need their help to protect their privacy and to accommodate them, and that accurate information about what job duties they can or can't do is the key. Suggest that an employee ask her doctor to omit a diagnosis from any information you receive. Be sure to document your attempts to arrive at a reasonable accommodation.

- *Don't let employees practice medicine.* Some people decide their own treatment without a doctor's advice. Don't accept an employee's explanation that she can't lift a certain weight, or needs extra breaks because of her disability. Ask to see a doctor's recommendation. If the employee hasn't seen a doctor, explain that everyone involved needs accurate medical information. (Likewise, require that employees who have been out for medical reasons present a doctor's release stating that they are fit to return to work.)

- *Monitor employee behavior.* Sometimes employees don't ask for an accommodation; they simply make one of their own. If you see that, don't assume that everything is okay. If, for example, an employee begins delegating work that they "can't do" to a coworker, you need to step in and find out whether the employee actually has a protected disability. Even if he does, you may prefer a reasonable accommodation that does not involve other employees directly.

You should also keep in mind that a disability and a workers' compensation claim can overlap. Generally, workers' comp applies to injuries sustained on the job. However, such injuries can aggravate existing disabilities, lead to long-term disability, or result from disabilities that were not accommodated.

Stay Out of Jail

- *Be consistent when accommodating employees.* Don't decide whether to make an accommodation based on the disability an employee has.
- *Keep information about an employee's disability confidential.*
- *Don't discriminate against employees known to have a relationship with a disabled person.* For example, it's illegal to discriminate against someone because he or she associates with someone who has HIV infection or AIDS.
- *If you're unsure whether an employee's situation is covered by the ADA, don't guess.* Consult your company's HR or legal department, or an attorney.
- *Document your attempts to reach a reasonable accommodation.*

Do at Least the Minimum

Take disabilities seriously. Meet your obligation to the company and employees.

Get More Information

Accommodating Employees with Psychiatric Disabilities: A Practical Guide to ADA Compliance, Allen Smith and Don Montuori, Thompson Publishing Group, 1998.

The Americans with Disabilities Act: A Primer for Small Business, U.S. Equal Employment Opportunity Commission, www.eeoc.gov/ada/adahandbook.html

Understanding the Americans with Disabilities Act, 2nd ed., William D. Goren, American Bar Association, 2007.

The ADA: A Primer

Even attorneys who specialize in the ADA struggle to master the nuances of the law. However, it's easy to grasp the basic concepts. If you know them, you'll know when you need a doctor to suggest an accommodation, and when you need legal advice.

Which Employers Are Covered by the ADA?

The ADA applies to all employers with 15 or more employees. However, the ADA sets minimal standards of protection. Many state laws are more stringent and cover employers with as few as two employees. The ADA does not mitigate or invalidate any laws that may provide greater protection. If you're unsure, check with an attorney or with your state employment department.

Which Employees Are Protected?

The ADA protects qualified individuals with a disability. With respect to an employee, the law defines a person with a disability as one who:

- Has a physical or mental impairment that substantially limits one or more major life activities (defined not exclusively as caring for oneself, performing manual tasks, walking, seeing, hearing, speaking, breathing, learning, working, and participating in community activities). The Supreme Court has ruled that a person is not impaired under federal law if medication,

continued

prostheses, eyeglasses, and so on can eliminate the effects of the employee's medical condition.

- Has a record of such impairment (this provision is intended to protect people who have a history of disability but are no longer impaired, such as cancer patients in recovery).

- Is regarded as having such an impairment (this provision protects people whose impairments don't actually limit major life activities, but who are treated by an employer as if they have such limitations).

The ADA Amendments Act of 2008 changes the way these criteria should be interpreted. The act expands the definition of "major life activities" to include:

- Most activities previously mentioned above, such as walking and seeing, as well as new ones, such as reading, bending, and communicating.

- Major bodily functions, such as "functions of the immune system, normal cell growth, digestive, bowel, bladder, respiratory, neurological, brain, circulatory, endocrine, and reproductive functions."

In determining whether one has a disability, mitigating measures (if you are able to use medication to eliminate the limitations of your medical condition, or successfully use a prosthetic, hearing aid, glasses, or other assistive device) other than "ordinary eyeglasses or contact lenses" will not be considered.

Impairments that may be intermittent or in remission will be classified as a disability if, when active, it would substantially limit a major life activity.

However, the ADA doesn't require an accommodation if an impairment limits someone in performing only a particular job or a narrow range of jobs. For example, an auto body welder developed carpal tunnel syndrome and was no longer able to do repetitive factory work. Her employer was not required to accommodate her in a

continued

welding job because her education, skills, and training made her eligible for many other positions. In order to qualify for an accommodation, an employee must show that her ability to perform a broad range of jobs is limited.

You may choose to accommodate a worker when it isn't required, but if you do so, be consistent—don't just accommodate the employees you like.

How Do You Determine Who the ADA Considers Qualified?

Determining whether someone is qualified under the ADA requires two steps.

First, he must meet the necessary prerequisites for the job, such as education, work experience, training, skills, licenses, certificates, and other job-related requirements (for example, has the ability to work with other people).

Second, you must determine whether a reasonable accommodation would permit him to perform the essential functions of the job. (See "Job Descriptions: How to Draft Blueprints for Results" in Chapter 4.) For example, if someone is qualified to work with people as a counselor but can't type documents, you need to decide how essential typing documents is to the job, and if it is essential, how the inability to type can be accommodated.

What's a Reasonable Accommodation?

Any effective accommodation that an employer can make without undue hardship is reasonable. It may include:

- Making existing facilities readily accessible to and usable by people with disabilities
- Restructuring jobs
- Modifying work schedules
- Reassigning a disabled person to a vacant position
- Acquiring or modifying equipment

continued

- Adjusting examinations, training materials, or policies
- Providing qualified readers or interpreters
- Making other similar accommodations

The ADA does not require an employer to modify or change a job to accommodate an employee if the employer can show that the change would alter the essential functions of the job. For example, a romantic, candlelit restaurant need not change its ambience by putting bright lights in the dining area to accommodate a server with poor eyesight. However, the same restaurant may have to install the very same lights in the kitchen as a reasonable accommodation to a chef with poor eyesight.

Are Accommodations Limited to Job-Specific Functions?

No. Accommodations may have to be made to address issues beyond the employee's job duties, such as access to:

- The facility
- Restrooms
- General communications (such as memos)
- Break and dining areas
- Company social events

What Is an Undue Hardship?

An undue hardship is anything that would require significant difficulty or expense. You should consider:

- The nature and cost of the accommodation needed
- The overall financial resources of the facility
- How many people are employed at the facility
- The effect on expenses and resources, and the impact on the operation of facilities
- The overall financial resources of the organization

continued

- The overall size of the business
- The number, type, and location of its facilities
- The type of the company's operations
- The composition, structure, and functions of the workforce

In other words, undue hardship includes any action that is unduly costly, extensive, or substantial, or that would fundamentally alter the operation of the business. Generally, larger employers are expected to make greater efforts than small employers to accommodate employees.

Beware, however, that the EEOC and the courts are very reluctant to conclude that an undue hardship exists. Both have defined the term very narrowly.

RELIGION: HOW TO RESPECT ESTABLISHED PRACTICES

Know the Issue

You're forgiven if you're confused. On the one hand, we want to know everything about the religious beliefs of our politicians. And we want them to have religious beliefs: a 2007 *Newsweek* poll found that 62 percent of registered voters would not vote for an atheist.

On the other hand, religion is a topic that we're generally advised to avoid at cocktail parties—or at work. But although religious beliefs are among the least-discussed topics in the workplace, when they do come up they can affect everything from schedules and job duties to dress and appearance standards. Suddenly, what we weren't talking about all is something we're talking about in depositions. What's the right thing to do?

Happily, managing this aspect of diversity is less complex than it seems. We'll share some of the specifics, but there's really just one simple rule: do your best to respect established religious practice.

Take Action

- *Make a reasonable effort to accommodate a range of religious beliefs.* Title VII of the Civil Rights Act prohibits discrimination on the basis of religion. That sounds broad enough to be intimidating, but over time the Supreme Court and the EEOC have clarified what it means.

  The court first said that those who have an "orthodox belief in God" are clearly protected. Later, it expanded the definition to protect moral and ethical beliefs that have the function of a religion in someone's life. This opened the door for the EEOC to state that the law's protection is not limited to traditional religion and religious practices. For example, a teacher won a judgment against a school district after she argued successfully that she was fired because of her New Age beliefs.

  Having said that, the law distinguishes between what a religion requires and what people simply prefer. For example, a former employee sued a department store after she was fired for going on a pilgrimage during the store's busy holiday season. The employee lost the case because although she "felt called to go," her religion didn't require it and there were pilgrimages at other times that she could have attended.

  In another case, an employer required its salespeople to live in the same area as their customers. A Jewish applicant was offered a sales job and accepted it. Later he asked to move 40 miles away because the town had no Jewish community. The company denied his request, and he sued for religious discrimination. He lost the case because the Jewish faith doesn't require living in a Jewish community, and he admitted that part of his motivation was to enroll his children in a better school district. The court found he simply preferred to live in a Jewish community.

The courts only ask that employers make a reasonable effort to accommodate religious beliefs; the courts specifically protect employers from undue hardship. As a manager, your job is to decide what's "reasonable" when it comes to scheduling, job tasks, appearance, and so on. Obviously, this decision can't and shouldn't be made in a vacuum; the courts and the EEOC have provided the framework.

- *Don't sacrifice business interests.* No accommodation should imperil your business. For example, an employer working to meet a deadline hired welders to work at least 10-hour days, six days a week, to finish the project. One welder sued after he was fired for refusing to work Saturdays on religious grounds. The employer won after proving that it had a shortage of welders and was unable to hire welders for just one day per week. Short one welder, the company would have missed delivery on contracts that included penalties for being late. The court concluded that giving the man Saturdays off would be a hardship for the whole firm.

- *Don't impinge on the rights of other employees.* After being offered a job as a sheriff's deputy, a woman told the department she was unable to work on her sabbath. She withdrew her application and sued when she was told that she would have to work on those days. The department explained that work assignments were based on seniority. The woman lost her case because the court said that the department's seniority system was fair, and that accommodating her would have impinged on the rights of other employees.

- *Explore the options.* The law requires that you consider how to accommodate an employee's religious beliefs. A temporary Department of Agriculture border inspector sued when he didn't get a regular position because his religion kept him from working Saturdays. The department argued that giving him Saturdays off would burden his coworkers and complicate scheduling. The employee won because the department had not considered any options, such as shift trading. The court also found that coworkers would not be burdened because the man was willing to work other undesirable shifts, relieving coworkers from having to do so. (Note, however, that the decision might have been different if scheduling was influenced by a collective bargaining agreement or an established seniority system.)

Stay Out of Jail

- *Don't make any hiring, promotion, or work assignment decisions based on someone's religious beliefs.*
- *If the only way to accommodate a religious belief is to break the law, don't do it.* Yes, it does come up. At one company, an employee believed that his Social Security number was the "mark of the beast" and refused to disclose it; he asked his employer to create one for him. At another company, a Sikh employee refused to wear the hard hat mandated by OSHA because his religion requires wearing a turban. Because both accommodations were illegal, employers didn't have to make them.

- *Don't permit religious harassment.* Allowing employees to advocate for their religious beliefs at work can create a hostile environment. Three examples illustrate this point:
  - A bailiff who was a Jehovah's Witness read passages from the Bible to prisoners and in public areas of the courthouse.
  - A police chief advised a dispatcher about her prospects for salvation; his conduct escalated to the point that eventually he suggested to her that suicide would be preferable to the sinful way she was leading her life.
  - An employee sent letters to her coworkers asking them to accept Jesus and criticizing aspects of their behavior.

  Remember, just as employees have freedom of religion, they also are entitled to freedom from religion.

Real-Life Example

Sometimes, the best way to deal with a religious issue is on its own terms. Take, for example, the case of the farm workers and the devil. Several women who picked crops were asked to use the portable restroom facilities provided. For a time they did, but then they began crossing the street to use the facilities at a neighboring gas station. That was dangerous, took them much longer, and angered the station owner. When they were asked why they weren't using the restrooms provided, they explained that the devil was living in it. They knew this for a fact because they could see his boots while they were in the stalls. No amount of logic persuaded them that the devil was elsewhere. Finally, the manager decided to deal with the issue head on: he called a priest to perform an exorcism on the facility. Problem solved.

Get More Information

> *Serving Two Masters? Reflections on God and Profit,* C. William Pollard, Collins, 2006.
>
> *What Color Is Your Parachute?* Dick Bolles, Ten Speed Press, 2009.

SEXUAL ORIENTATION: HOW TO INCLUDE THE INVISIBLE MINORITY

Know the Issue

Do your coworkers have pictures of their spouses and children on their desks? Do people talk about their weekend plans at the water cooler or in the elevator? Does the company host social events that include spouses? Has anyone ever stopped by your desk to collect money to send a gift to a newlywed colleague or the parents of a new baby? If the answer to any of those questions is yes, then sexual orientation is an issue in your workplace.

This issue can be either a big positive or a big negative. If it's a positive, people feel included and respected. They are more productive and more committed. If it's a negative, people feel excluded and disrespected. They are less productive and far more likely to quit and go work for your competitor. They're also more likely to file potentially costly harassment lawsuits.

Huh? How did we get from baby gifts to turnover and lawsuits? Here's how: your heterosexual employees take for granted that they can comfortably share important elements of their private lives at work. All those normal activities from pictures to weekend plans are reflections of that comfort. That's as it should be.

In many workplaces, however, gay men, lesbians, and bisexuals do not feel comfortable sharing anything of their private lives. Although they may have been with a partner for years (or—in several states—be legally married to a same-sex spouse), they do not have any pictures on their desk. If they talk about weekend plans at all, they probably talk about "I," but never "he" or "she," and probably not "we," because it invites too many questions. They probably attend social events alone, or they come with a friend of the opposite sex. In short, while their heterosexual colleagues have one life, they have two lives: work life and personal life.

Okay, but how is this your problem and not something for the U.N. Human Rights Commission to address? It starts as a productivity issue. Gay men, lesbians, and bisexuals still in the closet at work expend an enormous amount of psychic energy protecting their secret. If you doubt it, try this experiment: Go an entire day without saying or doing anything that reveals your sexuality. You'll see "Don't Ask, Don't Tell" in a whole new light. Odds are that you'll be exhausted at the end of the day. You'll have devoted a lot of thought and energy to protecting yourself that would have been better served solving a work problem.

So, if it's that much work to stay in the closet, then why not just be honest? A growing number of gay people are honest—out of the closet and comfortable being themselves. But many gay people are afraid to be honest, and for good reason. Gay men, lesbians, and bisexuals know too many friends who've been passed up for promotions or fired, or worse. They know people who've been called names, robbed, beaten up, and splashed with acid. Yes, at work. What started as a productivity issue has become much more.

People faced with quiet indignity or violent hostility have three choices: they can put up with it, fight back, or leave. Fewer gay men, lesbians, and bisexuals are putting up with it. Many take the issue to court. Others leave for jobs where they are accepted. It turns out that losing gay employees may be a real loss to your organization. The University of Southern California's Kirk Snyder did a five-year study of 3,500 professionals in more than 2,000 organizations and discovered something dramatic: employees who work for gay managers have 25 to 30 percent higher workplace satisfaction and morale. Snyder attributes this difference to seven characteristics generally shared by gay executives: inclusion, creativity, adaptability, connectivity, communication, intuition, and collaboration. Does it make sense to let talent like that walk out the door—or sue you?

You may have religious beliefs that homosexuality is wrong, or you may simply be uncomfortable with the idea. We're not asking you to change those beliefs, but we are asking you to recognize that as a manager it's often your job to set aside personal feelings and treat people fairly. That's good business sense. (And in this case, the greatest beneficiaries may be the least visible—those who actively suppress their sexual orientation at work.) Here's how to do it.

Take Action

- *Look at your company policies.* Most large organizations (and many smaller ones) have nondiscrimination policies. If yours is among them, does the policy prohibit discrimination based on sexual orientation? If so, be sure you follow the policy. If not, suggest to HR or senior management that the policy be expanded. A clear policy is an important foundation for everything else you do.

- *Review your benefit plan.* Most employer-sponsored health care plans offer dependent coverage. Usually, however, dependents are defined strictly as spouses and children. (Of course, as noted, in some states same-sex couples may be legally married.) A growing number of companies, however, offer health coverage to domestic partners as well. If your plan offers such coverage, be sure your employees know about it. (Tell everyone about the coverage, not just those you think may be gay, lesbian, or bisexual.) If not, advocate to HR or senior management that such coverage be offered. Having it offers a competitive advantage (Microsoft, IBM, and Disney are among the many companies that now offer the benefits). It's also a matter or fairness; married people are effectively earning more for doing the same work if health coverage is provided to their spouses without cost. Don't worry about costs either. Numerous studies have shown that only a small number of employees accept the benefits (many partners are covered by their own employers), and the claims made by unmarried partners generally cost less than those filed by spouses.

- *Don't permit a hostile environment.* Most people wouldn't think of telling a racist or sexist joke at work. Telling jokes about gays, however, is more often still accepted. It shouldn't be. If you overhear such a joke, take the employee who told it aside and make it clear that such humor is unacceptable. Don't allow cartoons or images that impugn gay men, lesbians, or bisexuals to be posted. And by all means don't allow any derisive or hostile remarks to be made to employees known or suspected to be gay. If an employee tells you about such behavior, investigate promptly and confidentially. (For more information, see the section "Sexual Harassment: How to Recognize and Prevent Inappropriate Behavior" in Chapter 5.)

- *Use inclusive language.* If you or the organization is hosting a social event for employees and their families, be sure that invitations include "partners" or "significant others," and not just spouses. If employees attend these events with partners, be sure to introduce yourself and welcome the employee's guest. If you have policies allowing employees to take time off to care for an ill spouse (and in many cases the FMLA mandates that you do) or for bereavement leave, be sure that partners or significant others are covered by the policy. An employee who loses a partner of 20 years should not have to be at work the next day because his partner "didn't count." It has happened.

- *Be consistent.* If some employees have photos of their spouses or children on their desks, don't tell gay, lesbian, or bisexual employees that photos of their partners are not allowed. (Yes, it happens.) If winners of a sales incentive program are sent on a trip to Hawaii with their spouses or significant others, don't tell gay, lesbian, and bisexual employees that their partners have to stay home. If ... well, you get the idea.

- *Hold everyone accountable.* You won't tolerate off-color jokes, obscene photos, or lewd behavior from straight employees. Don't tolerate it from gay employees either. Gay people are entitled to equal treatment, but not special treatment.

Stay Out of Jail

- *Don't discriminate.* Currently, no federal law prohibits job discrimination based on sexual orientation. However, such discrimination is illegal in many states and cities. Congress has considered a federal law barring discrimination based on sexual orientation, and most experts expect it to pass at some point. (Most Americans support the proposal.) To be prudent, do not make decisions about hiring, promotion, overseas assignments, or other work-related issues based on someone's actual or perceived sexual orientation.

- *Don't ignore harassment.* Harassment law from any perspective is complicated (see "Sexual Harassment" in Chapter 5). However, when it comes to issues related to sexual orientation, it becomes particularly complex. Two types of harassment are at issue here:

  1. *Sexual harassment of an employee.* There are two forms of such harassment: demanding sexual favors or relations in exchange for promotion, job security, or other work-related actions (known as quid pro quo or economic harassment), or allowing an environment in which sexually explicit language, humor, images, and so on are present (this can be seen as harassment because some employees feel they are working in a hostile environment). This kind of harassment is illegal no matter who does the harassing or is harassed; men harassing men or women harassing women is no more acceptable than men harassing women or vice versa.

2. *Harassment based on sexual orientation.* Sometimes employees are harassed based on their sexual orientation. In such cases, the harassment generally has nothing to do with sexual favors. Instead, employees are taunted, humiliated, or even physically abused because they are gay, lesbian, or bisexual (or perceived to be). Such harassment is similar to name-calling or threats to African-Americans, Latinos, or women because of their race or gender. Currently, there is no federal law against harassment based on sexual orientation, but it is illegal in some states and cities. And it's always bad business.

The prudent thing is to protect employees from harassment and promptly investigate any claims.

Real-Life Example

Gays were frequently the butt of jokes. Disparaging comments were common. No one at the office was "out," so the salesperson at the high-tech company decided not to let anyone know she was a lesbian. "I truly believed that if I came out, I could lose my job," she said. "At a minimum, I wondered about the territories I would get."

So she lived in the closet. She never mentioned the partner she went home to every night, the one offering encouragement, a sympathetic ear about difficult clients, and occasionally a shoulder rub. She never talked about her weekends or holidays. She often had lunch alone.

But professionally she was excelling. She surpassed sales goals and earned a bigger territory. The promotion required travel, and because everyone assumed she was single, she was asked to travel on weekends. Soon she was among the company's top salespeople. And the lying began.

Her job performance caught the attention of the CEO, who invited her to his home for dinner. In a panic, she called a good friend—a gay man with a partner of his own—and asked him to go with her as her "date." After that, her friend was her date for all company social events. People even began asking when they were going to get married.

Then she won a sales contest. The prize was a trip to the Caribbean. She took the trip with her friend; her partner stayed home. But that trip put a strain on her relationship and on her friend's home life. She was the company's top salesperson, producing more revenue than anyone else, but she quit; the strain had gotten to be too much.

"My boss never knew why I left," she says. "He still calls once in a while and tries to get me back. I loved that job, but I could never go back. Life is too short."

Do at Least the Minimum

Don't allow gay, lesbian, or bisexual employees to be treated with less respect than other employees.

Get More Information

The G Quotient: Why Gay Executives Are Excelling As Leaders—and What Every Manager Needs to Know, Kirk Snyder, Jossey-Bass, 2006.

Straight Jobs, Gay Lives: Gay and Lesbian Professionals, Harvard Business School and the American Workplace, Annette Friskopp and Sharon Silverstein, Touchstone Books, 1996.

Straight Talk About Gays in the Workplace: Creating an Inclusive, Productive Environment for Everyone in Your Organization, 3rd ed., Liz Winfeld, Routledge, 2005.

PARENTS: HOW TO HELP EMPLOYEES BALANCE WORK AND FAMILY

Know the Issue

The singular anguish of being a working parent takes many forms: getting to that important meeting and finding the morning's peanut butter on your tie, brushing the jelly beans and Barbie clothes off the front seat before your client can get in the car, or discovering that the minutes from yesterday's meeting made an excellent canvas for your toddler's masterpiece. However, being a working parent is more than living gags right out of the *Baby Blues* comic strip. The real anguish is loosening the arms of a screaming child and walking out the door of a preschool, or sitting alone in a hotel room while your first grader appears in her first school play. Those are the situations that make life tough for parents and their managers.

Most parents have jobs outside the home. Parents of young children face daunting emotional and financial duties. We can either pretend it isn't our problem (which is about as easy as pretending that the children screaming at the next table in our favorite restaurant aren't there) or we can accept the fact and find ways to make the situation work for both sides.

Take Action

- *Be flexible*. When job duties permit, give parents the latitude to come in late, leave early, take time out of the middle of the day, or work at home. Stop worrying about when an employee gets work done and focus instead on the quality of the work. When you do that, you can stop worrying about people abusing the system.

Of course, many jobs require people to be at work during certain hours, but there may still be room for creativity. At a large hotel, for example, several resignations had put pressure on the housekeeping staff and replacements were hard to find. Rather than just buy bigger brooms or extend the workday, the manager asked the housekeepers for ideas. To his surprise, they proposed taking turns caring for each other's children; just eliminating the challenge of finding reliable child care enabled them to get more done.

Yes, we know: in tough times, when layoffs have cut staffing to the bone and everyone is doing three jobs, indulging in flexibility to help parents is not easy. It certainly may be more difficult than it once was. But creativity can go a long way toward easing stress without sacrificing productivity. If you can't do everything you'd like, at least employees know that you are aware of the challenges. And try to make it possible for parents to participate in particularly important family events.

- *Be reasonable*. A few gestures can go a long way toward making life easier for parents. Whenever possible, for example, avoid scheduling meetings the first thing in the morning or the last thing in the afternoon; it's more difficult for parents with children in child-care facilities to be flexible at those times of day. If you schedule all-day meetings, build in breaks that allow parents to check in with their child-care providers. Ask your employees if there are other easy things you can do to reduce their stress.

- *Respect time at home.* Many parents take work home to make up for time out of the office. Don't add to that burden by calling parents at home with questions that can be answered just as well the next day. Also, try to permit parents to get home at a reasonable hour. Be careful that you don't reward only those employees who join the gang for an after-work drink or a weekend trip to the beach. If you do, you're sending the signal that sacrificing personal time is a requirement for getting ahead.

- *Don't make kids invisible.* Just acknowledging employees' kids goes a long way toward helping parents feel supported. If you sponsor social events for employees, include their children occasionally and plan activities for the kids. (If children's activities are about as familiar to you as hosting a state dinner for a foreign ambassador, ask the parents in your office.) When kids show up at the office (and they will!), smile and talk to them. No one's asking you to audition for a job on *Sesame Street*, but watch morale plummet if you pretend you don't even see the kids. Better yet, set aside a free office or a corner somewhere where kids can entertain themselves for short periods.

- *Don't overdo it.* Do what you can to help parents, but be careful not to do it at the expense of employees who don't have kids (see the section "Employees Without Children: How to Reap Rewards by Recognizing Personal Lives" later in the chapter).

Stay Out of Jail

- *Don't make hiring, promotion, or work-assignment decisions based on whether employees are parents.* It has no bearing on their ability to do the job.

- *Giving employees flexibility is easiest when they are exempt.* With nonexempt employees, you run the risk of violating overtime laws. Be sure that nonexempt employees accurately track their time in the office and that you approve any work schedule changes in advance. Note the approval in writing so there is no disagreement later.

- *Allow children to visit occasionally, but be sure they are not allowed anywhere that might be dangerous,* such as near an assembly line or in an auto-repair bay.

- *If you have an area where children may spend time in the office, be sure it's childproof and secure.* Have parents sign a release stating that they are responsible for their children. (An attorney or your legal department can draft the release.)

- *Remember the Family Medical Leave Act (FMLA).* If your company is covered and the employee is eligible, the law protects the employee's right to miss work to care for an ill child, parent, or spouse under many circumstances. Furthermore, if the employee is eligible for family leave, you will want to notify the employee of that fact so the company can deduct the time taken from the employee's annual allotment.

Real-Life Example

Wonderware, an Irvine, California-based developer of software for manufacturing firms, is a very parent-friendly place. Most employees set their own schedules. That means some arrive as early as 6 A.M. so they can have more time with their children after school. No one frowns if parents leave the office for school conferences or doctor appointments.

When parents get in a child-care bind, they're welcome to bring kids into the office. The Kid's Rooms (each of the company's four buildings has a room) are stocked with standard office supplies (paper, staplers, pens, pencils, crayons, rulers, tape), a TV, a VCR, and several older computers. The kids are also welcome to the free food: vending machine items, fresh fruit, string cheese, hard-boiled eggs, celery sticks, carrots, and a drink refrigerator that includes milk, fruit juice, and sodas. A telephone in the room makes it easy to reach Mom or Dad.

At Wonderware, kids are considered part of the company "family." At the annual picnic, they play on an inflatable mountain, a large slide, and a human Foosball field. They participate in the hula hoop endurance challenge, water balloon tossing, and sack races, and also enjoy the hired juggler/mime. Other annual family activities include an Easter egg hunt, a summer kickoff barbecue, and a Christmas crafts evening at which kids visit with Santa, frost cookies, and decorate mugs, glasses, and ornaments.

All of that makes the company an appealing place for parents to work. It's great for recruitment and retention, and it goes a long way toward building commitment.

Manage Up

If your boss has children, learn their names and ages. Say hello if they visit and make a point to ask about them occasionally.

Do at Least the Minimum

Don't pretend that parents aren't parents and make their lives diffi-
cult (by letting a meeting run long past normal hours, for example)
just because you can.

Get More Information

> *The Working Parents Handbook*, June Solnit Sale and Kit
> Kollenberg with Ellen Melnikoff, Fireside, 1996.

EMPLOYEES WITHOUT CHILDREN: HOW TO REAP REWARDS BY RECOGNIZING PERSONAL LIVES

Know the Issue

Max is Julie's prize collie. She has raised him from the time he was
a young puppy, investing thousands of hours in training and groom-
ing. Outside work, she and Max are virtually inseparable. She belongs
to a club of collie owners, and because she knows that not every dog
is as fortunate as Max, she volunteers at a local animal shelter. So
when Julie asks for a day off so Max can participate in a high-profile dog show, would you let her take it?

Before you answer, consider some other situations. What if Max
was her oldest friend, visiting from across the country and only in
town for one day? What if Julie is a Meals on Wheels volunteer and
Max is a housebound elderly man? Would you give Julie the time if
Max was her five-year-old nephew? Her grandfather? Her hospital-
ized boyfriend? Her 10-year-old son?

These situations are at the center of workplace skirmishes that
threaten to erupt into full-scale warfare because most employers will

only give Julie the time if Max is her son, and employees without children resent that. "Our company says it wants to help balance the demands of work and personal life," John says, "but they seem to think that personal life is the same as children. I'm tired of watching the parents walk out of here at five to pick up their kids while the rest of us stay here and work. It isn't fair."

This is a highly emotional issue. Parents argue that juggling work and family is tough. They face child-care crises, doctors' appointments, and family situations that require them to take time off. They say that their coworkers don't see the time they work at home after the kids are in bed. Besides, they argue, someone has to raise the next generation.

Fair enough, say those without children, but we're tired of feeling that our personal lives don't matter. "I get asked all the time to help out so someone can go to his kid's soccer game, or whatever," John says, "and I do it. But when I ask them to return the favor so I can do something that's important to me, they're always too busy." John also complains that his manager never interferes when employees need to do something for their kids, but subjects everyone else to the third degree when they want to take time off or alter their schedule. He adds that parents are asked to travel less often, they are forgiven for missed deadlines, and they earn the same money for working fewer hours.

As with most divisive issues, there is truth on both sides, which is a manager's nightmare. Ignoring the issue won't make it go away. (You might as well write job requisitions to fill the empty jobs you're about to have and start packing rations so you'll be ready for the open warfare.) You can make the whole problem go away by putting the focus back on job performance.

Take Action

- *Flexibility is flexibility is flexibility.* Let's assume you're managing exempt employees. If you're a cool boss who lets people slip out early or come in late occasionally, give everyone the same flexibility. Resist the temptation to ask what they'll be doing. If you give people time to deal with their personal lives, it doesn't matter whether they spend that time taking their kids to a soccer game, volunteering at a homeless shelter, or going to an antiques show; it's their business, not yours. Measure whether work is completed on time and done well; don't log every time Jane comes in late or leaves early.

- *Give people maneuvering room.* Even if you are a cool boss, it's tougher to give people in nonexempt jobs the flexibility to just cut out early. Often the work they do can only be performed on site (and not at home, for example), and you must also contend with overtime law. Still, we're talking about a job, not a prison camp. If your company policies allow it, let people use vacation or personal leave time in small increments (such as a half day at a time) provided they request the time in advance so you can plan. Track the hours used.

- *Accept that there will be emergencies.* Crises happen in everyone's life; treat them all equally. Don't reassure parents that "everything will be fine here, just go," and then make it tough for others to get away.

- *Don't make assumptions.* Don't assume that employees without children are more willing to travel, or that parents can't stay late. Make decisions based on who is best suited to the job.

- *Monitor work hours*. No one's asking you to track every hour exempt employees are at work, but watch general trends. Employees might leave at different times for many reasons. But if those leaving on time or early are always the same people, it's time to step in and coach them about sharing the burden.
- *Hold people equally accountable*. Once deadlines are determined, decide the consequences for not meeting them and hold everyone to the same standard. Don't cut parents extra slack.

Stay Out of Jail

- Don't make hiring, promotion, or work assignment decisions based on whether an employee is a parent.
- Remember the Family Medical Leave Act (FMLA). If your company is covered and the employee is eligible, the law protects the employee's right to miss work to care for an ill child, parent, or spouse under many circumstances. Furthermore, if the employee is eligible for family leave, you will want to notify the employee of that fact so the company can deduct the time taken from the employee's annual allotment.

Real-Life Example

Cancer patients often have extended hospital stays, and during that time they get to know the nurses and other members of the staff. The team at one California hospital helped that process with a bulletin board on the oncology floor. Each employee was invited to post something about him- or herself, which patients and their families could then look at. Although some people chose to post pictures of their children, the board was not just an oversized "Hey, look at my kid display." Some employees posted pictures of their spouse or significant other; others pinned up photos of themselves busy with their hobby or charity work. "I like the board because it shows we're all real people with real lives," one nurse said. "We're not just nurses or just parents."

Do at Least the Minimum

Don't routinely pick on employees without children to work late or take out-of-town trips.

Get More Information

> *Harvard Business Review on Work and Life Balance,* Harvard Business School Press, 2000.

Today's Diverse Workforce: A Glossary

The issues of workplace diversity and affirmative action are often hot buttons, and the emotions they elicit are often based on misunderstandings, so you and your employees may find these basic explanations helpful.

> *Affirmative action.* Describes an effort to achieve equality in employment. President Johnson introduced the idea in 1965 when he signed Executive Order 11246. The order requires employers that do business with the federal government to "develop affirmative action plans to assure equal employment opportunity in their employment practices." Initially, it simply
>
> *continued*

meant that companies pledged to take steps not to discriminate. Now, to ensure that federal contractors comply with the order, those employers are required to monitor applicant pools to make sure they include women and minorities. Employers evaluate the data themselves (though reports are subject to government audit), and when they spot problems, establish employment targets to ensure that women and minorities are represented in all segments of the workforce. Some employers that are not federal contractors elect to develop affirmative action efforts to improve the diversity of their workforces.

Equal Employment Opportunity Commission (EEOC). The agency charged with enforcing federal antidiscrimination laws.

Quotas. Commitments to hire or promote a specific number or percentage of people in protected classes. Quotas are often seen as part of an affirmative action plan, but they are not. In fact, quotas are illegal. The only exceptions are when quotas are imposed as the outcome of a legal dispute in which an employer is found guilty of active discrimination. (Only judges may impose quotas.) In such cases, the quotas must be met.

Set-aside programs. These set aside some government contracts in a pool for minority- and women-owned businesses. They allow such businesses to win contracts even if they don't submit the lowest bid.

Diversity. A concept recognizing that many kinds of people are in today's workforce. It is often misused to suggest only race or race and gender. In reality, there are many other kinds of diversity. They include age, religion, varying abilities and disabilities, sexual orientation, education, and so on. As opposed to affirmative action (which addresses the workforce yet to be hired), diversity generally refers to employees already in place. Some people speak of "managing diversity," a phrase that experts generally discourage because it suggests that diversity is a problem that somehow must be contained. A better phrase

continued

is "valuing diversity," which describes a process of recognizing and appreciating differences, and using those differences
for the benefit of the whole organization. It sees diversity as
an opportunity, not a problem.

Reverse discrimination. This a misnomer, because discrimination
for any reason is still discrimination. The phrase is used to
describe a situation in which someone outside a protected class
(a young white male, for example) is passed over for a job or
promotion in favor of someone less qualified from a protected
group. Such cases can attract a lot of attention, but in *Reverse
Discrimination: Dismantling the Myth,* author Fred L. Pincus
reports that only 9.1 percent of all Title VII race claims
resolved by the EEOC between 1995 and 2000 were reverse-
discrimination claims.

8

Making Successful Hires

Consider the typical process for buying a car. First, we eye every car on the road, picturing ourselves behind the wheel: Too Mid-Life Crisis? Too Soccer Mom? Enough "I Made It?" The process consumes us. Suddenly, car ads become more interesting than the articles in our favorite magazine. We postpone the microwave popcorn ritual to actually watch the car commercials. We talk to everyone we know about their cars.

Finally, we're ready to go hands-on. We peer in windows, open doors and trunks, and sit in drivers' seats. We picture how fast we'll be able accelerate or how much gas the hybrid engine will save. Then, in our minds, we customize with a sun roof and tasteful pin-striping, or a spoiler and eight-speaker stereo system. When we can no longer resist the charms of the hotshot salesperson, we agree to a test drive. Then we dicker over options and price and terms and credit and an extended warranty. Only then do we drive off the lot in our dream car.

If only a fraction as much time were spent in assessing the average job candidate. But too often someone is hired on little more than a cursory interview and a gut feeling. To be fair, hiring candidates is time-consuming and difficult. It requires us to turn off (almost) all our emotional responses to people to focus on objective data. It demands that we use listening skills usually reserved for talks with doctors, divorce attorneys, and traffic cops. The process is also constrained by legal straitjackets, large and small.

Don't despair. Great hiring skills can be learned. And with patience—and dogged determination to follow a fair, thorough process—you'll improve your odds of success far beyond any you'll find in Vegas.

SOURCING CANDIDATES: WHERE TO FIND THE RIGHT PERSON FOR THE JOB

Know the Issue

"I liked the old days," one manager told us. "If somebody wasn't pulling his weight or you didn't like him, you fired him. Then you went out to the line in front of the building and hired a guy to replace him. It was easy."

We aren't sure which "old days" he's talking about (during the Hoover administration?), but they were only "easy" if you didn't care anything about the quality of your workforce. But times have changed: there are almost no jobs left for which just anyone will do. Trust us: hiring the wrong person is worse than hiring no person.

Don't think of yourself as a fisher, casting a wide net and hoping for the best. Think of yourself as a chef, a jeweler, or a director. In any of these jobs, you'd be utterly reliant on the right resources.

In the end, all the talent and skill in the world won't matter if all you have to work with is bad meat, bad stones, or bad actors. All of your managerial skills won't matter either, if all you have to work with are employees who were compromise hires.

For all those reasons, sourcing candidates is crucial. Even when there are lots of people looking for jobs, you still need to find the best of those who are available. Think like a marketer, and then be diligent about making the most of all the sourcing options you have.

Take Action

- *Use social networking media.* Trying to fill jobs without using social networking sites would be a little like planning an evening of home entertainment without even considering DVDs or cable TV: You could do it, but why limit your options? At last count Facebook claimed that it had more than 30 million active users, and LinkedIn had more than 20 million—and both were growing exponentially. And they are just two high-profile social networking tools among many available to you. No wonder many employers rely on social networking to find talent. Of course, sheer volume promises nothing, so as with any source, you have to be smart about how you use social networking:
  - *Know the purpose of the social network.* While LinkedIn is a professional network, Facebook is primarily a social network. Accordingly, Facebook may be a great place to find college kids who want to serve drinks poolside, but not the best for hiring marketing professionals.
  - *Know the demographics of the social network.* Beyond a social network's purpose, different networks attract

different constituencies. MySpace, for example, is most popular with high school students and younger—not the best place to search for candidates if experience is important.

○ *Know what tools are available.* Because they have different purposes, different social networks also offer varying levels of help. LinkedIn, for example, has a formal jobs and hiring community and offers job-posting forms and a fee-based posting process. The network also offers a place to post a company profile.

○ *Develop and maintain your own network.* The operative word in social networking is "networking," so develop your own network and keep it current. Include friends, colleagues, former colleagues, peers you meet at professional events, and even people who sit next to you on the plane when you travel for business. The idea is to have a network of people who already are aware of and interested in your company.

○ *Don't overlook niche networks.* Sure, LinkedIn and Facebook are the big players. But there are numerous special networks out there serving specific industries or geographic areas. Those smaller networks may be a better choice. Think of it this way: If you were selling expensive kitchen knives, would you be better off advertising on *Dancing with the Stars* or the Food Network?

○ *Think fast.* Don't rely on new technology, but use it as if it's old technology. Users of social networks expect prompt responses and immediate gratification—younger generations will even find e-mail too slow and rely on texts or tweets instead. Know your audience and act accordingly.

- *Use the Internet.* A decade ago—when we wrote the first edition of this book—Internet recruiting was the new frontier. Today it may already seem old-fashioned when compared to social networking media. But the Internet—used smartly—can still be an effective sourcing tool.
  - *Think about the people most likely to apply for your job.* Do they have access to the Internet? (The Nielsen Company reported in December 2008 that more than 25 percent of homes in the United States did not have Internet access at that time.) Which recruiting sites are they visiting? The top sites can give you information about their audience. Find a good match.
  - *Find out whether your organization has a preferred site or sites.* If you work in a large company, HR may have already contracted with one or more recruiting sites. If so, follow their lead. If the company has no formal policy or agreement, network with other managers to see if they've had good luck with a site.
  - *Get information from several sites that match your needs.* Find out job posting options, pricing, audience demographics, traffic, currency of résumés, and site reliability. Get references.
  - *Post your job and track the responses.* Track how many responses you get, how quickly you receive responses, how qualified the applicants are, how many you interview, and how many (if any) you hire. If you use more than one site, compare how each performs.
- *Ask employees for referrals.* Who knows your business better than anyone? Current employees. Many companies have

a formal program in which employees refer people (friends, relatives, neighbors) who they feel would make good employees, and are rewarded if one of their referrals is hired. Study after study has shown that employees hired through referral programs perform better—and stay longer—than employees hired through any other source. Of course, for a referral program to work, you can't just send an e-mail to your staff and hope for the best. Instead:

○ *Decide which jobs you'll accept referrals for and who is eligible to participate.* (Hint: the broader the program, the better). Decide how the referrals will be made and how long the program will last.

○ *Decide how to reward employees.* (You can give a small prize, such as movie tickets, to every employee who makes a referral, but most programs offer more substantial rewards when hires are actually made.)

○ *Explain in advance that the hiring decisions will be business decisions, not personal ones.* Have a plan for contacting the referrals.

○ *Promote the program.*

○ *Monitor participation.* If interest in the program starts to flag, rejuvenate it with new prizes or fresh promotion. If enthusiasm wanes because referrals aren't being hired, think about why. Do people need more explicit information about the kind of people you're looking for?

• *Hang out where your candidates hang out.* Be the employer that candidates see when they do whatever it is they normally do. For example, where do disenfranchised software programmers hang out? The Dilbert Web page! So that's exactly where Cisco Systems placed job ads. Meanwhile, the approach at Olds Products, a mustard manufacturer, is about 180 degrees less irreverent. Representatives for Olds went looking for people at churches, synagogues, and mosques — trading $100 donations for job candidate leads.

- *Hire for attitude, train for skill.* If you were looking for an information analyst, you'd go to the Juilliard School and hire a violinist, right? That's just what Electronic Data Systems (EDS) did after realizing they were duking it out with their competitors for the same small pool of high-tech grads. It makes sense if you think about it: any violinist who gets into Juilliard is driven and detail-oriented. He can learn information analysis.

- *Take college recruitment a step further.* Going to college career fairs is swell, but to really stand out on campus, think big. EDS became the primary sponsor of the U.S. Sunrayce, an intercollegiate competition to build and race solar-powered cars. The company provided scoring and timing devices, location tracking systems, and even technical engineers. While students were winning races, EDS was shaking hands with several bright engineering graduates who eventually accepted job offers. But the race only happens once a year. What else could EDS do? Race down the ski slopes with flyers and T-shirts to recruit students on their winter break.

- *Use agencies.* There it is on your calendar: dinner with a client. Your spouse is unavailable, and your two-year-old will not be welcome. What do you do? Call a babysitter. Those woefully underpaid helpmates can do a lot — everything from making sure that teeth are brushed to keeping the kids alive all weekend. But no one—not even live-in help—can raise the kids for you.

The same applies when dealing with employment agencies. Depending on which you hire and the instructions you give, they can do a lot to make your life easier. But they can't and shouldn't do the hiring for you.

○ *Figure out what kind of help you need.* Plot out the hiring process. Where are you most likely to get bogged down? Finding candidates may be the toughest hurdle. On the other hand, just finding time to interview people may be a bigger challenge.

○ *Decide what kind of agency would be best to work with.* There are four primary types of agencies: temporary help agencies (which generally fill jobs on a temporary basis but may offer a temp-to-perm option); employment placement agencies (which generally fill lower-level jobs that don't require special skills); contingency search firms (generally used to fill mid-level jobs and only paid if you hire someone); and retained search firms (usually used for top-level or highly specialized jobs and paid whether or not you hire one of their candidates). Services, results, and fees vary. Choose the type that's best for the assignment.

○ *Find out whether others in your organization are already working with an agency.* If you work in a company with an HR function, some agencies may already have been chosen. If so, use them.

○ *Tell the agency what you want.* Remember, you're the boss. That means you can have things your way ("Don't call me Monday mornings during my regular staff meeting"), but it also means you're responsible for making sure the agency understands the assignment. Don't be stingy with information; the more the agency knows, the better.

○ *Clarify expectations.* Be sure that you and the agency are on the same page about how the process will work. Don't assume anything.

○ *Monitor your progress.* Once the process is under way, think about how it's going. Are you seeing the sort of candidate you expected to see? Is the agency responsive? Are you feeling supported or pressured? Do candidates seem too well-prepared? If you have concerns, say so.

○ *Follow up after the job is filled.* Give the agency feedback about the process, pro and con. Keep the agency apprised about how the candidate is performing—particularly if the placement is guaranteed.

○ *Read the contract.* Review the written agreement (that is, the contract) with the agency very carefully to make certain that your company's responsibilities and the agency's obligations are clear and accurate.

• *Don't disregard classifieds.* Many people hear "classified ad" and think "newspaper." And because newspaper circulation is in decline (and many younger people get all their information online), they then dismiss the classified ad as a candidate-sourcing tool. But a classified ad is a format, not a medium, and whether it appears in the *Arizona Republic,* on CareerBuilder, or on Craigslist, there are times when it's a very effective tool.

○ *Know your audience.* Sure, you might find the perfect person for your highly specialized job through a classified ad.

You might win the lottery, too. But classifieds work best for broader categories of jobs. You also should consider where to place the ad. An online site such as Craigslist may be great if you're seeking teens to deliver pizzas. A job board (such as Monster) or social networking site (such as LinkedIn) may be best for finding professionals, such as accountants. But many people still don't have Internet access at home, so a newspaper may be a better choice if you're seeking to hire housekeeping staff for a hotel.

○ *Sell the job.* Would you plunk down eight bucks at the multiplex to see something known only as *Action Flick*? Of course you wouldn't. If people won't invest two hours and eight dollars in an unknown, why would they bet their career on a mystery job? A classified ad in any medium is not an announcement—it's a marketing piece. So write it accordingly—sell what the job has to offer.

○ *Match the environment.* You want your ad to stand out as offering a cool job, but not to stand out because it's clear to the audience that you are completely out of touch with their world. For example, Craigslist is less formal than a newspaper, so your ad should also be less formal. It's usually easier and less expensive to run longer ads online, so make the effort to be more thorough and creative. Finally, keep in mind that some sites have established job-posting forms.

○ *Take advantage of the medium.* If you post an ad online, take advantage of what the Internet has to offer. Include a link to graphics, video, audio, and other tools that are not only interactive, but help sell your organization as well as the job.

○ *Learn what works.* Some job posting sites offer statistical analysis of job ads, showing how many responses an ad generated, for example. If they are available, use those statistics. Study the ads that work best. Track responses to your own ad. If it isn't pulling, try a different approach.

○ *Focus on key words.* Unlike newspaper classifieds, which readers scan visually, online ads are pulled from extensive databases. Users are in charge, and they only scan the ads that interest them. Therefore, whether your ad is seen or ignored will depend in large part on whether you include the "right" keywords. To figure out what the right words are, study other job postings on the site. (Some job sites publish keyword guidelines.) Also, consider what is most likely important to job seekers and use words that tag those concerns. Use synonyms whenever possible so your ad may be found through several different searches. Some Internet job boards offer specific fields and/or formats in which to place keywords, so be sure to check for such requirements when posting.

○ *Don't be coy.* It's a waste of everyone's time to be misleading (or evasive) about salary, job duties, and so forth in an ad. When posting online, the more information you provide, the better. The specificity helps job hunters determine how "real" the job is, and it will also slash the number of responses you get for unqualified candidates.

○ *Don't run blind ads.* Blind ads (in which you conceal the name of your organization) establish an atmosphere of second-guessing and distrust from the outset. Also, many top candidates won't respond to blind ads, reasoning that if they are sending personal information to someone, they want to know where they're sending it.

○ *If you're an equal opportunity employer (and you should be), say so.*

○ *Decide how you want candidates to respond.* Whatever you decide, include the information in the ad. Match the response to the media: don't post an Internet ad asking people to respond via mail, for example.

○ *Develop a plan to respond.* Once the ad runs, you need to be ready to respond. Once you have the plan, communicate it to anyone involved and then stick to it.

○ *Acknowledge all responses.* It's good form to acknowledge every application, even if you use a form letter. Anything less than that is disrespectful. And some candidates are receiving unemployment and need to prove that they are making a legitimate effort to find work.

Whichever source (or sources) you choose, remember that it's only the beginning of the process. No matter how promising your prospects are, you still need to assess their potential and follow a well-considered hiring process.

Stay Out of Jail

- *Don't discriminate in ad copy.* Don't even think about an ad (in print or online) that reads, "Seeking young women . . ." or "No Latinos," or "No one over 40 need apply . . ." or any other phrase that discriminates against a protected group or groups.

- *If you use an agency, remember, you are still the employer.* An agency can act on your behalf during the process, but you are still responsible. Be sure that background checks, tests, and so on are complete and done within the confines of the law. Ask to see copies of any material, and keep copies of the material in the employee file after the employee starts. Review any formal offer before the agency makes it. (Insist on that when you hire the agency.) Be sure the agency is not promising something you can't deliver. Be sure the employee understands the offer; do not assume the agency will take care of it. Be sure that employees hired through an agency have been subjected to the same tests, assessments, background checks, and so forth as employees hired from other sources. Be sure that the agency does not discriminate in its hiring practices.

- *Don't make promises.* Remember, you're expanding your options—not promising to hire anyone.
- *Keep hiring information confidential.*
- *Don't rely too much on any program if the result is that all applicants start "looking alike."* You could find yourself accused of discrimination if it effectively excludes applicants from protected classes.
- *Find out whether candidates have an employment contract or have signed a "do not compete" clause that prohibits them from working for a competitor in the same industry.* If they have, it could result in legal problems you don't need.
- *Be politic.* When networking, don't say anything about anyone else that you wouldn't want repeated.
- *Don't use the Internet exclusively.* Not everyone has access to the Internet. Those who are online are disproportionately

white and middle or upper class. Because of that, there's some concern that posting a job online only (as opposed to online and in traditional media) puts minority candidates at a disadvantage in getting those jobs.

- *Protect the privacy of applicants*. Do not sell résumés you receive over the Internet or forward them to other prospective employers without the candidate's permission.

Manage Up

- *If you try something creative and it works, be sure your boss knows about it.* Who wouldn't be happy with an employee who can solve problems creatively?
- *Don't forget to include your boss in your network.*

Get More Information

www.workplace911.com

www.careerbuilder.com

www.careermag.com

www.careerpath.com

www.dice.com (specializes in high-tech jobs)

www.flipdog.com

www.hotjobs.yahoo.com

www.imdiversity.com

www.jobs.com

www.linkedin.com

www.monster.com

www.therecruiterslounge.com

Smart Staffing: How to Hire, Reward, and Keep Top Employees for Your Growing Company, Wayne Outlaw, Upstart, 1998.

Zero Defect Hiring: A Quick Guide to the Most Important Decisions Managers Have to Make, Walter Anthony Dinteman, Pfeiffer, 2003.

APPLICATIONS: HOW TO GET THE BASIC INFORMATION YOU NEED

Know the Issue

You're at the hospital. All you really want is to be done with your test or procedure or surgery so you can go home. But before they ever get started, there's . . . paperwork. Lots of it. It's exasperating, but the forms make it possible for every doctor and nurse you encounter to get key information about you. Odds are that the form includes a release granting the hospital the right to treat you. Yes, there's a lot riding on those forms.

There's a lot riding on employment application forms, too, but most companies pay about as much attention to them as they do to the reading material in the lobby. In many cases, applicants who have résumés aren't even asked to complete an application. But applications can do much more than express a candidate's interest in working for you. They also standardize the information you collect (lawyers love that), and they provide a great place to give candidates important legal information (such as your at-will and nondiscriminatory hiring practices). The few minutes it takes a candidate to complete an application can be invaluable to you.

Take Action

- *Find out whether your firm has an application form.* If you work in a large or well-established firm, there's probably an existing form to use. Track one down. You should be able to get one from HR or from other managers.

- *If there is no form, create one.* If your company doesn't already have a form, you need one. Forms are commercially available. Or create a form yourself. If you do that, limit the information you collect to what's relevant to the job. Good forms ask for:
  - Name, address, and telephone number
  - Date of application
  - Social Security number
  - Position applied for
  - Previous applications to or employment with the company
  - Employment history (including employers' names and addresses, job titles, salaries, and dates of employment)
  - Special skills
  - Education, including school names and addresses, dates attended (except for dates of grammar school and high school), courses of study, degrees earned, and honors awarded

- *Good forms also ask questions to help employers comply with the law.* For example:
  - "If you are under 18 years of age, can you provide required proof of your eligibility to work?"

- ○ "Are you legally eligible for employment in the United States?"
- ○ "Have you been convicted of a felony (or a misdemeanor involving violent or fraudulent conduct)? If yes, please state the location, the date, and the crime(s) for which you were convicted." (Note: the form should include an advisory that a conviction will not necessarily disqualify an applicant from employment.)
- ○ "Have you ever been arrested for any criminal violation for which you are currently out on bail, out on your own recognizance, or otherwise on release pending trial? If yes, explain." (Note: different states have different laws relative to questions about convictions; check with a labor attorney before you put this question on an application.)

- *Applications may also ask for practical data*, such as when an applicant will be available to begin work and whether the applicant is available to travel, should the position require it.
- *Applications often advise candidates of employment requirements*, such as passing a drug test or background check. When permission is required (as when doing a background check), the form may ask candidates to grant permission and sign it.
- *Finally, a good application clearly states employment policies*, such as at-will employment, the necessity that the application be honest, the fact that the employer resolves disputes by arbitration, the employer's position on drug testing and background checks, and the following with respect to nondiscrimination:

We consider applicants for all positions without regard to race, color, religion, creed, sex, marital status, age, national origin, ancestry, physical or mental disability, medical condition, sexual orientation, or any other consideration made unlawful by federal, state, or local laws. We are an equal opportunity employer and we offer employment on the basis of ability, experience, training, and character.

- *Have every applicant complete the form—even if they have supplied a résumé that includes most of the information.*
- *Keep the completed applications in confidential files.*

Stay Out of Jail

- *If you create an application form, have an attorney review it before you use it.*
- *Verify the information provided, such as employment history and Social Security number.*

Do at Least the Minimum

Have every applicant complete a form before he or she is hired.

Get More Information

Hiring Smart! How to Predict Winners and Losers in the Incredibly Expensive People-Reading Game, Pierre Mornell, Ten Speed Press, 2004.

How to Spot a Liar: Why People Don't Tell the Truth . . . and How You Can Catch Them, Gregory Hartley and Maryanne Karinch, Career Press, 2005.

RÉSUMÉS: HOW TO SPOT THE HYPE AND FIND THE TRUTH

Know the Issue

When Lily Tomlin observed, "No matter how cynical you become, it's never enough to keep up," she probably didn't have résumés in mind. But you should, because too many people out there are, well, creative. Some submit résumés far funnier than anything you'll see on TV tonight. If you doubt it, Robert Half, a veteran of the temporary staffing industry and an expert recruiter, collects what he calls "résumania." A few samples:

- "Raised by a father who was a member of a military special operations group, I'm a man who doesn't intimidate easily."
- "Restaurant manager. Cleaned and supervised employees."
- "In my next life, I will be a professional backup dancer or a rabbi."
- "Qualifications: I have guts, drive, ambition, and heart, which is probably more than a lot of the drones that you have working for you."
- "Education: Watched the first season of *The Apprentice* and part of the second season."

Granted, few résumés are that entertaining, but they may not be very helpful either. Remember that what you see as basic information, the candidate sees as unabashed marketing; and marketing, as we know, isn't rich with truth. Robert Half reports that surveys done by his company, Robert Half International, show that 30 percent of job seekers lie on their résumés. Many of the rest exaggerate.

None of this gives you license to throw a stack of résumés down a flight of stairs and hire the people whose résumés get to the bottom. For one thing, enough résumés are totally legit to keep things interesting. For another, jurors are more kindly disposed to managers who hire using some sort of uniform rationale. Résumés are the best place to start.

Take Action

- *Give résumés a careful reading.* Here's how:
  - *Presentation counts.* Give priority to résumés accompanied by a cover letter. Look for résumés that are typeset or created in a word processing program (as opposed to handwritten carelessly), and printed on something other than an old napkin or the reverse side of a grocery list. Deduct points for changes made by hand or cute symbols like smiley faces.
  - *Beware of hyperbole.* Suppose, for example, a résumé states, "Set new sales record." It sounds impressive, but guessing all the things it might mean while still being 100 percent accurate could keep a frat house busy all weekend. "Set new record for lowest sales" and "Set a record for new sales while losing all existing clients" are two that come to mind.
  - *Beware of name droppers.* If a candidate cites experience at a brand name employer, make sure their experience is relevant. Flipping burgers or dressing as a giant mouse may not prepare them for the work you need done.
  - *Beware of job hoppers.* You want employees with ambition, but if a candidate has a history of changing jobs every

18 months, beware. Odds are that the employee wouldn't stay with you any longer, which means you'll never see a return on your investment in hiring and training. That said, our advice applies primarily to frequent job changes before 2008, when the economy took a dramatic downturn. In a rough economy, people grab what opportunities they can, and that may mean several short-term assignments. They may also be the unfortunate victim of several layoffs. If candidates have the requisite skills, use the interview to explore their job history.

- *Look for gaps.* Candidates who drop out of the workforce temporarily for legitimate reasons (a job search or protected leave) usually say so. If they don't, something has been omitted for a reason. Did the candidate spend time in prison as a convicted felon, or get fired for embezzling or sexual harassment, or spend a long time collecting unemployment because other people were smart enough not to hire him?

- *Beware of career students.* Recent college graduates have reason to emphasize their education. Candidates who have earned a degree while working full-time are justified for tooting their own horns. For everyone else, education should be given less emphasis than work experience. There's a reason they call life off campus the "real world."

- *Sweat the small stuff.* One HR pro told us that he always pays careful attention to the employment dates listed on a résumé. He says that many people give them a cursory glance, or less. But he finds that the dates often include discrepancies. Making such errors can indicate that a candidate either plays fast and loose with the truth or can't be bothered to pay attention to details. Either way, it's an indication that—at a minimum—you need further information.

○ *Beware of extraneous data.* Sure, you want a well-rounded candidate, but that doesn't mean you need to know about their pets, voting history, or must-see TV shows. It's helpful to know that she's joined professional associations to network or to hone her skills. It's less helpful for you to know about her membership in the Book of the Month Club or frequent-flier program.

○ *Logic counts.* Look for job history in chronological order. Organization by function or other order that makes you work to figure out job tenure and history has probably been packaged to conceal something.

• *Spot the top candidates by looking for the following:*

○ *Specific accomplishments.* Are there concrete examples of what the candidate has accomplished, or glittering generalities about his responsibilities? In sales, for example, look for dollar volume, market share, or increased percentage in sales. Market data and timelines are an added bonus: "As sales rep for one of five national territories, moved sales from lowest market share against four competitors to highest market share in 18 months."

○ *Training.* Does the candidate indicate any special training he has had? Depending on your business, anything from university extension courses to conference seminars could be helpful.

- *Customization.* Has the résumé been drafted for your job—or at least a similar job—or is it a generic one-size-fits-all résumé?
- *Career progress.* Has the candidate made job changes leading to progressively more responsibility and higher pay, or does he simply seem stuck? Does the candidate seem to have a career plan?
- *Bottom-line orientation.* Does he mention cutting costs or making money?

- *Beware résumé-scanning software.* Many large organizations today use résumé-scanning software in the hiring process. Résumés are scanned into the system, which in effect creates a large database that allows users to scan for keywords. For example, you could receive 25 résumés for a software programmer position and then search for experience in a specific programming language or application. Although such software can make sifting through résumés more efficient and objective, those gains come at some cost, too. Without the full résumés, you also can't really tell a candidate's full story. Specific experience isn't always as valuable as a candidate's job history or accomplishments. Think of it this way: Would you date someone based entirely on a list of keywords?

Stay Out of Jail

- *If candidates include personal information in their résumés, ignore it when evaluating their qualifications.*

- *Keep all the résumés submitted in application for the job.*
- *Be careful if you are fully reliant on résumés that have been scanned into databases.* There have been legal challenges to résumé scanning on the grounds the keywords used adversely affect protected minorities.

Get More Information

Hiring and Keeping the Best People, 2nd ed., Harvard Business School Press, 2003.

Hiring Smart! How to Predict Winners and Losers in the Incredibly Expensive People-Reading Game, Pierre Mornell, Ten Speed Press, 2004.

Smart Staffing: How to Hire, Reward and Keep Top Employees for Your Growing Company, Wayne Outlaw, Kaplan Business, 1998.

ASSESSMENT TOOLS: HOW TO BE SURE CANDIDATES WILL FIT IN

Know the Issue

Remember the Man in the Gray Flannel Suit—that '50s archetype of the corporation man? Today he's as extinct as the T-Rex. His habitat is now home to a variety of new species: Bernie Brainstorm, Natalie Numbers, Monica Meetings, Donna Deadlines, and Peter Policy among them. But evolution is a tricky thing. Although the Man in the Gray Flannel Suit is unlikely to survive as the fittest almost anywhere today, choosing the fittest of today's employees is a tough call. That's because today's leading organizations have distinct cultures, and in the best of them, the culture assumes cultlike dimensions. So Bernie Brainstorm may set runways ablaze at Southwest Airlines, for example, while Peter Policy almost certainly won't. That's both good and bad, but when hiring, it means that choosing a candidate who won't fit into the culture is a waste of time.

Furthermore, within each culture people are working together more closely than ever. As a manager, that can be challenging. Monica Meetings and Donna Deadlines may complement each other—may even need each other—but keeping them from killing each other is an art.

All of which, believe it or not, leads us to assessment tools. Ultimately, you can't change someone's personality, but you can identify it, and work hard to put the right person into the right job and the right culture.

The tools in question are most commonly called psychological tests or personality tests, but both are misnomers. These tools don't really measure personality; they measure values, thinking style, and behavioral preferences, among other things. By whatever name, they can help you figure out whether a candidate is likely a good fit with the open job and with your organization—or not.

Take Action

- *Review your culture.* What are the norms? What attributes are imperative for success? What behavior will really stand out?
- *Review the job description.* Pay close attention to the behavioral expectations. What sort of person are you looking for? An idea person? A doer? An enforcer?
- *Review your organization's assessment policy.* If there is a policy, follow it. If there is no policy, draft one for your

department. Have it approved by HR. If there is no HR department, have it reviewed by the legal department or an attorney.

- *Review assessment options.* American consumers can choose from 13 different kinds of organic catsup, so you can imagine how many choices you have to assess values and behavior. The task of sorting through them might be scary enough to permanently alter your own behavior, so let's state up front that there is no single right answer. Any number of professional tools are just fine. What's important is to find one that works for you. (See the sidebar "Assessment Tools: A Primer" later in the chapter for a look at some of the best-known assessment tools.) Although each approach is somewhat different, there's remarkable consistency in the results they produce.

- *Test the test.* Once you've identified an approach that seems right to you, take the test yourself. Do the results seem to describe you accurately? Do your boss, spouse, partner, or coworkers agree? If so, the test is probably a good choice for you. If not, you may wish to try another option.

- *Consider the practicalities.* How expensive is the tool? How long does it take to administer? Can the assessment be taken anywhere? How is it interpreted? Can you determine the results or must an expert do it? Choose a test you can live with long-term.

- *Use the tool.* Depending on which assessment you use, you can administer it either before any interview, between the first and second interview, or after all interviews. It's best to administer between the first and second interviews.

- *Tell the candidate how the assessment will be used.* Explain the assessment's role in your hiring process. Identify who will see the results. (It may be only you; if you're using team interviews, however, there may be occasion to show the results to other interviewers.)

- *See how the candidate reacts to the results.* Share the results with your top candidates during a follow-up interview. How does she react? We all have personality quirks; some people manage theirs while others indulge them. Is she most interested in learning about herself or in arguing with you about the results? Does she explain how she manages her quirks? Offer examples of how they surface on the job? You're not looking for a perfect person, but ideally you'll find someone self-aware and honest about who they are.

- *Discuss the results.* Use the results to help frame discussion. For example, suppose an assessment shows that a candidate craves variety, and you know the job won't offer much variety. Be honest and see how the candidate reacts. Can she see trade-offs (such as the chance to learn in exchange for limited tasks)? Does she really hear you?

Stay Out of Jail

- *Don't rely too heavily on assessments.* Look at results alongside credentials, the interview, and other data; don't make the hiring decision on assessments alone. Most tools measure preferences, not skills. For example, just because someone likes to work on several projects at once doesn't mean he is adept at it.

- *Be careful not to discriminate.* A June 2009, Supreme Court decision on tests generated a lot of headlines—and confusion. The case centered on a test used by the New Haven, Connecticut, fire department in determining the promotion of firefighters. After determining that African-American fire-fighters scored disproportionately poorly on the test, it threw out the results. The subsequent legal battle centered on the city's white firefighters, who claimed they were discrimi-nated against when their higher scores were disregarded. The Supreme Court ruled that it was unlawful for the city to reject the test results simply because the higher-scoring candidates were white, adding that the possibility of a lawsuit from minority firefighters was not a lawful justification for the city's action. Legal and civil rights observers noted that the decision lacked clarity, leaving employers in a seemingly no-win situation relative to discrimination; most predicted that many similar cases are certain to work their way through the courts.

  The case has most direct application to public employers using civil service examinations (the case did not address the types of assessments described in this chapter), but employers are cautioned that no test should reflect a racial (or gender) bias. (Most commercial assessment tools have been validated to ensure they do not reflect such bias; see the sidebar "Validation: A Primer" for more information.)

- *Have an attorney review the assessment you use.* Some candidates have objected to the questions asked on some tests, claiming they invade privacy. Some also claim that the questions are unrelated to job performance. In several instances the courts have agreed. In one case candidates complained about an assessment in which they were asked to decide how applicable certain statements were to themselves. The judge ruled in favor of the candidates. In his opinion, he cited these statements—among others—as objectionable:

- I shouldn't do many of the things I do.
- I often lose my temper.
- In school, I was frequently rebellious.
- I hate opera singing.

To further add to the confusion, what's acceptable in one state may not be in another. Bottom line: Run the test by an attorney.

- *Be sure the assessment you use is validated* (see the sidebar "Validation: A Primer" for more information.)

- *Get proof of the assessment's validity, and proof that it does not adversely affect a protected group*. Keep the proof on file.

- *Keep the results of all the assessments you administer in confidential applicant files*.

- *Be consistent*. Once you've chosen a tool, use it on all applicants; don't pick and choose. (If you assess for one job, you needn't test for all. But if one candidate for a job is assessed, then all the candidates for that same job must take the test.) Keep the environment and other circumstances as consistent as possible when the test is administered.

Do at Least the Minimum

Use behavior or values tests when filling the key jobs in your department. A lot is at stake in those cases.

Get More Information

Books

> *Hiring Smart! How to Predict Winners and Losers in the Incredibly Expensive People-Reading Game,* Pierre Mornell, Ten Speed Press, 2004.

Tests

> DiscProfile, PO Box 11238, Arrowhead Station, AZ 85318–1238; (623) 572–4067, 888/662–2424; www.discprofile.com
>
> The Hartman Value Profile, Value Partners, 3201 Bandera Street, Athens, TX 75752; (903) 677–5860; www.valuepartnersconsulting.com, www.hartmaninstitute.org
>
> Herrmann Brain Dominance Instrument, Herrmann International, 794 Buffalo Creek Road, Lake Lure, NC 28746; (828) 625–9153, (800) 432–4234; www.hbdi.com
>
> The Job Person Environment Assessment (JPEA), Human Productivity Systems, Inc. (HPS), 1817 W. Avenue K, Lancaster, CA 93534; (661) 949–7788; www.hpsonline.com
>
> Kolbe A Index, 3421 N. 44th Street, Phoenix, AZ 85018; (602) 840–9770, (800) 642–2822; www.kolbe.com
>
> The Myers-Briggs Type Inventory (MBTI) is administered by many organizations and professionals.

Assessment Tools: A Primer

- *Myers-Briggs Type Inventory.* The MBTI is the most widely used assessment in the world. It identifies people as one of 16 broad personality types, on the supposition that personality drives behavior. The 16 types are derived by measuring four traits (extroversion/introversion, sensing/intuition, thinking/feeling, judging/perceiving), each of which is assigned a scale. (For example, someone might be either an extreme introvert or extrovert, or be placed somewhere toward the center of the scale and have characteristics of both.) The 16 types reflect the dominant tendency in each trait. An INTJ, therefore, is an introvert, intuits, thinks, and judges. These personality types can help predict behavior in the individual alone and in relation to other personality types.

- *DiSC Profile.* This also profiles personality. It uses a four-dimensional model of behavior (dominance, influence, steadiness, and conscientiousness) and explores patterns of behavior in 15 combinations of those core behaviors.

- *The Job Person Environment Assessment,* in contrast, makes no claim to assess motivation or personality type. Instead, the three-part JPEA (each part may be used separately or all three parts used together) gauges the behavior people prefer to exhibit at work. The concept behind the instrument is that everyone seeks to meet their behavioral preferences in a job. The instrument's developers argue (convincingly) that the impulse is so strong that people work to change the job (or quit) if their preferences aren't being met.

  The first component of the JPEA measures several preferences, including autonomy (how much freedom do people want on the job?), task involvement (does someone prefer to focus on just one activity, or to do many different things?), and performance feedback (does a person rely on objective data such as a balance sheet, or on subjective feedback such as a

  continued

"Way to go!"). The tool places people on a scale for each measurement. (Therefore, Brian may be "high" on subjective feedback while MaryLou is "low.")

The second component assesses the behavior required to succeed in each job. For example, rocket scientists must process a lot of objective data while florists do not. The instrument measures the behavior required in each job (determined by a manager, the person in the job, both, or a team of people). If the two components are used together, an individual profile can be matched against the job demands to identify potential stressors and challenges. (The third component measures perceptions about the level of support that the environment provides.)

- *Kolbe A Index.* Where the JPEA measures overt or known behavior preferences, the Kolbe A Index measures instinctive behavior—how we actually behave, particularly under stress. The tool identifies cognitive strengths in four zones (Fact Finder, Follow Thru, Quick Start, and Implementer). The results show how we solve problems, and what we will or won't do on the job. The results also offer advice that may not be 100 percent flattering but is realistic ("turn to others to institute procedures, and cut a deal to avoid most of them").

- *Herrmann Brain Dominance Instrument.* The HBDI doesn't measure behavior at all; instead it measures thinking style. It looks at the brain in four quadrants (quadrant A is logical, for example, while quadrant D is artistic). The tool acknowledges that we all use all four quadrants, but identifies which quadrant is our dominant thinking style and how the quadrants influence one another (More than 30 different profile types are identified using the HBDI, which can be used to help identify thinking styles best suited to particular professions or organizational cultures. For example, someone whose thinking style uses very little of the artistic quadrant may not be suited to an advertising career.

continued

- *Hartman Value Profile.* This assesses personal values (rather than personality or behavior), so it gets at work ethic and attitude, for example.

Finally, many organizations also use assessments of emotional intelligence (see "Emotional Intelligence: How to Recognize and Use the Data in Your Emotions" in Chapter 6) during the hiring process.

Validation: A Primer

If you're doing virtually any kind of preemployment testing, validation is a concept you should be familiar with—and no, we're not talking about a group hug. Validation is the process of proving that a test is relevant to a job, that it test only what it claims to test, and that it doesn't discriminate against any protected groups or individuals applying for the job.

To understand validation you must first know about the Uniform Guidelines on Employee Selection Procedures. The guidelines were created jointly in 1978 by several federal agencies, among them the EEOC, the Department of Labor, and the Department of Justice. The guidelines were written to help employers hire without discriminating. What does that mean for testing? It means that if you use a test to make hiring decisions, you must look at the people who have been hired after taking the test. Look first at the people who were hired most often—say people with blue hair. To make the math easy, say that 100 people with blue hair were hired. If fewer than 80 of any other group (say people with red thumbs) were hired using the test as a basis, then the selection rate is considered substantially different and therefore unacceptable. Of course, we don't live in a world where people naturally have blue hair or red thumbs, so the government looks instead at race, sex, religion, and national origin.

continued

Validation is proof of any test or procedure's nondiscriminatory job-relatedness. Generally, the process begins with an analysis to identify the job requirements. The next step is to identify selection tools and standards that will isolate the applicants who meet those requirements. (Testing current employees and applicants without using the results to make hiring decisions can help measure the test's effectiveness.) Validating a test takes place over a long period of time and is applied to a large sample population. The final stage is to draft a report that outlines the steps taken and the results. Industrial and personnel psychologists with specific expertise in such research usually validate tests.

Three methods can demonstrate validity:

- *Criterion-related validity* is a statistical correlation between test scores and the job performance of a sample of employees.
- *Content validity* demonstrates that the content of a test represents important aspects of job performance.
- *Construct validity* shows that a test measures something believed to be a basic human trait (such as honesty) and that this trait is important for succeeding in a job.

Of these, content validity is used most often.

As with flame throwing and stunt skateboarding, validating a test is probably something you shouldn't try at home. Buying a validated test is easiest. If you decide to develop a test yourself, have it reviewed by an attorney; you may ultimately need to have it validated. After all, the Uniform Guidelines apply to all private employers with 15 or more employees, state and local governments, labor organizations, and

Types of Drug Tests

Although some state laws dictate which types of tests can be used, several options are technologically feasible. Urine is the most commonly used specimen for illicit drugs (reflecting Substance Abuse and

continued

Mental Health Services Administration guidelines), and breath is the most common for alcohol, reflecting Department of Transportation (DOT) guidelines.

Urine. Results of a urine test show the presence or absence of drug metabolites in a person's urine. Metabolites are drug residues that remain in the body for some time after the effects of a drug have worn off. Therefore, a positive urine test does not necessarily mean a person was under the influence of drugs at the time of the test. Instead, it detects and measures use of a particular drug within the previous few days and has become the de facto evidence of current use. Because alcohol passes rapidly through the system, urine tests must be conducted very quickly after alcohol consumption in order to ensure any degree of accuracy. For this reason, urine tests are generally not helpful in detecting alcohol use; illicit and prescription drug use is more easily traced in urine.

Breath. A *breath-alcohol test* is the most common test for finding out how much alcohol is currently in the blood. The person being tested blows into a breath-alcohol device, and the results are given as a number, known as the Blood Alcohol Concentration. The BAC shows the level of alcohol in the blood at the time the test was taken. BAC levels have been correlated with impairment, and the legal limit of 0.08 for driving has been set in all states. Under DOT regulations, a BAC of 0.02 is high enough to stop someone from performing a safety-sensitive task for a specific amount of time (usually between eight and 24 hours), and a BAC reading of 0.04 or higher is considered to be a positive drug test and requires immediate removal from safety-sensitive functions. In addition, a person who tests at the 0.04 BAC level may not resume job duties until a specific return-to-duty process has been successfully completed.

Blood. A blood test measures the actual amount of alcohol or other drugs in the blood at the time of the test. Blood samples provide an accurate measure of the physiologically active drug

continued

present in a person at the time the sample is drawn. Although blood samples are a better indicator of recent consumption than urine samples, there is a lack of published data correlating blood levels for drugs and impairment with the same degree of certainty established for alcohol. In cases of serious injury or death as the result of an accident, the only way to determine legal intoxication is through a blood specimen. There is also a very short detection period, as most drugs are quickly cleared from the blood and deposited into the urine.

Hair. Analysis of hair provides a much longer "testing window," giving a more complete drug-use history going back as far as 90 days. Like urine testing, hair testing does not provide evidence of current impairment, but rather only past use of a specific drug. Hair testing cannot be used to detect alcohol use. It is the least invasive form of drug testing, therefore privacy issues are decreased.

Oral fluids. Saliva, or oral fluids, collected from the mouth also can be used to detect traces of drugs and alcohol. Oral fluids are easy to collect (a swab of the inner cheek is the most common collection method), harder to adulterate or substitute, and may be better at detecting specific substances, including marijuana, cocaine, and amphetamines/methamphetamines. Because drugs do not remain in oral fluids as long as they do in urine, this method shows promise in determining current use and impairment.

Sweat. This type of drug test consists of a patch, which looks like a large adhesive bandage, applied to the skin and worn for some length of time. (Because of the length of time required, this test is perceived as more invasive than others.) A gas-permeable membrane on the patch protects the tested area from dirt and other contaminants. Although relatively easy to administer, this method has not been widely used in workplaces and is more often used to maintain compliance with probation and parole.

continued

> *Nonmedical tests.* Another option is to test for impairment, rather than for the chemical presence of illegal drugs. Such tests include *balance and reflex performance checks* and *critical tracking tests,* which measure hand-eye coordination and quick reaction time. Beware, however, that these tests could discriminate against people with certain disabilities or impairments.
>
> *Source:* Working Partners for an Alcohol- and Drug-Free Workplace, U.S. Department of Labor; *The AMA Handbook for Employee Recruitment and Retention,* American Management Association, New York, 1992.

PHYSICALS: HOW TO BE SURE CANDIDATES WILL BE ABLE TO DO THE JOB

Know the Issue

Around the turn of the last century, a young Scottish man chose his bride by considering which of the eligible young women was healthiest. He planned to emigrate to the United States and wanted a companion who would survive the trip and be strong enough to work hard after they arrived. Not exactly the romantic fantasy of a Julia Roberts movie, it's nonetheless an honest reflection of the economic realities the young couple faced.

Although no employer today would openly seek the healthiest girl in the village, many do require physical exams. Sometimes they should. None of us wants to board an airliner wondering whether the pilot is at high risk of suffering a heart attack.

But it would take an unabashed fan of managed care to really love preemployment physicals. The laws are complex, confidentiality is paramount, and the emotional stakes can be high.

If you decide a physical is warranted, focus on what's relevant to the job. Remember, the purpose of a preemployment physical is not to get the complete medical history of the candidate. You have three responsibilities:

1. To protect employees from on-the-job injuries
2. To protect coworkers and customers from injury
3. To protect the company against false claims that it is responsible for an employee's disability or medical condition by having a "baseline" test on file

Take Action

- *Revisit the physical requirements for the job noted in the job description.* Most white-collar jobs don't require much physical activity, so there's little reason to require a physical. The cost probably outweighs any value to the company. If, however, the job requires something more, a physical might be appropriate. Consider whether the job requires:

  ○ Heavy lifting. Here's the test: Can the employee, without difficulty or with a reasonable accommodation, perform the essential job functions without endangering his or her health or safety, or the health and safety of others?

  ○ Exertion, such as climbing stairs or walking long distances.

  ○ Working at elevated heights; for example, on ladders or a multistory construction site.

  ○ The ability to respond to safety warnings (such as flashing lights, alarms, or other devices).

- Licensing that requires specific physical abilities.
- Normal vision (employees who work with color-coded electrical wire, for example, could be in danger if they are color blind).

Or anything else beyond the norm.

Stay Out of Jail

- *Asking a job candidate to have a complete physical is legal.* However, the ADA prohibits requiring a medical exam before an offer of employment is made. Extending a job offer must be based on the candidate's experience and skills, but conditional on passing the job-related physical. As far as the law is concerned, a physical may be far less than an exam by a doctor. None of the following is permitted before a job offer is made:
  - Any procedure administered and/or interpreted by a health care professional
  - Any procedure intended to reveal the existence, nature, or severity of an impairment
  - Any invasive procedure (such as requiring the drawing of blood or urine)
  - Any test that measures physiological or psychological responses
  - Any procedure that employs medical equipment or devices
- *Limit the tests to job-related functions.* This is one case in which less is more. If, through whatever means, you know that a candidate is pregnant, suffers from migraines, or is a

cancer survivor, you may be accused of discrimination if you do not hire that person. Even if the charges are unfounded, defending yourself will be time-consuming and expensive. Stick to what's relevant to the job.

- *Physicals must be required of all applicants for a job; you can't pick and choose who gets one.*

- *Information obtained must be maintained and collected on separate forms and in confidential medical files separate from an employee's or candidate's primary personnel file.*

- *Medical information may not be disclosed.* Your organization may require that physicals be administered through HR or an employee health department. If so, do not expect to see the results yourself. Legally, you have no right or reason to know the particulars of an employee's medical condition. Therefore, you're likely simply to get a report stating whether the candidate can perform the essential job functions. If somehow you do see other information (such as a diagnosis), tell HR there has been a breach that must be corrected, and keep the information to yourself.

- *There is one exception to the confidentiality*: candidates may ask to see the results of their own physicals.

- *If the physical discloses a disability, and you decide not to hire a candidate because of that disability, you must show that the disability cannot reasonably be accommodated and that the job tasks you require that cannot be performed are core functions of the job.* It is a very difficult standard.

- *You may require a candidate to see a specific doctor.* In theory, this prevents the employee from unduly influencing the results. If you exercise this option, however, do it consistently. And remember that doing so sends a signal that you don't trust people.

- *If the applicant refutes the results of a physical, he or she may opt to have another doctor do a physical.* If those results are different, you aren't obligated to accept them. However, if the applicant is otherwise a good choice for the position, or simply to show good faith, you may wish to get a second opinion. Make it clear that doing so is at your discretion, and isn't a precedent for the future. (Note: in a few selected cases — such as truck drivers — a neutral third doctor may be required to settle the dispute.)

Do at Least the Minimum

- *Require physicals for jobs in which employee health and safety (or the health and safety of others) may be at risk.*
- *Limit tests to job-related abilities.*
- *Keep any medical information you have confidential.*

Get More Information

The Employer's Legal Handbook, Fred Steingold, Nolo, 2009.

REFERENCE CHECKS: HOW TO GET THE WHOLE STORY

Know the Issue

There's a body on the floor of the parlor: The owner of the manor has been murdered and his priceless heirloom painting is gone. The security log shows that other than the victim, no one was in the house that night except the maid—and she denies she did it.

Would Hercule Poirot or any other self-respecting detective simply accept her statement? Of course not! He would talk to witnesses to get their version of events, comparing each person's story to the others in an effort to find the greater truth.

Most job candidates aren't hiding smoking guns, buried ransom, or forged wills. But they are working hard to present themselves at their very best, and you owe it to yourself to be sure you've heard the whole story. Sure, Ms. Perfect might have been the most accurate checker at the supermarket. But was she also the slowest? References can help answer questions.

A warning: it won't be easy. Because of some successful lawsuits filed by candidates who felt they were defamed by previous employers, many companies have limited references only to confirming dates of employment and job title. That makes it tough even to get positive references, let alone cautionary ones. Just working through voice mail to find the right person can be overwhelming. If Sam Spade had so many obstacles to overcome, we still might not know who stole the Maltese Falcon.

Stick with it. If you persevere, checking references can be very worthwhile.

Take Action

- *Figure out what you want to know.* Calling references to ask generic questions ("How long have you known Nancy?") isn't likely to yield much that's worthwhile. Review your interview notes. Has the candidate talked about an accomplishment you'd like to confirm? Would you like to know more about the environment she worked in? Are there pieces of the puzzle that don't fit? References can help answer whatever questions you still have.

- *Ask the candidate for references.* Some candidates list references on their résumé. Others provide them in a cover letter. However you get them, ignore them if the candidate volunteered them. Applicants choose people ready to tell you how wonderful they are, but those may not be the people who can answer your questions. Tell the candidate the areas you'd like to explore ("I'm interested in finding out more about the events you organized") and ask her who you should call. That way, she knows who you'll be calling, and you won't waste time speaking to people who can't help you anyway. Just don't give away too much about what you'd like to ask; you don't want the candidate to prep the reference.

- *Tell the candidate whom you're calling and when.* Too many bosses have found out that their employees were job hunting when a potential boss called for a reference. Don't put a candidate in that situation.

- *Don't limit yourself to the candidate's boss.* Yes, the candidate's current or previous boss can answer questions, but don't stop there. Is the candidate a member of a professional association? Call another member to find out how the candidate participates. Has the applicant published in professional journals? Call the editor and ask how it was to work with the candidate. Be creative in your thinking. Just be sure to limit questions to job-related topics. Develop some specific questions related to these issues:
  - Technical competence

- ○ People skills, where relevant
- ○ Motivation
- *Use voice mail.* If you're pressed for time, Dr. Pierre Mornell has a great suggestion. Call references during their lunch hour and leave a message. Tell them that Joe is a candidate for a job in your firm, and ask them to call back if Joe is outstanding. What happens next is telling. If Joe is great, most people will happily call back. If no one does, you've learned something without anyone saying something negative.
- *Be persistent.* If references agree only to confirm employment, at least do that. Then keep calling. Eventually, someone will talk. People are more likely to answer specific questions ("What percentage of Jane's students were promoted to the next grade last year?") than generic ones ("Did Jane's students like her?").
- *Meet in person.* It's often not possible, but if you can, meet key references face-to-face. Buy them lunch or a morning latte and have a conversation. You're more likely to get anecdotes and better examples of the candidate's work in a relaxed environment without distractions.
- *Take the focus off the candidate.* If a reference can't—or won't—tell you more than the basics, try another approach. Ask about the qualities she was looking for in the person hired to replace your candidate. Are the qualities she mentions consistent with what you've seen in interviews with the candidate? Or is she describing someone who sounds like the opposite of the person you've been talking with?

- *Talk to your own staff.* Don't ignore your own internal references. If someone else scheduled the interview, talk to that person. Talk to the receptionist, the parking garage attendant, and anyone else the candidate interacted with. Did they see the same qualities you did? Or did they meet someone rude or who was telling inappropriate jokes?

Stay Out of Jail

- *Should there ever be a problem after a candidate is hired (such as violence or sexual harassment), the better your due diligence was up front, the better off you'll be.*
- *Keep your questions focused on the job—don't get personal.*
- *Keep whatever you hear from a reference confidential.*
- *Keep a record of which references you spoke with and when. Take notes during the conversation.*
- *Don't tape-record your conversations.*
- *Never claim to be someone else, or misrepresent the call. Be up front about who you are and why you're calling.*

Real-Life Example

One executive has a strategy for hiring sales talent. He asks job candidates to identify their toughest sale, and then he calls that client. The information can be invaluable. How long did it take to close the sale? How did the candidate keep the conversation open? What information did he give the client? How did his performance compare to his competitor's sales pitch? After the sale, did the candidate offer good service or disappear?

Do at Least the Minimum

Verify employment dates, titles, and salary.

Get More Information

> *The Employer's Legal Handbook*, Fred Steingold, Nolo, 2009.
>
> *Hiring Smart! How to Predict Winners and Losers in the Incredibly Expensive People-Reading Game*, Pierre Mornell, Ten Speed Press, 2004.

BACKGROUND CHECKS: HOW TO FIND OUT WHAT CANDIDATES DON'T WANT YOU TO KNOW

Know the Issue

You've found your dream house and you can't wait to move in. But during escrow the extras begin: title searches, termite inspections, radon gas tests, and on and on. It can be irritating and expensive, but it can also save you from making a $400,000 mistake.

Odds are, a background check won't uncover wood rot in your top candidate. But it might uncover something else that you really need to know before you make a job offer. Protect your employer—and your reputation. Do a thorough check to verify the facts.

Take Action

- *Find your employer's policy and follow it*. If you work in a large firm, there's probably a policy on background checks. If so, follow it. The firm may also require that the HR department conduct or monitor any background checks. If there is no policy or HR function to help, then follow these guidelines.

○ *Make sure the candidate is who he says he is.* Verify his name, address, and Social Security number.

○ *Determine the credentials the job demands.* Review the job description to see whether a high school diploma or a college or postgraduate degree is required. Then consider other requirements. Many positions—from attorneys to cosmetologists—require licenses. Others (accountants, for example) require certification of their skills. Still others (such as teachers) require periodic training to keep current. Make a list of everything necessary.

○ *Verify his credentials.* Did the candidate really earn the college degree he claims to have? You may want to know simply to test the candidate's honesty. In other situations, the data may be more critical. If you require a degree for a particular job, it's best to get proof of the degree. (Universities generally verify enrollment dates and degrees earned.)

If the job demands other credentials, verify those, too:

○ Licenses (including a driver's license if the job requires driving)

○ Certification (a prominent hospital was embarrassed when a physician on its staff turned out not to have the board certification he claimed, which imperiled his license to practice)

○ Training hours, if required

• *Identify work-related risks.* An employer assumes some risk every time an employee is hired. But some positions carry specific risks that should not be ignored. For example, if the job requires management of money (cash or credit), it's prudent to check a candidate's credit history. A credit check, however, isn't relevant when hiring an appliance repair technician. (Or, in truth, most other jobs. Although a growing number of employers are checking applicant credit histories, they are usually not relevant. And during an economy in which many hardworking, honest people are facing financial crises not of their own making, you may miss out on the best person for the job if you rule out someone who's made late payments on a credit balance.) On the other hand, recent felony convictions may be relevant if a position requires an employee to interact with customers or other members of the public, either at the workplace or in customers' homes. Stick to the facts (not hearsay or opinion) and make sure inquiries are job-related. But get the information you need.

- *Collect the data.* Much of this information (such as licenses) is a matter of public record. Other information (such as credit history) can be obtained from reporting agencies. But collecting data can be tedious and time-consuming, particularly if you're filling several jobs at once. Therefore, you may want to hire a professional firm to conduct the check for you. If you elect to hire a firm, be sure you hire a reputable one:
  - Ask for a list of clients and call some of them.
  - Find out how the firm gets its information.
  - Does the firm do a national check, or merely a local one?
  - Does the firm guarantee its work?
  - Keep the data in a confidential candidate file.

- ○ Comply with the federal and state legal requirements when you use a third party to get information.

- *Resist the temptation to search the Internet.* Given that background checks can be expensive and cumbersome, it's only natural to think about getting information through the back door by using an online search engine to collect data on candidates. Although the temptation is often irresistible, it isn't the panacea it may seem. For one thing, the Internet is a big place. And although search engines are a huge help, you may still have to look in numerous places to find what you're looking for. When you find it, it may or may not be true— even if created by the candidate him- or herself. Yes, some people seem happy to share all the details of their youthful (or not so youthful) indiscretions. But many people also carefully craft their social networking pages to present the most flattering portrait possible.

  Beyond that, the law encourages organizations to be as objective as possible when hiring, and most of what you can find on the Internet is counter to that principle. For example, you may learn a candidate's marital status or how many children he or she has. You may also discover that a candidate is active in a political or social cause, holds certain religious beliefs, or is a diehard Trekker. You can't ask about any of those issues in an interview, so you have to ask yourself what you'll do with the information if you find it online. Using it may be very risky—even illegal. Some employers are getting around it by asking candidates for their permission to do Internet searches about them, but if you choose to follow that path, you should consult an attorney first.

Stay Out of Jail

- *Be consistent.* Verify the same information for every candidate for the same job. For example, don't conduct a check on some candidates and not others. What you check may vary from job to job, but in each case there should be a business rationale for your decision.

- *Limit what you inquire about.* For example, it may be illegal—or evidence of unlawful discrimination—to explore:
    - Arrest records or misdemeanor convictions
    - Workers' compensation claims
    - Legal activity (including employment-related lawsuits)
    - Marital status
    - Physical or mental disabilities
    - Political activities
    - Bankruptcy
    - Sexual orientation

- *Comply with the Fair Credit Reporting Act.* The FCRA governs the retrieval and use of consumer information from credit reports, criminal records, and department of motor vehicle reports (among others) when it is obtained by a consumer credit-reporting agency. The law is complex, and the definition of a consumer credit-reporting agency is broad, but you should know about certain provisions:
    - You may not use consumer reports unless (1) the report is used for a permissible purpose, and (2) you receive oral, written, or electronic authorization to use the report.

- Before you use any background check as a reason (either as the whole reason or as a contributing factor) not to hire someone, you must provide the candidate with a copy of the report and a summary of his rights under FCRA. Copies of the rights usually are provided by the reporting agencies.
- Before taking any adverse action based on the report, it's best to allow candidates a reasonable time to explain or fix any information that may not be correct in the report. The law does not specify what's reasonable, but courts have held that five days is acceptable.
- Be prepared to explain how adverse information obtained in a report is job-related and sufficient to render an applicant unsuitable for a particular position.

Real-Life Example

She seemed too good to be true. A manager in a small business was searching for a new employee, and the woman across from him had every qualification he hoped to find. She seemed to have all the answers to his questions before he even asked them and she seemed reliable—she had made very few job changes.

Her résumé did include a four-year gap in employment, which she explained by stating that she had chosen to stay home and care for her young children until they started school. Now she was ready to reenter the workforce.

The manager hired her and she was one of the best employees the company ever had. She quickly learned every position in the office. Everyone thought she must have been sent from heaven.

Then one day the perfect employee took a day off. As it happened, the owner's wife was filling in that day and answered the phone. It was a call from the bank, inquiring whether the company was aware that its checking account was overdrawn.

The call led to an investigation, which revealed that the perfect employee had been embezzling for six years. She had stolen more than $400,000. Later, the police told the manager that the perfect employee had not spent four years at home caring for her children; she had spent that time in prison for stealing from a previous employer. For the second offense, the perfect employee was sentenced to six years in the state penitentiary. She lost her home, her husband, and her family, and has been paying the company $50 a month in restitution.

The manager who hired her wonders what her résumé looks like today, and is glad he wasn't fired for his failure to do a background check on the employee.

Do at Least the Minimum

- *Be sure the candidate is who he claims to be.*
- *Verify that the candidate has any valid licenses or other certification required by law.*

Get More Information

The Employer's Legal Handbook, Fred Steingold, Nolo, 2009.

Hiring Smart! How to Predict Winners and Losers in the Incredibly Expensive People-Reading Game, Pierre Mornell, Ten Speed Press, 2004.

INTERVIEWS: HOW TO GET THE INFORMATION YOU NEED

Know the Issue

Just be quiet. That's our first and best advice for doing an effective interview.

The whole point of an interview is to find out what and how the candidate thinks, yet most managers barely come up for air once the interview starts. They rattle on about the company, the job, their own work history, or the basketball playoffs. They do it because they're nervous (admit it—it's not just the candidates who find interviews stressful), because they like the candidate and try to sell the job, because they find silence uncomfortable, or just because they like to talk.

Whatever the reason, the impact on the interview is almost entirely negative. Here's what happens. Chatty Hattie is filling a key job in her department. The more she talks, the better she likes the candidate. The conversation is easy. They joke. They laugh and nod. The candidate, when she's allowed to talk, says just the right things.

Hattie likes the candidate because she's had a good time during the interview. In other words, Hattie has decided she likes herself! And the candidate says all the right things because Hattie gave her more lifelines than if she were answering questions on *Who Wants to Be a Millionaire?*

Hattie may be a swell lunch date, but she's a bad, bad interviewer. Remember: an interview and a conversation are *not* the same thing.

An interview has one purpose and one purpose only: to get information to help you determine whether the candidate is qualified to do the job. Getting that information means consistently following a well-structured, objective plan. It may not be as much fun as a three-brewski lunch, but you're much less likely to hire a loser or end up in court.

Take Action

- *Take time to prepare.* Without preparation, any job interview you conduct has all the downsides of a blind date and none of the potential upsides. Without preparation, the odds that you'll get the information you need are slim to none. And any canny interviewee will hijack the meeting and have you follow her agenda. There is a better way.

   ○ *Interview fewer people.* Most managers interview too many people and then let disastrous interviews drag on too long. Spend the time up front narrowing the field, and then give your two or three top candidates their full due.

   ○ *Limit interruptions.* Preparing for an interview takes your full concentration. Do what you need to do to get some quiet time. Close your door, let voice mail answer the phone, and focus. If you absolutely can't limit interruptions at work, then prepare offsite.

   ○ *Ask the candidate to reconfirm your appointment.*

   ○ *Prepare questions.* You've already carefully read the résumé and made notes. Review them now, and write some sample questions. The goal of your questions should be: to answer any questions you may have (such as what was happening during the two years that are unaccounted for on the résumé); to check the accuracy of any conclusions you may have reached ("It looks as though you were promoted twice during a relatively short period of time at your previous employer. Is that right?"); to ask the candidate to relate her experience to the open job; and to explore behavioral issues (for example, if punctuality is a hot button for you, ask about it).

○ *Reserve a room in which to meet.* Neutral places are better than your office.

○ *Plan your schedule.* Allow about an hour for your meeting. Pace yourself. If you're meeting with several candidates in a single day, allow at least a half hour between meetings in which to make notes and catch your breath. Also work hard to be prompt.

One proviso: these guidelines assume that you're interviewing for a position that requires at least some experience. If you're hiring counter staff at a fast-food store or janitorial help at a hotel, you can limit your prep time, but all candidates deserve the courtesy of a prompt meeting in a comfortable environment.

- *Control the interview.* Yes, you'd like the candidate to be relaxed and comfortable. But the interview is about your agenda, and you should use the time wisely to get the information you need. To do that:

○ *Set the stage.* Candidates are more likely to relax and focus if you set their expectations. Thank the candidate for coming. Introduce yourself and briefly explain your role in the organization. Let the candidate know that you will be making the hiring decision. Tell the candidate how much time you anticipate spending. Offer a brief overview of the topics you'll be covering.

○ *Don't start with the big questions.* Ask simple questions first to help candidates relax. Just don't ask, "What's your sign?"

○ *Follow a logical train of thought.* Jumping around confuses everyone, but yes, you can revisit a topic if you forget something or later answers raise questions.

○ *Vary the questions.* Give candidates some variety by asking both close-ended questions ("What was your salary in your last position?") and open-ended ones ("What is there about this job that appeals to you?").

○ *Limit your role.* Throughout the interview, keep this rule in mind: the candidate talks 80 percent of the time; you talk 20 percent of the time. Here's a second rule: anything you say should be said almost entirely at the beginning of the interview and at the end. Tell the candidate up front that you'll answer questions at the end of the interview. Interviews get offtrack when candidates jump in with questions and interviewers answer them. You want answers that are as genuine as possible, not answers shaped by information you've provided. If candidates ask anyway, gently remind them that you'll be happy to answer their questions later.

○ *Tolerate silence.* If candidates struggle to answer a question, don't rescue them. Let them think. If you must say something, simply encourage them to take their time.

○ *Find your own tricks to keep quiet.* One interviewer trained himself to take a drink of water every time he wanted to say something. Find a way that works for you.

• *Find out what the candidate is really like.* The more you know about how candidates behaved before, the more you know what to expect should you hire them. And at the risk of sounding too Marin County, you also want to know how they felt about their work.

- *Ask the candidate to describe a typical day in his current or previous job.* Then listen and probe for specifics: What excited him? What bored him? Who did he interact with? How did he respond to interruptions? What was his greatest frustration?

- *Explore how she likes to be managed.* Her potential working relationship with you is paramount. Ask what she likes most about her current boss, and what she likes least. Ask her to describe her ideal boss.

- *Skip the greatest strength/greatest weakness question.* It's too abstract and most candidates have rehearsed the answers. Instead, try the following: "If I were to ask your current boss what she values most about you, what would I hear?" and "If I were to ask your boss what about you drives him crazy, what would I hear?" (One candidate answered the latter question by admitting to sneaking into the boss's office after hours and rearranging everything because "the way she kept things on her desk didn't make any sense.")

- *Ask how he makes decisions; how he establishes priorities; when he asks for help rather than working alone; where he goes for information; when he makes a decision independently and when not; how he learns from mistakes.*

- *Identify some recent situations in your department that you thought were especially well handled or were not handled well at all.* Give the candidates the background and ask how they would have handled the situations.

- *Leave candidates with the best impression.* It takes years of sacrifice and hard work to get to the Olympics, but in the end the difference between a gold medal and no medal is often just hundredths of a second. In other words, how you finish counts. Your "finish" is the last impression a candidate has of your meeting. Don't squander the opportunity.

  ○ *Let the candidate ask questions.* Once you have asked the candidate all your questions, let her know how much time is left and invite her to ask her own. (Time the interview so there will be time for the candidate's questions. If the interview is running long and you'll need extra time, ask for it; that shows respect.)

  ○ *Answer questions honestly.*

  ○ *Stay focused.* During this initial interview, the primary goal is to determine whether the candidate is a serious contender for the job. If he is, he'll be invited back for another interview and will have the chance to ask many questions then. If he isn't, you don't want to waste either his time or yours answering detailed questions about the job now. However, to be fair to the candidate, be sure he leaves with enough information to decide whether he's interested in pursuing the job further. Be sure to address basic concerns:

    - Salary (offer a range, not a specific figure at this stage)
    - Overtime or travel requirements
    - Appearance standards (including uniforms)
    - Work hours (particularly if you are hiring for night, weekend, or other nonstandard hours)

- ○ *Offer a five-minute warning.* Let the candidate know when time is almost up. When time is up, bring the interview to a conclusion:
  - Explain the next steps in the process. (For example, if there will be a second or third interview, now is the time to say so.)
  - Offer an estimated time frame for making your decision.
  - Make yourself available for follow-up questions. Give the candidate your card.
  - Take care of any incidentals (parking validations, for example).
  - Thank the candidate for coming.
  - Review. After the candidate leaves, allow time to review your notes, and make sure they're clear while the interview is still fresh in your mind.
- *Keep candidates interested.* Too many candidates complete an interview only to face deafening silence. Has the job been filled? Are they still in the running? Has the interviewer fled to Cancun with embezzled funds? Even in a plentiful labor market, the times in which you're the only one courting a qualified candidate are about as rare as good airline food. The longer you're silent, the more likely your dream candidate will accept another job. So do yourself a favor and keep the lines of communication open.
  - ○ *Keep your commitment.* Ideally, you gave the candidate an estimate of when you would hire someone. Stick to that schedule if possible.

○ *Let candidates know when the schedule changes.* Times will occur when it isn't possible to stick to your original schedule. When that happens, let the candidate know there has been a delay, why it has happened, and what your new target is.

○ *Respond to candidate inquiries.* If candidates call or send e-mail inquiring about the status of the job, respond or be sure someone responds on your behalf.

○ *Enlist the candidate's help.* If a delay is caused by an inability to connect with references, or another situation in which a candidate might help, ask for that help. Remember, candidates have a vested interest in the outcome.

○ *If a candidate receives another offer during this stage, take it seriously.* The market is competitive and other offers are likely. Without making promises, give the candidate a realistic sense of his or her chances. Then let the candidate decide whether to remain in consideration for your job. Don't be pressured into making a premature decision, but don't cost someone another opportunity either.

Stay Out of Jail

• *Take notes.* You won't remember everything, and it may be helpful later (should there be a legal dispute) to have a record of the interview. Make notes of what you say in addition to what the candidate says.

• *Base your questions on work-related situations, not the candidate's personal life.* (See the sidebar "Don't Get Personal: Toxic Questions and Antidotes later in the chapter.")

- *Be careful not to say anything that might be construed as a promise.* If a candidate asks about career development opportunities, for example, offer some examples of career paths other employees have followed. Be clear, however, that if you hire the candidate, her performance will be evaluated individually and that you can't guarantee a promotion. If she asks a question and you do not know the answer (about the benefit plan, for example), say so and offer to get the answer. Don't make something up.

Real-Life Example

Ann Perle, of Crossroads Consulting in Houston, stresses the importance of looking behind the info on the résumé. She tells the story of two recent college grads. One graduated in four years with a high grade-point average and had several extracurricular activities to his credit. The other candidate took five years to complete her degree. She had a mediocre GPA and no extracurricular activities. On paper one seemed to be the more ambitious, accomplished choice.

The interviews, however, told a different story. Both were asked to describe their college experiences and to summarize how they felt about them. The first candidate explained that he had had a great time. His father paid for school, he managed to find the easiest classes to take, and he hadn't worked hard. In effect, he had been at one long party. The other candidate might never have been to a party during school. She had been responsible for helping her mother keep up the mortgage payments and raise her younger siblings. She worked two jobs to put herself through college. She challenged herself throughout and felt proud of what she had been able to learn and do. Guess which candidate got the job?

Perle suggests that one way to get at this perspective is to ask candidates, "What is there about you that made that possible (or made that happen)?" When someone tells you, for example, "I always meet my deadlines," you may find out that the person is well organized and plans ahead, or that she is simply able to persuade others to help.

Manage Up

- *Let your boss know that you've scheduled interviews.* Give her a sentence or two on the strengths of the candidates. Explain what you hope to find out during the interview.
- *Trust us: there's something your boss will really want to know about your top candidates.* Find out before your interviews what it is.
- *Let your boss know what time frame you're working within.* Keep her informed if things change. You don't want her thinking that nothing is happening or that you can't make a decision.

Get More Information

Hiring Smart! How to Predict Winners and Losers in the Incredibly Expensive People-Reading Game, Pierre Mornell, Ten Speed Press, 2004.

Don't Get Personal: Toxic Questions and Antidotes

Okay, wouldn't you think common sense would tell you that drinking drain opener is a really bad idea? But there is still the danger that people will drink it, which is why manufacturers label it carefully and point out that it is toxic. And people still ask pointless, and often illegal, interview questions. So we feel compelled to label them with a skull and crossbones and point out that asking personal questions is hazardous to your legal health. Fortunately, you can ask safe questions instead.

TOXIC QUESTIONS	ANTIDOTES
"How old are you?"	"If hired, can you show proof of your age?"
"When were you born?"	"Are you over 18 years of age?"
"What is your date of birth?"	"If you are under 18, can you, after employment, submit a work permit?"
"When did you graduate from high school?"	A statement that being hired is subject to verification that the candidate meets legal age requirements
"When did you go to elementary school?"	
"Where were you born?"	"Can you, as a condition of employment, submit verification of your legal right to work in the United States?"
"I love your accent. Where are you from?"	
"Is your husband [or wife] from around here?"	
"Are you a U.S. citizen?"	
"May we see your naturalization or alien registration papers?"	

continued

TOXIC QUESTIONS	ANTIDOTES
"What's your maiden name?"	"Have you ever used another name?"
"Is any further information relative to a name change or use of an assumed name or nickname needed for us to verify your education or job history? If yes, please explain."	
"What's your native language?"	"What languages do you speak, read, or write?" (Even then, don't ask unless the answer is relevant to the job.)
"I see from your résumé that you're fluent in Spanish. Did you learn that in high school?"	
"Has your family been in this country a long time?"	
"That's an interesting last name. What nationality is it?"	
"Do you have a big family?"	There's no legal way to ask about family status. Just don't go there.
"Are you currently using birth control?"	
"Planning to have kids someday?"	
"How many children do you have?"	
"How old are you kids?"	
"Who takes care of your children while you're at work?"	
"Who lives with you?"	
"Are you gay?"	

continued

TOXIC QUESTIONS	ANTIDOTES
"What's your husband's [or wife's] name?"	"If you are under 18, what is the name and address of your parent or guardian?"
"What are your children's names?"	"Do any of your relatives work for this organization? If so, what are their names? What positions do they have?"
"What race are you?"	A statement that, after employment, a photograph may be required for the candidate's personnel file or ID badge
"So, are you 100 percent African-American or mixed race?"	
"Wow! Do you sunburn easily at the beach?"	
"Is that your natural hair color?"	
"Do you have any physical disabilities or handicaps?"	A statement that a job offer may be contingent on the candidate passing a job-related physical
"Are you sick much?"	
"Have you been paid a lot of workers' comp money?"	
"Have you ever had cancer?"	
"Do you have AIDS?"	
"Have you lost a lot of weight lately?"	
"Have you tried dieting?"	
"Do you see a shrink?"	
"Are you religious?"	A statement of regular days, hours, or shifts to be worked

continued

TOXIC QUESTIONS	ANTIDOTES
"Do you go to church? Which one?"	
"Do you pray?"	
"Have you been baptized?"	
"Does your religion prevent you from working weekends or holidays?"	
"Do you observe any religious holidays? Which ones?"	
"Do you belong to any clubs?"	"Are you a member of any job-related organizations, clubs, or professional associations?" (Please exclude the name or character of any organization that indicates the race, color, creed, sex, marital status, religion, national origin, or ancestry of its members.)
"Are you a member of any organization?"	
"When you registered to vote, which political party did you choose?"	

continued

TOXIC QUESTIONS	*ANTIDOTES*
"Have you ever been arrested?"	A question on the application asking whether the candidate has been convicted of a felony, within the past x years (check state law), along with a notation that a conviction will not necessarily eliminate the possibility of employment. (Note: employers that have a direct responsibility for the supervision, care, or treatment of children, mentally ill or disabled persons, or other vulnerable adults may, depending on the law of the state in which the employment occurs, have greater latitude to inquire into an applicant's arrest and conviction record.)
"Have you ever been in trouble with the law?" "Have you ever been to jail?" "Have you ever been convicted of a crime?"	
"What is the name and address of a relative for us to contact in case of accident of emergency?"	"What is the name and address of a person for us to contact in case of accident or emergency?"

JOB OFFERS: HOW TO STRUCTURE AND NEGOTIATE A WIN-WIN PACKAGE

Know the Issue

There's a gentle tug on the end of the line; then a stronger one. You've hooked a fish! It begins to thrash, and as it breaks the surface of the water, you can see it's a beauty—easily the best catch of the day.

What do you do next? Settle back onto your seat and pull a hat over your eyes to nap while the fish swims to the boat and leaps into a waiting bucket? Only if the fish on the line is a Disney creation. Otherwise, you'll use all your fishing expertise, and a lot of hard work, to reel it in.

When you get to the end of the interviews, assignments, tests, and reference checks and found the candidate of your dreams, it's easy to just exhale and think your job is done. But this is no time to kick back and assume the candidate will happily flop into your boat and accept an offer.

You'd be far better off developing a Captain Ahab complex and pursuing your top choice with relentless intensity. Okay, maybe Captain Ahab is a little scary, but you should work hard to close the deal. Even after your top candidate says yes, you need to negotiate a deal that will work for everyone involved.

Take Action

- *Structure a win-win package.* The consequences are much higher, however, if we use our hearts instead of our heads when we determine a job offer. In hiring, we're spending someone else's money and we're paid to spend it wisely. So using our hearts instead of our heads—and offering a candidate more than he or she is worth—can have several repercussions. It can throw your budget out of whack, raise fairness issues, put pressure on you to raise all salaries, and give you no maneuvering room to give the employee a raise. No matter how appealing a candidate is, we still need to be rational when it comes to shaping an offer.

- *Start with base salary.* Some pay rates—such as those for entry-level fast-food jobs, jobs covered by collective bargaining agreements, and most government jobs—are fixed. But most are not, which puts the burden on you to figure them out. If you work in a large organization, you probably have established salary grades, which gives you a head start. If there aren't published grades, at least you can look to salaries for precedents.

    Most smaller organizations do not have fixed pay grades so you have more options—and therefore more work. If you're filling a job that already exists (hiring a second retail clerk, for example), use existing salaries as a guideline. If it's a new job, or one that's unique in your organization, be sure you know the going rate for comparable jobs. You may get a good sense just by asking candidates about their current salary during the interview process, but if you're unsure, look at a salary survey. Certain companies specialize in salary surveys, and trade associations and consulting firms also conduct them. You'll probably have to pay for the data, but it's worth it. Just be sure the data is current and that you understand what's included in the figures. (Some surveys, for example, report base salaries only, while others report total pay packages.)

Once you know the general parameters, you can set a specific salary. The rate shouldn't be arbitrary. Base it on the following:

- ○ The education, experience, and skills the candidate brings to the job
- ○ The job's responsibilities (for example, two retail clerks may have essentially the same job, although one has responsibility for opening the shop)
- ○ Hardship (you may offer a shift differential, for example, to people who work nights)

- *Correlate salary with experience and responsibility.* That said, even in an employer's labor market, it's self-defeating to pay at the bottom of the range; top people are always in demand. You should also avoid offering salaries at the top of the range. If you start at the top, you'll have nowhere to go if you need to negotiate to close the deal, and you'll have a harder time giving the employee a raise if he excels. So where does that leave you? In the middle. Just to make the math easy, assume a job has a range between $20,000 and $30,000. Offer someone with less experience $22,000 and someone with more $27,000. Whatever you decide, be sure you have objective reasons to explain it.

  An ethical aside: don't ever bring in someone new with the same or less experience at a higher pay rate than a current employee. If you find that you have to move to a higher rate to compete for talent, then adjust the rate of your current employee as well.

- *Look at variable pay.* Base pay compensates people for their skills, consistent job performance, and value in the labor market. Variable pay has become a popular way to compensate for specific results. It may include bonuses, profit sharing, stock options, and commissions, for example. If a new hire will be eligible for such variable pay, you should present it as part of the offer.

Most variable pay is linked to specific business goals and is not something to create or amend when determining an offer. This rule has a couple of exceptions, however: signing bonuses and commissions.

If you discover that established salaries in your company are more than 10 percent below the market, you can't compete for talent. In those cases, negotiate with your HR department, or if there isn't one, with the CEO for a signing bonus to boost the package. The signing bonus should bridge the gap between the salary you're offering and market pay rates. (After the hire, push to have the grades revised.)

Signing bonuses are sometimes used deliberately to bring in new hires at market rates or above without raising salaries of existing employees. In effect, it's a technique to "hide" unfair disparities. It's a bad idea, though. Not only is it dishonest, but it sets a poor precedent. What will you do the following year to keep the new employee at the higher overall rate?

The other variable pay to determine at this stage is sales commissions. Any job offer to a salesperson should be explicit about the commission structure. Be sure to address these issues:

○ What is the basic commission rate?

○ Does the rate apply to all sales, or is commission higher on some sales (such as new accounts, accounts "stolen" from competitors, or accounts of a certain size)?

○ When are commissions paid? When the sale is made or when the client pays?

○ Are any commissions shared (as in shared territories or split accounts)?

○ When does the salesperson begin earning commission? (Does he earn commission on sales that he services but were actually made by his predecessor?)

○ Are there house accounts that do not earn commission?

○ What happens when the employee leaves the job? Does he earn commission on business sold at that time even if the transaction hasn't yet happened (standing orders, for example) or only on transactions complete when employment ends?

If the commission plan is not in writing, it should be. It should address exactly what the salesperson must do to earn the commission. It also should state that customers and territories can be assigned and reassigned at the employer's discretion, and that the plan itself is subject to change. Consider reiterating your at-will policy and stating that disputes about commission will be resolved by arbitration.

• *Remember benefits.* When is a $40,000 job not a $40,000 job? When it's a $40,000 job. That's because salary is only the beginning. The employer's actual cost also includes payroll taxes, the employer's contribution to Social Security, and benefits. Those expenses generally add 30 percent to the total package. In other words, a job with a $40,000 salary actually costs the company $52,000.

Get the figures on how much your company spends per employee on benefits and include this in your offer. Health insurance, vacation pay, 401(k) matching funds, and other perks are part of total compensation. A $52,000 job is easier to sell than a $40,000 job.

- *Decide a start date.* The final part of the offer is the job's start date. Think about what you really need. Is the job tied to a project with a distant deadline? Or do you want someone in the office yesterday? Remember that you need to give the candidate time to make the transition. People who are leaving jobs usually require more time that those who aren't working, for example.

- *Timing is everything.* Once you've decided whom to hire and put your offer together, you're probably chomping at the bit. But impatience can backfire. Not many candidates will listen carefully to an offer that comes while someone is listening to the conversation.

  Call the candidate to make an appointment. Ideally, you should present the offer within a couple of days; if you delay, all your top choices will have been snapped up. Try to present the offer face-to-face, so you can convey interest and gauge the candidate's reaction. If that's not possible, at least arrange to have the candidate's undivided attention during a phone call.

  Friday is the best day to make an offer because it gives people the weekend to talk with family and friends and to think without the distraction of their current job. And, yes, that means that Monday is the worst day.

- *Put it in writing.* Even a face-to-face offer isn't enough. Your offer should also be in writing. A written offer gives the candidate something to review (because she won't be able to remember everything), leaves less room for misunderstanding, and offers you some protection if there's a dispute later. The written offer should include the following:

- ○ Job title, location, proposed start date, and duties and responsibilities
- ○ The job the position reports to
- ○ Base salary
- ○ Specifics of any variable pay (including sales commission if appropriate)
- ○ Employment benefits (include dates when employees become eligible for specific benefits, such as health care coverage)
- ○ Special considerations (such as reimbursement for moving expenses or signing bonuses)
- ○ Dates when the employee's performance will be reviewed
- ○ Any legal documents that will be required (such as proof of eligibility to work)
- ○ Any contingencies to the offer (such as passing a physical). The letter also should cover certain legal ground:
  - If you are an at-will employer (and you should be), the offer is the place to say so. The concept is simple: at-will employment means that either the employer or the employee can end employment at any time for any reason. Make it clear that the employment offered is at-will and not for any definite term.
  - State that no promises have been made other than those in the letter.

- If you call for arbitration to resolve disputes (and more and more employers have concluded this is a must), have the applicant review that language as well.

Finally, the offer also should include a written copy of the employee handbook or policies and procedures manual, and it should be clear that the employee will be bound to the terms of the handbook if she accepts the position.

- *Keep the meeting upbeat.* If you're having a bad day, don't carry that baggage into the offer meeting. Convey your enthusiasm about the company, the job, and the future. Talk about ways in which you think the candidate can contribute, and make him feel wanted.

  During the meeting, the offer letter and attachments may seem intimidating to the candidate; with its legal details, it may feel like a contract from a police state, but don't apologize. Explain that it's comprehensive so there won't be any surprises later.

  Allow time for her to ask questions, and make yourself available should she have questions later.

- *Give the candidate time to think.* Accepting a new job is a big decision that affects not only the candidate, but also her family and the people at the job she would leave behind. Allow the candidate a few days to consider the offer, but don't leave the door open indefinitely. (One candidate asked if he could have a month to think about it. A month is long enough to lose all your other prospects for the job if he turns you down.)

- *Be prepared to negotiate.* The candidate probably won't see the offer as an all-or-nothing proposition. Expect to negotiate.

- *Set a money ceiling.* If the candidate wants to negotiate money, know your limits going in. Remember the range you set at the outset. Resist all temptation to exceed the range. Although you may "win" in the short term, in the long term it won't be worth it. (One executive eventually had to raise the salaries of every secretary in the firm after he broke down and hired one for a salary outside the established range.) If you've left yourself some room, you can bump the offer up somewhat if you think the candidate's experience warrants it. Sometimes all candidates really want is a good-faith gesture.

  Don't get suckered into making promises that will haunt you. Too often, managers buckle in the heat of the moment and promise big raises in the future. Unless you have a crystal ball, don't do it. There are too many unknowns, starting with how the candidate will actually perform.

- *Look for other money.* You've topped out on salary? Get creative and hunt for other money. One candidate was enrolled in a master's program, for example. The manager couldn't offer a higher salary, but he did have money in his training budget to help offset the candidate's tuition. Another manager found out that a candidate's family lived near the host city for the industry's trade show; he tagged money in his travel budget and offered to send her on a trip home as long as she attended the conference while she was there.

- *Be careful with benefits.* Candidates think you have control over benefits, but often you don't. Insurance carriers usually decide the eligibility requirements for health care coverage, and company policy often limits you in other ways. In rare cases it's possible to get around the rules, but don't try to negotiate without checking first.

- *Little things count.* All candidates want to be wanted. Although we often think the grand gesture or big bucks are the only way to show our interest, smaller gestures are often enough. If you can't meet some demands, ask what else a candidate might like. Managers have landed top talent with cell phones (around $300), membership fees in airline clubs (around $400), or software. You don't want negotiations to become *Let's Make a Deal*, but a little creativity can go a long way.

- *Focus on flexibility.* You usually have more room to negotiate with things that cost little or nothing. For example, one manager won the bidding war for a graphic artist when she offered to let the artist work earlier hours. The candidate had another offer with a higher salary, but the flexibility cut her commute and let her spend more time with her kids. Ultimately, those benefits were more important than money. Look to flex hours, telecommuting, and other options that might help close a deal.

- *Listen to the candidate.* What does the candidate really want? It's one thing if he's genuinely trying to strike a reasonable deal, but sometimes a candidate's true motivation surfaces only during the negotiation stage. Is he truly interested in the job, or in meeting his own agenda? Listen for:
  - Whether the candidate is trying to find a way to take the job or a reason to turn it down.
  - Whether he's interested in a career move or a financial windfall. If all the questions are about perks and none are about job challenges, he may not be the passionate employee you're hoping for.

- ○ Whether the candidate can see beyond the next six months. Does she have the patience to earn the long-term rewards of the job?

- *Go back to basics*. During negotiation, it's easy to get distracted by the trees and lose sight of the forest. Remember, the candidate initially was interested in the job, before she even knew about the salary, benefits, and so forth. Focus your energy on what excited her initially: job challenges, increased responsibility, the chance to work with cutting-edge technology, or whatever it might be.

- *Don't meet counteroffers*. Once a candidate accepts your job, he may call to say that his current employer has made a counteroffer. A few things might have happened. The candidate may be a stellar employee, and his current boss may be stricken at the thought of losing him. It's also possible the candidate initiated a job search expressly to get a raise in his current job. Or the candidate might be "auctioning" his services to the highest bidder. Whatever's going on, don't match the offer.

  By this stage of the process, you've negotiated a fair package and the candidate wants the job. To squabble about money again smacks of extortion. It may be good for the candidate, but not for your business. The bidding war often doesn't stop after one round either. The current employer may best your counter to the counteroffer, and so it goes. Where will it end?

  A good preemptive strategy is to raise the issue of counteroffers yourself. Warn the candidate that he may get one, and remind him of all the reasons he sought your job in the first place. Counteroffers rarely address the root issues.

(Recruitment guru Robert Half says that seven of 10 people who accept a counteroffer from their current employer have left that company within a year precisely because the root problems are still there.) If candidates are prepped to expect a counteroffer, they're more likely to reject it.

- *Revise the offer letter.* If you negotiate any changes to the offer, revise the offer letter. You and the candidate both need an accurate one.

- *Find out whether a noncompete agreement is an issue.* Ask candidates whether they have an agreement with their current or former employer that includes a noncompete clause. If the answer is yes, ask to see the agreement and have a lawyer look at it. Many noncompete agreements are written in ways that are not enforceable or will not hold up in court. Your lawyer can advise you about this, but even if the agreement is not enforceable, you need to decide if this candidate is worth the risk of possibly having to argue the agreement in court. If the agreement is enforceable, your prior knowledge of it will be a liability in court.

Stay Out of Jail

- *Be sure your offers aren't arbitrary.* Don't expose yourself to discrimination charges by appearing to play favorites or basing pay on subjective factors. Tie pay to experience and responsibilities.

- *Make sure that people in comparable jobs earn comparable pay.* Be careful, for example, that women aren't being offered lower salaries than men.

- *Be consistent in presenting offers.* Although the terms will vary from job to job, the format should be consistent.

- *Don't say anything that could be construed as a promise other than what is expressly set forth in the offer letter.* Such comments as "we've been very successful in the past two years and fully expect to continue to be successful" and "we expect to go public in the next year" and "we always pay more than our competitors" and "there will be stock options" have led to lawsuits.
- *Be specific about exactly what benefits are included in the offer package.*
- *Double-check before you make the offer that the need still exists for the new hire and that you still have the authority to fill the position.*
- *If you don't know the answer to a question, say so and get the answer.* Don't make something up.
- *Don't ask a new hire for any confidential information*, trade secrets, client lists, or other sensitive data. If an employee offers it, decline.
- *You can't control who applies for jobs in your firms, but you may run into trouble if you actively solicit applications from your competitors' employees.*

Real-Life Example

The candidate had impeccable qualifications and seemed to have people lining up to offer glowing references. He had so much going for him that the manager decided to fly him from the Midwest to California for an interview. During his visit, he won over everyone he met and the manager offered him a job. But after thinking about it over the weekend, the candidate turned it down. He didn't want to uproot his family. The manager was crushed.

Then, two days later, the candidate called. He was reconsidering. After accepting another offer in his hometown, he learned that he would have to wait six months for medical coverage. His wife was undergoing treatment, and he couldn't wait six months. Could the manager in California get him coverage any sooner?

Yes, the manager in California could have him covered in 90 days. "But I thought about it long and hard," the manager said, "and then I called him back and told him I couldn't help him. He had decided against our job for some profound reasons, and now it was all about medical coverage. None of his other thinking had changed. I ended up hiring my second choice. Her qualifications weren't as impressive, but she really wanted the job. That counts for something."

Manage Up

Take responsibility for closing the deal. Find out in advance what maneuvering room you have in shaping an offer. If you run into trouble, look for solutions. Don't whine, "Our pay scale is too low. I can't hire anyone." Instead, present research proving that your salaries are out of step. Be prepared to make cuts in other parts of your budget if your boss can't just throw money at the problem.

Get More Information

> *The Employer's Legal Handbook*, Fred Steingold, Nolo, 2009.
>
> *Hiring Smart! How to Predict Winners and Losers in the Incredibly Expensive People-Reading Game*, Pierre Mornell, Ten Speed Press, 2004.

CLOSING THE DEAL: HOW TO TURN CANDIDATES INTO EMPLOYEES

Know the Issue

The star athlete was wooed by every college big enough to have a team, and he's chosen yours. You can already count the money that will pour in from alumni. Maybe this is the year for a berth in the NCAA tournament. Now that the press conference is over, all that's left is for him to show up. Or is it?

Not quite. There's still all that pesky paperwork: registering for classes, getting a parking permit, getting a dorm assignment, and on and on.

So it is with your star hire. She accepted the offer. Now, shake her hand, shout "Hallelujah!" and get back to your real job until she starts, right? Not so fast. Hiring is a complex process that doesn't just stop; you need to finish it. You also need to take a few steps to make sure nothing goes wrong between now and the hire's start date.

Take Action

- *Get it in writing.* Just as you need to make the offer verbally and in writing, the candidate should accept verbally and in writing. The offer letter also should make clear that he's read your company policies and employee handbook, understands them, and agrees to abide by them. Have the candidate sign the offer letter; his signature indicates that he understands and accepts the offer.

    You and the candidate should keep signed copies of the letter. Put your copy in the candidate's brand-new personnel file.

- *Tie up loose ends.* If employment was at all conditional, make sure the conditions are met. If you require a physical, for example, make sure the candidate gets the physical and that you (or someone in HR) has a copy of the report.

- *Make sure all employees are legally entitled to work.* In a large organization, HR will make sure that all employees are legally entitled to work. In smaller organizations, it's probably up to you. This is not a trivial concern. The penalty for knowingly hiring unauthorized workers is as great as $10,000 per employee and six months in prison. Fortunately, the law includes a mechanism to help protect you. It requires that every new employee complete a Form I–9. Have the candidate complete the form when he accepts the job. (For details on how to comply, see the sidebar "Form I–9: A Primer.")

  Three groups of people are lawfully permitted to work in the United States:

  - U.S. citizens
  - Permanent resident aliens (green card holders) who have an unlimited right to work in the United States
  - Other non-U.S. citizens who have some type of time-limited work authorization (which may or may not be limited to a specific employer)

  Everything should be in order before the candidate's first day.

- *Notify the other candidates.* Once you've made an offer and someone has accepted it, let the other candidates know that the job has been filled. Notify them in writing. (Other candidates includes *all* other candidates. Even if you choose not to interview an applicant, she deserves an acknowledgment of her interest. It's easiest to send letters as you eliminate people from consideration, but if you haven't already done so, do it now.)

The letter should thank people for their interest. If you interviewed them, or they completed an assessment of some sort, thank them for their time. Do not offer other information about why a candidate wasn't hired.

If you would consider them for a future opening and you think such an opening may exist, say so. Otherwise, don't raise false expectations.

Keep all the rejected applicants' cover letters, résumés, tests, and so on in a file for at least three years. (How long you're required to keep the material varies from state to state; check with HR or an attorney if you're unsure.) Cumbersome? Yes, but this protects you in case a rejected candidate sues for discrimination or your decision is otherwise challenged.

- *Don't share too much information.* Candidates often want to know why they weren't hired. If they got far enough in the process to be seriously considered, you probably like them and are tempted to help. Don't. Sharing your perception of their weaknesses invites hurt feelings and arguments about why you're wrong. Some disgruntled candidates might even make a complaint. Besides, the information isn't as helpful as candidates think it is. Something you considered a weakness in comparison to other candidates for that job may be irrelevant in the eyes of another boss hiring for a different job.

Don't share anything about the hiring process either. One young manager called her favorite applicant to tell her that she had wanted to hire her but was overruled by her boss. The manager's impulse was probably to help the candidate feel appreciated. That's a nice idea, but such a call may leave the candidate with the feeling that she was the most qualified for the job and was discriminated against. At a minimum, she might call the boss to argue; she could go further and file a complaint. Sometimes silence is golden.

Stay Out of Jail

- *Be sure all offers are accepted in writing and include the candidate's signature.*
- *Make sure all conditions of employment have been met.*
- *Verify eligibility to work.*
- *Be sure the applicant agrees in writing to be bound by the employee handbook and company policies before actually being hired.*
- *Don't make comments about information supplied on the I–9.* If something doesn't look right, ask about it and postpone hiring until it's clarified.

Get More Information

Form I–9 is available on the Internet at www.uscis.gov/files/form/i–9.pdf.

Form I–9: A Primer

Employers face substantial penalties for knowingly hiring unauthorized workers. Therefore, they are required to have all new hires complete a Form I–9 and to review documents that substantiate an employee's right to work. The United States Citizenship and Immigration Service (USCIS) periodically audits I–9 forms, so it's important that they be completed and stored properly.

Who Should Complete a Form I–9?

All new hires, including those hired after November 6, 1986. This includes anyone who gets paid for work performed on a regular schedule. (Technically, the law requires homeowners to verify the status of the kid who mows the lawn once a week.) This includes any person who receives wages or remuneration (anything of value given in exchange for labor, such as food or shelter) for labor to be completed in the United States. I–9s are not required for independent contractors.

Who Should Not Complete a Form I–9?

- Anyone hired before November 7, 1986, who is continuing employment and reasonably expects to be employed at all times
- Anyone employed in a private residence to perform informal or irregular household duties
- Independent contractors
- Employees of temp agencies
- Anyone not physically working in the United States

When Should It Be Completed?

On an employee's hire date, which the USCIS defines as "the actual commencement of employment for wages or other remuneration."

continued

Is an Employee's Statement That He Is Eligible to Work Enough?

No. In addition to attesting under penalty of perjury that he is not an unauthorized alien, the employee must produce documents to prove his identity and authorization to work. Employees may choose a single document to prove their identity and eligibility, or may prove each separately. The USCIS lists more than 20 acceptable documents, ranging from the obvious (a U.S. passport) to the obscure (USCIS Form I–766). (Employers may not insist that employees choose a specific one.) Most people will produce a passport or green card. If you're unsure about which other documents to accept, check with the USCIS.

So It's All Up to the Employee?

No. The employer must look at the documents. The law doesn't require that employers be experts in fraud or counterfeit documents; it only asks employers to use their best judgment as to whether the documents seem genuine. The employer must then, within three business days, complete section two of the form.

Should Copies of the Documents Be Included with the Form?

The law says that copies may be attached to the form but don't have to be. Employers must be consistent, though. If they attach copies to one form, they should attach them to all. If an employer is using E-Verify and employees present documents used in the photo screening tool (such as Permanent Resident Card, Form I–551), the employer must keep a photocopy of the document the employee presents. If you are not an E-Verify participant, you do not have to keep a copy of the documents.

If an employer would like to photocopy documents, the employer should do so for all employees and retain each copy with Form I–9. Employers should not use the photocopies for any other purpose. Photocopying does not relieve the employer of the obligation to complete Form I–9.

continued

What Is E-Verify?

E-Verify is an Internet-based system operated by the Department of Homeland Security in partnership with the Social Security Administration that allows participating employers to electronically verify the employment eligibility of their newly hired employees. E-Verify is free and voluntary, and is the best means available for determining employment eligibility of new hires and the validity of their Social Security numbers. For more information, visit www.uscis.gov/e-verify.

What Happens to the Form When It's Complete?

Employers should keep the forms in their files. (The forms should be kept separately from personnel files.) Forms should be kept for three years or until one year after termination of employment, whichever is longer. Agricultural associations/employers and farm labor contractors must retain Form I–9 for three years after the date of employment for recruited persons and those who are referred for a fee.

If an employee is hired when he has a temporary permit to work in the United States, who is responsible for verifying that the permit has been renewed at the appropriate time?

The employer.

FIRST DAYS ON THE JOB: HOW TO LAY THE GROUNDWORK FOR SUCCESS

Know the Issue

Imagine this vacation: Instead of going to work one morning, you drive to the airport. You buy a ticket for the first available flight. When you arrive, you hunt for a place to stay and then ask the concierge for suggestions about what to do and where to eat. Dinner is fabulous and life is great, until you reach into your wallet and realize you've left your credit card at home. Sound like fun? To a few spontaneous souls, perhaps, but most of us like to plan ahead. Anticipation can be half the fun, and there's some comfort in knowing we have a place to sleep.

Yet many of the same managers who make absolutely sure they never leave home without their American Express card don't give a moment's thought to preparing for an employee's first day. The attitude seems to be, "She's hired, she'll show up, what's to do?"

There's nothing to do if you don't mind employees being frustrated, unproductive, or even literally lost. But if your goal is to have energetic, focused employees who are making a contribution, then you can make that much more likely with a thorough orientation program—beginning before a new employee even shows up for work.

Take Action

- *Get things started even before the first day.* The most common image there is of the first day at work is—wow!—paperwork. Wouldn't that really get you excited about your new job? We didn't think so. Take a tip from many cruise lines and:
  - *Send paperwork in advance.* Most forms, which capture emergency contact information, tax withholdings, and so on, can be filled out any time. Let employees arrive the first day with the forms completed. (Note: In some states, you may have to pay employees for the time spent filling out the forms, even if they do it at home. Even so, it may be worth it to help give them a running start.)
  - *Make access easier.* Help the new hire get her security badge or parking permit before the first day. It's more

welcoming and makes it easier for the hire to be fully productive.

- *Set up a work area.* Having nowhere to work, or getting a workstation that has no supplies or is still full of someone else's junk, isn't what employees signed up for. Personal space is important. Having a clean, functional, well-stocked workstation ready when an employee walks through the door is the best thing you can do to help him feel he belongs. Don't stop with a working telephone, a comfortable chair, and a few paper clips. Be sure to organize paper files and delete unneeded files from the computer. (One secretary spent much of her first day trying to make sense of letters to God left on the hard drive by her predecessor.)

- *Let existing staff know that the new employee is coming.* New employees will begin wondering immediately whether they can really make a contribution if their position is so unimportant that no one even knows they're starting. Take time to let your existing staff know:
  - That you've made a hire
  - When the person starts
  - The nature of the person's job duties (especially if the job is new or has been changed since the previous person left)
  - Something about the person's qualifications (don't share personal information, but give people an idea of what you think this person can contribute)

    It's best to make this announcement in person, so you can convey your enthusiasm and answer any questions. Remind people the day before that the new employee is starting.

- *Don't get too hung up on the calendar.* You've agreed on a start date for your new hire. Now don't get tunnel vision about that date. Suppose your annual planning meeting falls before that date? Give the new hire the chance to attend the meeting. Just be sure that hires for nonexempt jobs get paid for that time.

- *Arrange your schedule around the new hire.* The worst thing you can do on an employee's first day is not be there. The next worst thing is to be so busy that you can't take any time with the person. New employees deserve at least some of your undivided attention on the first day. If something comes up and you absolutely must be out, call to arrange an alternate start date.

- *Offer a thorough orientation.* There's nothing haphazard about boot camp. Turning a new recruit into a Marine is a deliberate, consistent process that's been proven effective for decades. But the Marines spend more time on the right way to make a bed than many companies spend on the entire orientation process. What a wasted opportunity. The Marines understand that the first few days and weeks lay the groundwork for everything to follow.

  Although you needn't have your new employees crawl through the mud, they'll appreciate it if finding the bathroom isn't the biggest accomplishment of their third day. After all, you never get a second chance to make a first impression.

  A good orientation program should cover three key areas: the organization, the product (or service), and operations. Within each of those areas are specific issues to address. (See "Orientation Program Overview" later in the chapter.)

- *Introduce the new employee yourself.* Take time to introduce the new employee to as many coworkers as possible. Doing so shows respect for the new employee and for your current employees. It also makes it clear that the new employee is important. Don't delegate this task to someone else who has "more time."

- *Review expectations.* You've spent a lot of time writing a job description and thinking about the expectations you have for new employees. Now don't forget to share them!

- *Don't go it alone.* You're probably thinking, "Yeah, I'd love to orient my new employees, but I don't have the time." Well, who said you've got to do it all yourself? You might want to do the goals and strategies sections yourself, but assign other sections to seasoned employees and/or teams. (In fact, asking employees who are about to complete their first year to give a portion of the orientation for you is a great way to test how much they know.)

  This strategy will save you time and offer other rewards as well. New employees will meet their coworkers, they'll get different points of view, and veterans will value the chance to help new employees succeed.

- *Schedule the orientation.* Once you've developed the program and assigned "teachers," don't just hope the plan gets implemented. Assign dates for each part of the program and determine who should teach that part of the program. Work all your new hires into the schedule.

- *Don't rush.* People can only absorb just so much information at a time, so it doesn't make sense to try to tell people everything in 48 hours. Orientation works best when you allot several hours each week for the first month. That frees up most hours for employees to focus on their jobs.

- *Give employees the schedule.* On an employee's first day, give him the dates and times for each part of the orientation. Make it his responsibility to follow through, and hold other employees accountable for meeting their commitments as scheduled.

- *Be consistent.* Once your orientation program is developed, use it for every new hire. Don't cheat and decide that some employees are smart enough to get along without it, or that because of a pressing deadline you'll do the orientation "later."

- *Take advantage of support materials.* If you're in a large organization, your HR department may have materials (such as videos) to help in the orientation process. If not, use product brochures, catalogs, annual reports, and other material to supplement your information.

- *Assign a buddy.* As your new employees' manager, you're their number one source of information, and that's great when it comes to sharing overall department goals. But because you're the boss, new employees won't come to you about many things, either because they don't want to look stupid or because they think you're too busy. Assigning a buddy gives them another resource.

  Choose employees who have been around at least a year. If you can, select people who are outside the employee's immediate work group. Logic might tell you to choose someone in the work group, since those people are closest to the work, but new employees will interact with those people anyway. Having a buddy further removed will expose him to other parts of the company and give him someone to talk to about his coworkers ("What's the best way to approach Henry? Does he prefer e-mail or should I talk to him in the coffee room?").

Buddies are also information resources. They can answer everything from "Is there anywhere nearby where I can drop off my dry cleaning?" to "What's the best way to present ideas?" Most of the buddy time should be informal and spontaneous, but give them structured time, too. Buy them lunch once a month for the first six months so they can get away from the office and talk.

And don't put any limits on what they can talk about, including you. Current employees are the best source of insight on how to work with your quirks. (Yes, you do have some.) Don't ask buddies to share what they hear from new employees; nothing will undermine the buddy system faster. (The only exception should be situations you really need to know about, such as threats by a new employee.)

Stay Out of Jail

Employee information is confidential. If new hires complete forms in advance, ask them to mail them directly to HR or to bring them directly to you on the first day. Don't take a chance that the forms will end up where anyone in the office can see them.

Real-Life Example

The workstation assigned to the new employee had been empty for a few months, and no one thought to look through it. As the new employee got assignments, information, and backup material, she looked for somewhere to put it. The file drawers in her workstation were full. When she asked about it, she was told to "make room." So she did; she threw out most of what was in the files. Only weeks later, when someone came looking, did it become apparent that she'd thrown out work samples, invoices, and contracts. Oops.

Do at Least the Minimum

- Be there the employee's first day.
- Be sure the employee has a workstation ready.
- Tell existing employees to expect a new coworker.

Get More Information

Love 'Em or Lose 'Em: Getting Good People to Stay, 4th ed., Beverly Kaye and Sharon Jordan-Evans, Berrett-Koehler, 2008.

Orientation Program Overview

A good orientation program gives new employees a thorough overview of the organization, its operations, and its products or services. Here are some areas you should be sure to address:

The Organization (Allow about six hours)

Company history
Key stakeholders
Organization chart

- Roles and responsibilities of each department

Corporate culture

continued

Corporate goals

- Immediate
- Long-term

Revenue

- How does the company earn money?
- What are key expenses?

Policies and procedures
The benefit plan

- Components
- Enrollment procedures

Products and Services (Allow about eight hours)

Your industry/market

- Brief history
- Overall size

Projections

- Is the industry growing? By how much?

Regulatory issues
Market or industry lingo or vocabulary
Specific products produced or services provided

- Their relative importance to the company

Strategy for key products
Market position

- Chief competitors
- Who are they?
- What do they produce?

continued

Operations

Facilities

- Tour
- Hours
- Security

Handbook review
Time cards
Communication

- Mail and fax processes
- Telephone system
- Voice mail
- E-mail

Schedules and deadlines
Operating processes and procedures
Workflow
How departments interact

THE 90-DAY REVIEW: HOW TO DECIDE WHETHER THE EMPLOYEE SHOULD STAY—OR GO

Know the Issue

The offers for trial subscriptions to magazines arrive in your mail by the pound, and every one of them promises a risk-free experience. If, after three (or six or nine) issues you aren't completely satisfied, just write "Cancel" on your invoice and owe nothing.

But at some point you have to decide whether to subscribe and write the check. And so it is with new employees. At some point you have to decide whether they have become a fully functioning member of the team (ready to be managed like everyone else) or are not performing and need to be replaced.

If only it were as simple as writing "Cancel" on an invoice. It isn't, of course. If the employee has done well, you must meet with her to say so, and to set goals for the coming months. If she hasn't done well, the decision has profound implications for her, of course, but it also has implications for you and your company. The prospect of beginning the hiring process again can be daunting and costly; if the situation isn't handled right, it can lead to legal problems. You may feel that as a manager you've failed, and word may get out that your company has terminated new employees.

To postpone the decision as long as possible, employers have long relied on probationary periods. "Probation"—usually 90 days, but sometimes six or even 12 months—is a term that suggests two things: (1) a new employee must prove herself, but that once probation is over her employment is secure, and (2) probation gives employers a legal out, a period in which they can fire an employee without the risk of lawsuits.

Unfortunately, both of these ideas have seen their day, for we live in an era of at-will employment: a legal concept that says either the employer or the employee can end employment at any time for any reason (or no reason). At-will employment is increasingly popular because, as long as employees are told they're working at-will from the outset, employers have more latitude (refer to "Job Offers" earlier in the chapter). But at-will employment and probation are redundant. If employment can end any time for any reason, what status does an employee assume when he "passes" probation?

So where does this leave you as a manager? You still must decide whether a new employee should stay, and the end of 90 days is a good time to do so. Once you've made it, meet with the employee—she deserves to know where she stands.

Take Action

- *Don't call the first few months "probation."* Avoid using the word "probation," especially if you have an at-will employment policy (and, unless a collective bargaining agreement prevents it, you should). New employees need to know that employment is never guaranteed. If you insist on a similar concept, use the phrase "introductory period." Just be sure the introductory period is tied to something other than the employee's at-will status, such as her ability to earn or use vacation time or to qualify for portions of the benefit plan. Even then the downsides may outweigh the benefits of a defined period, because delaying vacation accrual or benefits enrollment may hurt your recruitment efforts.

- *Assess performance.* Evaluate the first 90 days. If the employee is doing well, consider her a successful hire. If performance problems have been an issue from the start and still haven't been resolved, however, then it's probably time to fire her. (Note: if the employee has significant performance problems, meet with her as early as 30 days after the start date so she has time to improve before you get to the 90-day mark.)

  In rare cases you may want to postpone the decision another 30 days, but don't take that step just because the decision is uncomfortable. Prolonging the decision can make it more difficult to terminate the employee in the future. Postpone the decision only if the employee has shown substantial progress and you think he will succeed given more time.

You may also postpone the decision if the employee did very well the first few weeks but you've seen a sudden decline in her performance. (If that happens, you're back to setting targets and monitoring performance.) In any case, you owe it to the employee and your company to make a decision within 120 days.

- *Set new goals.* After an introductory period, employees should move into the standard performance review period. That's usually annually, assuming they stay in the same job. Now is the time to set goals for the next nine months, even if the goal is as simple as meeting the expectations outlined in the job description.

  There's no point twisting yourself in contortions to find goals for employees, particularly nonexempt employees whose jobs are focused and routine. However, professional employees who have career paths need incremental goals to keep them challenged and growing.

- *Meet with the employee.* If an employee is succeeding, let her know that you're pleased with her performance. Identify areas of particular strength, and take time to celebrate her accomplishments. Share the goals you have for her, and give her the chance to share any goals she may have for herself. Make sure that her goals won't conflict with yours, distract her from your goals, or demand resources that you can't commit.

  If an employee is not succeeding despite the reviews and warnings we've described, then you need to make a change. If your company has an HR function, review the termination with them in advance. When you meet with the employee, treat her with respect (see "Termination: How to Let People Go Fairly and Legally" in Chapter 9). Don't begin your search for a replacement until you've let her go.

- *If you hired through an agency, pay attention to your contract.* Most agencies guarantee the placements they make, meaning that if the hire doesn't work out within a specified time, they will either refund the placement fee or apply the fee to a new search. Be mindful of the guarantee period when making a decision.

Stay Out of Jail

- *Be consistent.* If you give employees a 90-day review, be sure that all employees get the review.
- *Document performance.* Be sure your comments (pro and con) are in writing. Include a space for the employee to add comments, if any. Have the employee sign a copy to indicate that he got the review and understands it. Keep a copy in the employee's file.
- *Keep performance issues confidential.* An employee's performance is between you and the employee and, if appropriate, HR; others don't need to know.

Manage Up

After 90 days, let your boss know how the new employee is doing. If the new employee is doing well, let your boss know what she has accomplished and how she's contributing. If you fire the employee, let your boss know that it's happening and share your plan for replacing her. Take responsibility for the situation, especially if it is a hire that didn't succeed.

Get More Information

Business: The Ultimate Resource, Perseus, 2002.

9

Discipline and Termination

As drivers, we all know what we're supposed to do, but we don't always do it. That's why occasionally the police step in. They issue friendly (or not so friendly) warnings, write tickets, suspend or revoke licenses, and even send drivers to jail. We need them to do these things to protect the public safety, and state regulations ensure that their actions fit the crimes.

If you set expectations and effectively manage performance, employees know what they're supposed to do, too, but, like drivers, they don't always do it. That's when you need to step in and take action. Your safety and liability, along with that of your company, demand it. Like the police, you have many options to choose from, and like the state, your company should have policies to help you match your action to the "crime."

DISCIPLINE: HOW TO CHANGE PROBLEM BEHAVIOR

Know the Issue

If you were ever spanked as a child, you probably heard your parents say, "This is going to hurt me more than it's going to hurt you." As you felt the sting of the swat, you probably thought, "Yeah, right."

As an adult, you may better understand what they meant. The pain they felt was emotional, not physical, and it probably was harder on them. None of us likes to see another person's spirit diminished, even temporarily, and none of us likes to be the bad guy.

That's part of why discipline at work is often done so poorly. Other reasons are because it's done emotionally (usually in anger), because it's applied inconsistently (different disciplinary measures for the same infraction), because the company has no discipline policy (so managers don't know what to do when an infraction occurs), and because managers forget the real purpose of discipline (which is not to punish, but to change a person's behavior).

Administering discipline is never easy, but it becomes far less difficult if you do it fairly. That means know your options. Use them appropriately. Act rationally, not emotionally. And keep your eye on the big picture—reforming the behavior, not giving the employee "the business."

Take Action

- *Use the employee handbook.* Understand the policies and procedures outlined in the employee handbook (see "The Handbook: How to Use the Rules to Your Advantage" in Chapter 4). It's important that any discipline be consistent with the handbook. You don't want to discipline any employee for taking a long lunch hour on voting day, for example, if the manual says she may.

- *Listen to employees.* There's no excuse for some behavior, such as harassing a coworker or stealing, but you must hear the accused's side of the story before you take action. The employee may offer a credible denial or admit to the behavior. She may have logical explanations for apparent lapses. Was an employee late because she stopped in the parking lot to help an injured colleague? Ask before you assume the worst. Most jurors will consider you unfair if you don't give the employee a chance to explain.

- *Know your options.* At-will employers reserve the right to use whatever discipline—including immediate termination—they believe is appropriate. Many potential options, and combinations of options, are available, including:
  - Oral admonishment, warning, or instruction
  - Written admonishment, warning, or instruction
  - Training
  - Suspension without pay
  - Indefinite or temporary demotion
  - Indefinite or temporary transfer
  - Indefinite or temporary loss of benefit(s)
  - Termination

  The key is to choose the option that effectively changes inappropriate behavior or poor work performance, deters or prevents unlawful conduct, and shows your concern for the

rights of your employees. Sometimes an immediate termination is necessary (such as for sexual harassment or stealing), and sometimes a milder action is more appropriate. An
at-will employer reserves the right to make the decision at
its discretion. Nevertheless, because legal as well as management or labor relations issues lurk behind these decisions,
always consider consulting with HR or your boss before
imposing any discipline.

Be careful not to open the door to charges of discrimination. Be certain, for example, you know how your company
has treated similar cases in the past. You aren't tied to the
same discipline that was previously imposed, but if you vary
from precedent, do so only for legitimate, business-related
reasons. For example, the same offense can have different
consequences for a 20-year employee with an unblemished
record than for a six-month employee previously warned for
the same behavior.

- *Discipline effectively.* Ninety percent of all the discipline you
  impose will be warnings. To be effective and complete, a
  written warning must:
  - Communicate what the problem is. Describe what the
    employee has done that is inappropriate, against the rules,
    or not productive.
  - Communicate what your expectations and requirements
    are. Describe what the employee must do in the future.
  - Communicate the consequences of failing to meet your
    expectations or requirements. Describe what will happen,
    such as suspension without pay or termination. (Beware:

You may be limited to consequences you have communicated. Was the employee fairly put on notice of the consequences?)

○ Provide space for the employee to object or answer.

○ Be signed by the employee.

Extra credit is given to warnings that explain why the employee's behavior is a problem: "Your tardiness puts an unfair burden on other employees in the department, who must not only do their own work, but who must also, unexpectedly, rearrange their responsibilities to handle the work they were expecting you to perform."

- *Exercise restraint.* No rules exist that dictate which form of discipline to use for which circumstance. (Exceptions may arise if you are governed by a collective bargaining agreement or your employee handbook limits your options.) However, certain guidelines should be considered:

  ○ Unless the problem is serious, start with an admonishment. If you start with harsher discipline, it could limit your options in the future if the problem persists, and the employee may feel you're unfair.

  ○ Don't feel you have to use every option available. In some cases (excessive tardiness, for example), there isn't any training that's likely to help. In other cases, you may need to respond to new circumstances. Suppose you overheard an employee calling a coworker a fool. Giving the employee an oral admonishment might be appropriate. If the employee continued to call his coworkers names, a written warning would be the next logical step. But if the employee instead threatened a coworker or even hit someone, you'd need to impose harsher discipline, such as a suspension or even termination, right away.

○ Discipline usually becomes progressively harsher. It's uncommon to suspend someone and then backpedal to a warning.

○ See every step of discipline as the last one. Some high school principals create a self-perpetuating problem. They tell certain students that they expect to see them again, and so they do. People tend to meet your expectations for them. Inappropriate behavior is more likely to stop if you expect it to stop. See every step as an opportunity to teach.

• *Meet with employees.* Meet privately. Remain calm and respectful. If necessary, take some time before the meeting to collect yourself and your thoughts. Getting angry or emotional is liable to provoke a confrontation. Allow the employee to leave if he asks to. Have a witness present so there's no argument later about what was said.

• *Don't lose sight of the positive.* When we have to discipline an employee, it's easy (and natural) to let the problem blot out all else. But almost no employee is all bad; for the most part, employees perform well and try to do a good job. When you meet with an employee, try to remember what you like about her and what she does well. That will help keep the meeting constructive, instead of punitive.

• *Revisit the problem.* Don't discipline an employee and then forget about it. Remember, the goal is improvement. Review the situation again (30 days may be a good target): Has it improved? If so, commend the employee for improving. If not, further discipline may be needed.

Stay Out of Jail

- *Be consistent.* If something is against the rules, then all employees who break the rule should be subject to discipline. Although other factors (such as previous infractions) can inform your actions, don't impose harsh discipline on some employees while letting others go unpunished. Be especially careful not to consistently impose harsher penalties on members of protected groups (such as older employees or racial minorities, for example).

- *Document all discipline and keep records in the appropriate file.* Always remember that documentation is a potential exhibit in a lawsuit. Draft it, read it, and read it again before you give it to the employee. In the documentation, limit yourself to legitimate, business-related issues. Don't say anything that may be construed as discriminatory or reflecting a stereotype.

- *Don't let it be personal.* Focus on work-related behavior, not personality or psychology. For example, let an employee know that he's expected to complete assembling 10 swing sets each day; don't tell him he's "lazy."

Get More Information

The Progressive Discipline Handbook: Smart Strategies for Coaching Employees, Margie Mader-Clark and Lisa Guerin, Nolo, 2007.

TERMINATION: HOW TO LET PEOPLE GO FAIRLY AND LEGALLY

Know the Issue

Juries, doctors, and paramedics are among those who face life-altering moments of truth: Is the defendant guilty? Is there still value in treating the patient or has the disease progressed too far? Can the accident victim be rescued in time to save her life? These are wrenching decisions that deserve the utmost care and solemnity.

Your role as a manager means that you, too, may be in a position of facing a moment of truth: Is it in the best interests of the business to terminate an employee? Deciding "Yes" is one of the hardest things you will ever do as a manager. Most terminations will feel like a loss to you, to the employee, and probably to others in your company. Even if the employee "deserves it" because of poor performance or insubordination, it is still one of the most stressful events in a manager's life. Expect to face anger, hurt, and fear, and no matter how many times you terminate someone, it doesn't get easier.

There is nothing we can offer to make terminations easy or pleasant, but doing the wrong things can certainly make terminations harder and open the door to legal challenges. There are actions you can take to preserve an employee's dignity, limit the damage to the organization, and reduce your legal exposure.

Take Action

- *Take the decision seriously.* An employee's job is her livelihood and a large part of her identity. Do her the courtesy of considering a termination decision very carefully. Never decide to terminate an employee in the heat of anger, or because you think it would be easier than trying to improve her performance, because you don't like the person, or just because you can. Any decision should be based on a legitimate business reason:

- The employee has consistently not met performance standards and has not shown improvement despite warnings and the opportunity to do so.

- The employee has either violated company policy consistently (such as missing too many days without a legitimate reason), has not changed his behavior in response to any discipline offered, or has violated a policy in such a serious way (attacked a coworker, for example, or embezzled) that you are compelled to protect the company, its employees, or its assets.

- The nature of the job has substantially changed over time, the employee no longer has the skills to perform it, and there's no way you can alter the job or find another position for the employee.

- A downturn in business necessitates reducing the size of the workforce.

Just because you have an at-will employment policy and you can terminate an employee at any time for any reason doesn't make it a good idea.

Being fair and focusing on business concerns is how to best avoid wrongful termination claims. "Wrongful termination" is a broad term that refers to a termination a former employee contends should not have happened. The employee may claim he was terminated:

- In violation of an express contract to terminate only for cause.

- ○ In violation of an implied contract to terminate only for cause.
- ○ In violation of antidiscrimination laws.
- ○ For exercising a right (such as going to the labor commissioner with a concern).
- ○ For being a whistle-blower (reporting or threatening to report the employer to the IRS, SEC, or some other agency).
- ○ For refusing to violate a law (illegal dumping, lying under oath, or illegally terminating an employee).
- ○ For a combination of or a variation of any of these reasons. Good labor relations, good documentation, good disciplinary action, good employee handbooks, and good management are your best defense against any of these charges.

- *Take steps first.* Except in some instances of a workforce reduction, a termination should never be a complete surprise. If an employee's performance does not meet standards, she should be given the opportunity to improve. The same may also be true if an employee innocently violates a policy and does not cause harm to the company or to a coworker.

- *Tie up loose ends.* Don't terminate an employee without collecting all the data you need:
  - ○ Find out how much sick time, vacation time, or personal leave the employee has accrued. Determine whether your employee handbook or state law requires that the employee be paid for those benefits and when. California, for example, requires that accrued vacation be paid at the time the employee is terminated.

- ○ Calculate how many hours they have worked during the current pay period, including any applicable overtime. People must be paid for that time.
- ○ Calculate any commission owed the employee.
- ○ Determine whether the employee is eligible for continuing benefits coverage under COBRA (see the sidebar "COBRA: A Primer" later in the chapter").
- ○ Determine how much severance, if any, to give the employee. You may not want to give employees being terminated for poor performance (for cause) any severance, or you may want to give two weeks salary as a goodwill gesture and obtain a release against legal claims. Whatever you do, be consistent. Don't use the whim system.

If an employee is being terminated for other reasons (such as a downsizing or the elimination of a department), you'll probably want to offer severance. Whatever you decide, follow some logical rationale, such as a week's pay for each year employed with the company. (Beware: if you have a set "plan" with respect to severance, there are ERISA requirements that may apply.)

Also decide whether you'll offer any other help, such as out-placement counseling. If so, define the terms up front, put them in writing, and obtain a release in exchange.

- • *Determine the employee's final date of employment.* If employees are being fired for cause, it doesn't make much sense to keep them around after they are terminated. They will likely be angry and therefore disrupt morale in the office, or worse. In addition, they will want to focus on getting a new job. It's best for them to leave the day you notify them, even if you give them severance pay for a subsequent period. People being laid off or discharged for reasons other than performance may appreciate the chance to stay while they look for other jobs. Be consistent in what you decide, particularly for all employees in the same group.

- *Consider the timing of your meeting.* If you can avoid it, don't fire employees on Friday. It's harder for them to begin looking for a new job on the weekend, which may make them feel angrier or more frustrated.

  Also avoid waiting until the last hour of the day to fire people. They may have obligations they must meet, such as getting to a child-care facility, which will preclude a person from staying to clean out his desk. Avoid the awkwardness of the employee having to come back in the morning to face that task in full view of the office.

- *Meet with the employee.* Never fire someone by e-mail or voice mail, or send a not-so-subtle hint by changing the locks on the office door. Doing so is cowardly and guaranteed to make the situation worse. Meet with the employee. Respect the employee in the process:

  ○ Prepare exactly what you are going to say before the meeting begins, and then meet privately or with one witness. Don't fire someone in front of the whole office.

  ○ Give them time to collect themselves. If they cry, for example, let them calm down and dry their tears. Don't force them to walk back to their desk in their most distressed state.

- Give the employee a copy of the termination letter (see "Termination Letters: How to Write a Document That Protects Your Company" later in the chapter). Also, give the employee a copy of the severance agreement, if there is one.
- Never argue with the employee about the merits of your decision to terminate. Explain that you understand he may have a different opinion, but you are not meeting to discuss the issue at that time. (Of course, you have already investigated the reasons for the termination and you already heard the employee's position with respect to it.)
- Never require an employee to stay in a room or building with you. Make it clear the door is being shut for the employee's privacy, but that she may leave at any time if she wants to do so.
- Remain calm and respectful at all times no matter what.
- Keep the meeting brief and to the point. Have an agenda and stick to it, but avoid being abrupt. Don't ever be rude.
- Make no admissions, asides, excuses, or remarks about the employee, the company, or your boss. This meeting should be respectful, but all business.
- If need be, debrief on the status of any pending work so you know where to find material and understand what still needs to be done.
- *Manage their departure.* Under certain circumstances (such as when an employee is being fired for embezzlement or you think sabotage is a possibility), it makes sense for you and/or a security guard to follow the employee to his desk and watch

as he packs to leave. Don't give the employee the chance to destroy evidence by deleting or altering computer files.

Except in such extreme circumstances, however, we suggest you don't escort an employee out. Unless she is actually a criminal, she shouldn't be treated as such. That would unnecessarily undermine her dignity. It's also more likely to do serious damage to overall morale because other employees will be uncomfortable.

Let employees know when you expect them to have collected their things, and then leave them alone to do it.

Before they go, be sure to collect any company property, such as computers, keys, or credit cards.

Ideally, you should present employees with their final check in the termination meeting. If you can't do that, let them know when they can expect it. Make it available as soon as possible and meet that commitment. (In some states you must have the final paycheck ready and available at the time of the termination.)

Stay Out of Jail

- *If you have an HR department, review any termination and your supporting evidence with them before you act.* If you don't have an HR department, consider having an attorney evaluate the situation.

- *Keep your meeting brief and to the point.* If the employee is being terminated for a particular cause, you should have had several meetings about the situation. This is not the time to rehash those discussions. Don't argue with the employee about whether he deserves it. If need be, simply keep repeating calmly that you have made your decision. Generally, the less said, the better.

- *Be consistent.* Do not give some employees better severance or more notice simply because you like them. And never terminate someone simply because he has a different ethnic background or for other reasons that may be seen as discrimination.

- *Do not talk about the termination with other employees.* They do not need to know why someone was fired, how many chances she had to improve, what happened when you fired her, and so on. Simply say that anything that happened is between you and the employee, and that you would respect the same policy if they were the employee in question.

- *Be aware of your responsibilities under COBRA* (see the sidebar "COBRA: A Primer" later in the chapter).

- *Explain relevant COBRA provisions to the terminated employee, but don't promise more than you need to, or can, deliver.*

Real-Life Examples

- One boss worked so hard at making an employee feel better that the employee came to work as usual the next day. He didn't realize he'd been fired.

- Another boss invited employees to a Christmas party and handed them envelopes as they arrived. During the party, people opened the envelopes and found pink slips. When he was confronted, the boss said he felt the party would take some of the sting out of the situation. It didn't.

- One Workplace911.com reader suggests that the best way to fire someone is to let him make that choice himself. The manager calls the employee into his office to discuss the issues that led to the meeting. The boss shares specific examples of the problem and outlines the behavior that the employee needs to demonstrate in a timely manner.

  Next, the boss asks the employee if she really likes her job. Most answer "Yes." He asks the employee to think about how she can improve her performance. Then he advises her to take a paid day off to think about how to eliminate the problems. He also asks her to write down 20 ways she feels she can improve her performance. The employee is then told that if the problems continue she will be terminated.

  The employee is also told that if she chooses not to return, two weeks pay plus any monies owed her will be ready upon request. "Every time I used this system, the employee chose not to return," the manager says. "Listing how they would improve their performance wasn't something anyone wanted to put on paper. The employee was given a way out, with the option of retaining their dignity and having enough money to make a transition."

Get More Information

The Employer's Legal Handbook, Fred Steingold, Nolo, 2009.

The Progressive Discipline Handbook: Smart Strategies for Coaching Employees, Margie Mader-Clark and Lisa Guerin, Nolo, 2007.

COBRA: A Primer

The Consolidated Omnibus Budget Reconciliation Act (COBRA) was designed to ensure that employees and their families would not lose their health insurance coverage when they lost their jobs. Although the concept is simple, like most laws, it's complex and challenging. For expert advice in complying with COBRA, consult with a benefit plan expert or an attorney. Here are the basic provisions of the law:

Who Is Eligible for Coverage?

All employers (except churches) with 20 or more employees must give employees the option of maintaining health-care coverage under COBRA when they are terminated. (Some states have "mini-COBRA" laws that apply to employers with fewer than 20 employees.)

Employers don't have to offer COBRA to employees terminated for willful misconduct. (Because the risk of penalties for not complying with COBRA is so great, most employers ignore this option, even when an employee is terminated for stealing and confesses.)

In addition, COBRA must be offered under specific circumstances triggered by "qualifying events."

What Are Qualifying Events?

In addition to an employee's termination, other situations trigger entitlement to coverage. These include:

- The death of a covered employee (his or her dependents must be offered COBRA coverage)
- A reduction in an employee's schedule (as when you ordinarily provide coverage only to full-time employees and an employee who has worked full-time assumes a part-time schedule)
- The divorce or legal separation of the covered employee from the employee's spouse (the spouse must then be offered COBRA coverage)

continued

- A dependent child of an employee ceases to be a dependent (the child then must be offered COBRA coverage)
- An employee becomes entitled to coverage under Medicare (in which case dependents must be offered COBRA coverage)

Keep in mind that COBRA is intended to extend existing coverage; it is not intended to create new classifications of covered employees.

How Long Does COBRA Coverage Last?

Eighteen months, or 29 months for people with disabilities. However, if another qualifying event happens during that time, then coverage is extended for another 18 months, for a total of 36 months. For example, if a former employee died during the initial 18 months, then his dependents would be eligible for an additional 18 months.

Does Coverage Last That Long No Matter What?

No. Coverage may cease before 18 months pass if:

- The employee becomes covered under another employer's plan (unless the new employer's plan has a preexisting conditions clause that directly affects the employee)
- All employer-provided health plans are terminated (in other words, no employees receive health-care benefits)
- The covered individual doesn't pay the required premium (see the following section)
- In the case of a former spouse, the individual remarried and is then covered under another health plan

Who Pays for COBRA Coverage?

Individuals may be required to pay a premium. The cost may not exceed 102 percent of the applicable premium paid on behalf of active employees. (The additional 2 percent theoretically offsets the employer's cost.)

CONSTRUCTIVE TERMINATION: HOW TO PROTECT YOURSELF FROM CLAIMS THAT PEOPLE WERE FORCED TO QUIT

Know the Issue

Be careful what you wish for. Sometimes, when an employee is performing poorly, we wish to ourselves (or even out loud to colleagues or friends) that the employee would "just quit."

But if the employee does quit, she may be able to argue that she was actually fired. Yes, fired. Of course, we're not talking about a situation in which an employee leaves to pursue a better opportunity to accompany her relocating spouse, or has another amicable reason. We're talking about employees who quit in response to what they believe is an intolerably negative environment. That's because of a little-known legal concept called "constructive termination."

Sometimes this happens because an employee is the victim of specific behavior, such as sexual harassment or racial slurs. By not improving the working situation, the employer has, in effect, forced the employee to leave and she may be able to sue her former employer successfully.

In other cases, the employee may feel literally hounded by her boss, micromanaged or criticized, for example, to the point where being at work is unbearable. Sadly, in some cases this behavior is deliberate. The idea is that if we make a poor employee's life miserable enough, she will leave and we'll be spared having to fire her. Not so fast! The courts frown on such tactics (it's hardly taking the high road in dealing with a performance problem) and will deal with it accordingly.

So beware. Your employee's discomfort can become your legal problem. Don't let that happen.

Take Action

- *Encourage employees to come to you.* You don't want to face a constructive termination lawsuit over a problem you didn't even know existed. Suppose, for example, an employee feels he must quit because he can no longer face the racial epithets being left in his voice mail or e-mail. That's a problem you could have taken steps to correct if you knew about it. Make yourself accessible.

- *Investigate all claims.* If an employee comes to you with a complaint, take it seriously. Investigate to figure out, as best you can, what's really going on. Don't hope the problem will just go away.

    If you find that an employee's complaint is valid, take action to solve the problem; ignoring it may be seen as condoning the behavior. Deal with the problem directly, openly, and honestly. Offer training to employees who are causing the problem or, if need be, discipline (including terminating) those responsible.

- *If an employee has a performance problem, deal with it.* Meet with the employee and counsel her for improvement or, if need be, discipline her. Never resort to giving an employee the cold shoulder, ignoring her at meetings, leaving her out of events, or otherwise passively expressing your displeasure.

Stay Out of Jail

Never assume that forcing an employee to quit will end all employment problems and prevent a lawsuit for wrongful termination.

Get More Information

The Employer's Legal Handbook, Fred Steingold, Nolo, 2009.

TERMINATION LETTERS: HOW TO WRITE A DOCUMENT THAT PROTECTS YOUR COMPANY

Know the Issue

There's a reason that Dear John letters are the stuff of movies and songs much more often than, say, Dear John telephone calls. Having the message in writing makes it more final and less ambiguous. Whatever it says is right there in black and white.

Termination letters are important for the same reasons. They make the finality of your decision absolutely clear. They leave no room for an employee to wonder why he was fired, and they offer a stronger defense in court should an employee file suit over his discharge. Termination letters are one of the most important pieces of documentation you must draft.

Take Action

- *Always put it in writing.* Just because a termination seems inevitable or obvious to you doesn't mean an employee will see it that way. Even if he does, it doesn't mean he won't seize on an ambiguity to make a case in court. Always give an employee a letter when he or she is terminated explaining the reasons for the termination. The letter should include:
  - Employee's name and position.
  - Date the termination is effective.

- ○ Severance the employee will receive (including any vacation or personal leave time on the books that the employee must be paid for).
- ○ Information about benefits coverage (how long any existing coverage will continue).
- ○ Explanation. The letter also should include the reason(s) the employee is being fired. Without a clear (and substantiated) reason, the employee's attorney can argue in court that the reasons her client was fired were made up "after the fact" in response to the lawsuit, and that he was actually fired because of discrimination or whistleblowing.

In addition, if you don't give your reasons for firing someone, you may never even get the chance to defend those reasons in court because some arbitrators and judges compare termination letters to an "indictment" requiring all "charges" to be clearly stated or they will be "lost." Think of it this way: you can't be called into court to prosecute a man for burglary if he was never charged with burglary.

- ○ *Give the employee a copy.* During your meeting, give the employee a copy of the letter. Have the employee sign the letter to show receipt, and provide a space on the letter for the employee to respond in writing.
- ○ *Keep a copy in the employee's personnel file.*

Stay Out of Jail

- • *Stick to legitimate business reasons.* When explaining an employee's termination, stick to legitimate business reasons, such as, "Because of a downturn in business, the company is reducing its workforce" or "The employee is being terminated for failure to follow a direct order on January 12, 2009, when she was ordered, with a witness present, to work on the sales account, but she refused to do so for no legitimate or stated reason."

- *Do not include anything in a termination letter based on your personal feelings* ("The employee is not well-liked," for example). Also do not mention anything that reflects a stereotype, such as, "Like many older people, the employee cannot learn things quickly." Focus on the unacceptable outcome, not a supposed reason for the employee's behavior.

- *Focus on what you can prove.* Don't include claims against an employee that you can't prove. For example, don't state that the employee was fired for poor attendance if you have no records to show when and how often the employee was absent. It will be very difficult to defend any claim that you can't substantiate.

  In addition, if you can't prove one of your claims, you may lose the chance to claim any of them. Suppose, for example, you fire an employee because he was tardy, swore at a coworker, and attempted to burn the facility down. If you can prove the employee swore at a coworker and tried to burn the building down, but you can't prove that he was tardy, a judge or arbitrator may rule that you failed to prove your case and reject your entire explanation.

- *If the letter doesn't make it clear that an employee's employment was at-will or that he was given prior discipline or that he gave you his promise he would never repeat his offense, you may compromise your ability to establish those facts at trial.*

- *If you have an HR department, have someone in HR review the letter before you give it to the employee.* If you don't have an HR department, consider having an attorney review the letter.

Get More Information

The Employer's Legal Handbook, Fred Steingold, Nolo, 2009.

RESIGNATIONS: HOW TO GET CLOSURE WHEN PEOPLE MOVE ON

Know the Issue

Dinner was great until you realized that you were being dumped. Now you're a mass of emotions: surprise, hurt, anger, confusion, maybe even relief. You may want to bolt from the table and seek succor in a double scotch or a three-scoop hot fudge sundae. But first you probably want to know what went wrong and how the dumper can be so stupid. You'll want to know what hideous character flaw you need to hide on your next date. You'll want reassurance you aren't a total loser. In short, you'll want closure.

Surprisingly, you may feel many of these same feelings when an employee dumps you by resigning. No, the emotions aren't as strong. You aren't likely to build a bonfire with everything in your office that reminds you of the employee. But a resignation is a loss, and it's only natural to want to learn from the experience and to get some closure. Unlike even the worst dates, you also need to consider the legal issues on behalf of your employer.

Take Action

- *Get it in writing.* If an employee resigns, ask him to write a letter of resignation, or better yet, help him draft it. Be sure to include the fact that his resignation was voluntary and not due to anything the employer did or did not do. Doing so can help mitigate the risk of a constructive termination claim (see the previous section, "Constructive Termination: How to Protect Yourself from Claims That People Were Forced to Quit"). Assuming the reason isn't one that can be considered a constructive termination, put it in the letter: "I'm quitting to take a better position" or ". . . for family-related reasons," or ". . . to travel" or ". . . to go back to school." The letter also should state the employee's position and the date the resignation is effective. Keep a copy of the letter in the employee's personnel file.

- *Accept the employee's resignation in writing.* Keep the letter brief and to the point. Simply acknowledge receipt and acceptance of the resignation. Include the employee's name and position, and the date the resignation is effective.

- *Consider whether you want the employee to stay after the resignation.* If the employee is leaving for personal reasons, you may want to let him work the last two weeks (if he's given you that notice) and put things in order during that time. If an employee quits in hostility ("I hate you and I have to get out of here!"), however, it's better to accept the resignation immediately and let him leave that day. If he offers two weeks notice, pay him for that time and tell him the notice is appreciated, but his presence isn't needed. You're better off doing that than having him poison the atmosphere in the office for two weeks.

- *Do an exit interview.* Unless you had a terrible relationship with the employee, ask for constructive feedback about the company and about you:
  ○ If you want her to reconsider, ask if there's anything you can do that would prompt her to change her mind.
  ○ What did she like best about the job and the organization?
  ○ What did she like least?
  ○ If she was the boss, what's one thing she would do differently?
  ○ Does she have any suggestions for improving work flow or productivity?
  ○ Are there any problems that she thinks you're unaware of? Of course, you hope employees always feel free to talk to you about these things, but sometimes employees who are leaving feel they have nothing to lose and may be more candid. You may learn a lot that no current employee would want to tell you.
- *Tie up loose ends.* Debrief with the employee about the status of pending projects. Be sure you know where to find relevant information and material. Collect any company property, including keys and credit cards. Get a number where he can be reached in the event you must call to get some information.

Stay Out of Jail

- *Meet with the employee to discuss her reasons for leaving.* If you learn something you would rather not know, you cannot ignore it. If you hear about sexual harassment, for example, do an investigation right away (see "Sexual Harassment: How to Recognize and Prevent Inappropriate Behavior" in Chapter 5). If the person quitting says she was harassed, explain to her that harassment is against company policy, that you will investigate whether she stays or not, and that you would like her to reconsider her decision to quit. Document your statements in a letter to the employee and follow through with the investigation.

  If the investigation concludes that there was harassment and effective remedial action is taken (the harasser is terminated or moved), let the employee know via letter (even if she quit months earlier) and encourage her to come back to work.

  What you are trying to do is to turn a possible constructive termination into a more positive situation. The same applies to other improper actions that bothered the employee.

- *In some states, employees who quit must be paid all wages, bonuses, vacation, and other amounts due within 72 hours* of quitting or at the time of quitting if the employer was previously given 72 hours notice. Be sure you know what your state requires.

Get More Information

The Employer's Legal Handbook, Fred Steingold, Nolo, 2009.

ALTERNATIVES TO LAYOFFS: HOW TO KEEP TOP TALENT (AND STILL CUT COSTS)

Know the Issue

The western wildfires during the summer of 2008 were some of the worst anyone had ever seen, and water trucks were dispatched from neighboring states to combat the flames. As the trucks raced across Idaho, were they greeted with open arms? No! State troopers busted them for exceeding the weight limit on state roads. The trucks were forced to dump water by the side of the road before proceeding.

You think that's a head smacker? Well, now consider that Idaho officials care more about protecting their roadways than many companies care about protecting longtime employees. Budgets get tight, and companies dump their most valuable assets faster than that water. But wait. There *are* alternatives to layoffs. If you pursue those alternatives, not only do you retain key employees, you can still trim labor costs, keep morale high, and put yourself in a position to prosper when the economy bounces back.

Take Action

- *Ask employees*. Go direct to the source and ask employees for ideas on how to cut costs. Trust us: they know where the excess is hiding.

- *Consider making some jobs part-time*. Some employees will leap at the chance to cut their hours while maintaining full or partial benefits. Offer this option voluntarily and you may be surprised at how many come forward. Later, when business improves, you'll be in a strong position to ramp up.

- *Offer job sharing.* We've all heard that two heads are better than one. Job sharing well done proves how true that is. Two employees, each working part-time, voluntarily share one position, bringing double energy and double smarts to the job. The challenge is to make sure you've got the right people and the right jobs. Some jobs are better handled singly, and bad pairing leaves you with more pain than gain.

- *Offer phased retirement.* Neil Young sang that it was better to burn out than fade away, but boomers closing in on retirement may feel differently. Offering phased retirement allows them to settle gradually into a new lifestyle and it gives you continued access to their brains and experience.

- *Offer leaves or sabbaticals.* Offering time away from work without a reduction in benefits, seniority, or employment rights can help you keep top talent while temporarily reducing costs.

- *Get creative.* One company granted stock options to employees who voluntarily reduced their salaries. They offered two dollars worth of options for every one dollar in reduction. Twice the anticipated number of employees accepted the offer—and worker morale soared. What "perks" can you offer that will make employees *want* to help you?

Real-Life Examples

- Paul Levy, the CEO of Beth Israel Deaconess Medical Center in Boston, called employees to a meeting. He stood before the gathered nurses, technicians, secretaries, therapists, administrators, and others and told them the truth: the hospital was facing tough times. But it wasn't merely an announcement; it was in invitation to dialogue.

"I want to run an idea by you that I think is important, and I'd like to get your reaction to it," Levy said. "I'd like to do what we can to protect the lower-wage earners—the transporters, the housekeepers, the food service people. A lot of these people work really hard, and I don't want to put an additional burden on them. Now, if we protect these workers, it means the rest of us will have to make a bigger sacrifice. It means that others will have to give up more of their salary or benefits."

He had barely gotten the sentence out of his mouth when employees erupted into loud, enthusiastic, sustained applause. And then they offered ideas. *Lots* of ideas. Levy says that at one point he was getting 100 e-mail messages an hour.

The consensus was that the workers didn't want anyone to get laid off, and were willing to give up pay and benefits to make sure no one did. A nurse said her floor voted unanimously to forgo a 3 percent raise. A guy in finance who got laid off from his previous job suggested working one less day a week. Another nurse said she was willing to give up some vacation and sick time. A respiratory therapist suggested eliminating bonuses. And so it went. Levy himself took a pay cut.

Ultimately, the cost-cutting moves that employees suggested weren't enough to save every job. But by working with employees, Levy was able to reduce the number of necessary job cuts from 600 to about 150. Together, the hospital team saved more than 400 jobs.

- John Brown, president of Primary Freight Services, a shipping and logistics company in Rancho Dominguez, California, had similar thoughts. Brown saw his family-run firm's revenues drop 24 percent, and despite many of his competitors slashing 30 percent of their workforces, he decided to buck the trend. He chose instead to cut executive pay, including his own, and moved his staff to a four-day work week, thus saving 18 jobs and medical coverage for his employees.

  "It would have been a lot easier to look better if I laid off staff," he says about his company's balance sheet. "But service is all I have," he explains. "If I took away the core of what I have, I would have taken away from what made the company successful in the first place—my employees."

Get More Information

Managing in a Flexible Workplace, Barney Olmsted and Suzanne Smith, Amacom, 1997.

Responsible Restructuring: Creative and Profitable Alternatives to Layoffs, Wayne F. Cascio, Berrett-Koehler, 2002.

LAYOFFS: HOW TO CUT THE RISK OF LAWSUITS

Know the Issue

In any economic slump, layoffs dominate the headlines. And sometimes they make headlines even when there *isn't* an economic slump. Unfortunately, layoffs have become a hair-trigger solution to any real or perceived economic squeeze. Jobs are slashed, Wall Street rewards the downsizing company, everybody gets back to work, and life is good.

Except that it isn't. Layoffs are rarely the only real cost-cutting option (see the previous section, "Alternatives to Layoffs"). And even when they are, they even more rarely yield the expected results. Morale plummets. Confusion reigns. Work falls through the cracks. Customer service suffers. It often takes months for a company to recover. Some never do: Circuit City lasted just 20 months after deciding to lay off its top-earning salespeople.

The Circuit City example is an obvious case of failed leadership, but the truth is that *most* layoffs are the result of failed leadership. They happen because management failed in manpower planning (and hired more people than were necessary or appropriate) or failed to anticipate the possibility of adverse circumstances and to develop contingency plans for those circumstances.

Even when layoffs really are the last (and only) resort, they are painful and, for at least the short term, disruptive. And whatever the impetus for the layoff (a downturn in business, an upturn in expenses, a change in ownership, a change in business direction), the risk of litigation can be high. Not only do employees claim that the layoff should never have happened, but individual employees—even if they see the need for a layoff—also argue that the company was wrong to lay *them* off.

With all that said, we know that sometimes you are forced to implement layoffs or that business realities demand them. If you do have to lay people off, you can at least do so as humanely as possible. When you meet with employees, follow the guidelines outlined earlier in the chapter. Because layoffs are so charged and put the company at risk of a lawsuit, there are additional steps to take.

Take Action

- *Ask employees.* Go direct to the source and ask employees for ideas on how to cut costs. Trust us: they know where the excess is hiding. They may help you find alternatives to layoffs.

- *Make certain the reasons for the layoff are obvious, documented, discussed at the highest levels of the company, and considered as a last (or near-to-last) resort.*

- *Base layoff decisions on objective, work-related criteria.*

- *Support the reasons for the layoff decision* (for example, the employee refused cross-training in an important area where his skills are now needed) with reviews, disciplinary records, and personnel files.

- *Don't take action that conflicts with the employee handbook, the collective bargaining agreement, written employment agreements, published company policies, and so on.*

- *Consider having outside experts, such as accountants, economists, and business consultants, involved in the decision.* If such an expert is involved, a written recommendation, consistent with the company's eventual action, can be very helpful.

- *Make certain (or advocate) that the people (for example, the committee), or the person, deciding which employees leave and which stay, will be effective witnesses, able to explain why the layoff was necessary and why each employee was chosen for layoff.*

Stay Out of Jail

- *The WARN Act applies to employers of 100 or more full-time employees if there is a plant closing resulting in employment loss of 50 or more employees (not including part-time employees) or a mass layoff (defined as loss of employment of 500 or more employees, or of 50 to 499 employees if they make up at least one-third of an employer's active workforce).* If WARN applies, 60 days notice of the layoff must be given to the employees' labor representative (union), or if there is no representative, to the employees directly, and to state and local governmental entities.

- *Ask employees to sign a release waiving the right to file wrongful discharge claims in exchange for their severance.* Remember, the federal Age Discrimination in Employment Act (ADEA) requires special language in the release if employees who are 40 or older are offered exit incentives or are terminated as part of an employment termination program. The special language must advise employees of their right to consider whether to agree to the release (and therefore the waiver of a federal age claim) for 45 days, and their right to rescind the agreement within seven days after the 45-day consideration period.

- *Be careful about the laws against discrimination.*

- *Remember that ERISA covers such benefits as severance, if given in accordance with a severance plan.*

Get More Information

The Employer's Legal Handbook, Fred Steingold, Nolo, 2009.

Postscript

Eric Moussambani, a swimmer from Equatorial Guinea, was in over his head. Moussambani was at the Sydney Olympics, swimming a heat in the 100-meter freestyle. Through a series of weird circumstances, all the other swimmers in his heat had dropped out or been disqualified; Moussambani was alone in the pool.

Not only had he never won a race of that distance, Moussambani had never swum that far before. Ever. With almost half the race to go, he was exhausted—gasping for air and doubting he'd make it to the wall.

Moussambani was in Sydney through an outreach program to help athletes from disadvantaged countries. Unlike the other competitors, he had no coach, no corporate sponsors—he didn't even practice in an Olympic-size pool. Now he was swimming alone, watched by a stadium full of spectators and the television eyes of the world. He had no chance of winning a medal, or even of qualifying for the final. The best he could hope for was to finish the heat. It was more likely that his reward for flying halfway around the world was to be laughed at.

As a manager, you may sometimes feel like Moussambani felt in that pool. You haven't been fully prepared for the experience.

You're exhausted and struggling to get through the day, and everyone is watching. You suspect people are laughing, and you know there's no way you can do everything right.

When you have those days, think about Eric Moussambani. He willed himself to the finish of the heat. He had an Olympic experience that no one who saw the heat will ever forget. When he climbed out of the pool, the crowd in the stadium was cheering. Moussambani knows what he can do now, and he'll swim another day. There's glory in doing the best you can.

HELP IS ON THE WAY

Almost every section of this book includes sources for additional information. We encourage you to check out the books, magazines, Web sites, associations, and other material referenced. In addition, www.workplace911.com is chock full of free resources that address all aspects of today's workplace.

Finally, WorkplaceFairness.org is also a great resource for laws and policies about the workplace. Workplace Fairness is a nonprofit organization that makes comprehensive information about workers' rights—free of legal jargon—readily available to workers and to advocates and organizations that assist workers, completely free of charge and available 24/7 on the Internet.

Index

About the Authors

Bob Rosner is a bestselling author and award-winning journalist who has personally responded to over 50,000 e-mails from bosses and employees. He's learned that many bosses struggle to listen, that many employees struggle to speak up, and that there is precious little empathy between the two. Bob has been called "Dilbert, with a solution" for his creative answers to workplace challenges. He is the founder of Workplace911, a comprehensive Web site offering help for whatever ails you at work. He also is a popular speaker to corporations and associations and at weddings and bar mitzvahs. With over 3 million frequent-flyer miles, chances are that Bob will be passing through your city soon.

Allan Halcrow first focused on management issues as editor and publisher of *Workforce*, a leading magazine for human resources professionals. Although denied the Pulitzer Prize, Allan and the magazine nonetheless won numerous awards during his tenure. He is coauthor of the bestselling first edition of *The Boss's Survival Guide* and *Gray Matters: A Workplace Survival Guide,* which was selected as one of the year's best business books by *Fast Company* and still has the potential to be a hit movie. These days, Allan is a consultant and trainer with Help Jim, and, although he wears many hats, he most often helps people develop their emotional intelligence and business-writing skills (not necessarily at the same time).